Soul with A Mind

You, Your Life and Your Souls Mind.

Soul with A Mind
You, Your Life and your Souls Mind
By
Gerry Coleman.
Illustrations by Audrey Mulhall
Cover design by www.cmorefilms.com
Copyright © 2012 by Gerry Coleman

All rights reserved. No part of this publication may be reproduced or transmitted in any form or by any means, electronic or mechanical, including photocopy, recording, or any information storage or retrieval system, without permission in writing from the publisher.

www.gerrycoleman.ie
www.astralhealing.net

ISBN 978-1-908882-00-4

Mind Body Spirit Publications
Kildare Town,
Co. Kildare.
Ireland
0035345530387

Dedicated to Doreen and all on their Spiritual Path.

Contents

	Introduction	vii
1.	Understanding Energy Psychology.	9
2.	Learning your Craft as a Therapist Healer.	25
3.	Utilising Spiritual and Earth Energies.	49
4.	The Chakra System: Human Development in a Physical Body.	61
5.	The Emotional Light Body.	81
6.	The Cauldron System of Human Development.	101
7.	The Tree of Life Human Energetic System.	109
8.	The Creation of Human Essence & Human Sexuality.	115
9.	Spiritual Laws that Govern the Experience of Mankind.	151
10.	Personality Development.	169
11.	The Hierarchy of the Processing of Human Emotions.	201
12.	Sending Discarnate Spirits to the Light.	209
13.	Past life Chakra Energetic Bands.	223
14.	Psychic Attack.	233
15.	How to Meditate Energetically.	243
16.	Meditation to Connect to the Wild Green Man.	249
17.	Sexual Abuse Healing Methodologies.	253
18.	Understanding and Treating Depression.	267
19.	Understanding and Treating Bereavement.	285
20.	Understanding Abundance.	293
21.	The Magic of the Inner Child & Soul Retrieval.	299
22.	Dream Analysis: Subconscious and Energetic Dreams.	323
23.	Parasitic Entity Removal.	331
24.	Mediumistic and Psychic Unfoldment.	337
	Energetic Therapeutic Healing Methodologies.	
25.	Astral Trance Healing	345
26.	Somatic Healing	359
27.	Removing Imprints within the layers of the Light Body	361
28.	The Eyes as a Radar Screen of the Light Body	365
29.	Connecting A Person to Light and Wisdom During a Treatment	369
30.	Repairing a Crack in a Crown Chakra.	371
31.	Dissociation of Light Body from Physical Body.	375
32.	Dismantling Energetic Chords Between People.	379
33.	Repairing Major Holes in a Person's Aura.	383
34.	Etheric Crystals in the Third Eye	385
35.	Energetic Breath Work	387
36.	Healing the Heart Chakra (1) & Removing Extreme Sadness (2)	391
37.	Healing a Damaged Chakra	395
38.	Measuring the Functioning of a Chakra through Dowsing with a Pendulum.	397
39.	Removing Imprints Left by Living People.	403
40.	Reconnecting a Person's Energetic Roots.	405
41.	Distant Healing.	407
	About Gerry Coleman	416

"There comes a time when the mind takes a higher plane of knowledge but can never prove how it got there."

Albert Einstein

Introduction.

Soul with a Mind is an exploration of the process of personal development through the discipline of energy psychology. Energy psychology is the name given to the mergence of two disciplines: psychology and spiritual energetic healing. By psychology we mean the influence of the work of Ericsson on how we mature into adulthood and the work of Jung and his archetypal theories of consciousness. On closer examination of spiritual science we find that it is in agreement with psychology as to the evolution of human consciousness.

Spiritual energetic healing as presented in this book is approached with the same logic as that of any science. Spirituality or more specifically, energy healing has been utilised to bring depth of emotionality to the often cold scientific world of psychology. The goal after reading this book is that you will have a better understanding of the experience of life on Earth.

Theories of human suffering are presented through psychological and spiritual science but are then shown how to be treated energetically through the human light body. The human light body or aura is the very fabric of our Soul. We utilise the four energetic systems that constitute our light body to alleviate present and future emotional suffering. The energetic storing of past negative emotionality recreates through the spiritual laws of mankind the same emotional experiences in your future. Therefore, you can only create a better future for yourself and mankind by understanding and releasing the emotionality of the past. The four energetic light body systems are the chakra system, the emotional light body, the tree of life system and the cauldron system of human development. Energetic spiritual healing heals on the Soul level of the individual which filters into the emotional, physical and mental levels of the individual.

The light body or the soul of the individual which exists within each of the three energetic worlds is healed through the utilisation of our helpers that exist within the realm of the Spiritual worlds. From the Angelic realm or the astral plane, we utilise Angels, Guides, Teachers and Masters. From the lower world we utilise Earth energies such as Morgan, Power animals and the Fairy realm. Living as spiritual beings within a human body in the middle world on planet earth allows us reap the benefits of transformation on the Soul level of our being. Through using the term 'soul level' we mean the astral plane which is the plane of existence within the spiritual realm upon which we hold the emotionality of our past and present incarnations. Through the spiritual laws of mankind, we resonate, mirror or reflect our stored emotionality from within the astral plane which creates the emotionality of experiences of our present life here on earth. In other words you are a God in the creation of your life on Earth whether it concerns money, relationships, career or happiness. The trick is how do you influence what you are creating within your life on Earth?

It is through integrating our ego and shadow aspects that we become a blank canvas vibrating at the correct frequency of our true essence. It is through understanding the emotionality of our energetic experiences that we use astral trance healing as an energetic tool to transmute the negative imprints of our past. We take back our power by developing our vibration in which we give birth to our true Self. We can let go of fear and the illusion of what we think is our reality and realise that we can achieve the life we came here to live. This is the utilisation of the law of attraction when we are in alignment with our true soul's purpose.

The dawn of the new energies of the Divine Feminine as predicted through the 2012 Mayan prophesies means that we have no choice but to develop in tandem with the vibrations of Mother Earth. The history of the evolution of mankind has brought new science, treatments and healing as befitting the times that we inhabit. Astral trance healing, as described in this book is one such healing that integrates the Divine Feminine within our light body because it is a treatment and science that befits the vibration of the dawn of our true essence.

Astral trance healing is both a science and a healing methodology that can be utilised for the development of self or others. More importantly, that science is also a way of life.

Jung said with reference to therapy and healing that you can only heal what you can understand. Soul with a Mind describes how we can interpret the emotionality of our past experiences but also how we can release those patterns to be free in our own essence. It is time for mankind to fully partake in their own evolution and embrace their essence. Mankind is but a Soul with a Mind.

1. Understanding Energy Psychology.

I originally trained as a hypnotherapist which is practising psychotherapy through the medium of hypnosis. I saw the wonderful healing that was available to people if they connected to the emotionality of their past experiences and hypnotherapy provided a fast, efficient medium by which their negative emotions could be accessed and released. Hypnotherapy, as practised by a professional and ethical therapist has the ability to remove crippling fears and phobias in less then an hour and hand people back their lives. I knew nothing of energy healing or what I now term energy psychology. I completed a Reiki course and could feel energies but I was content to abandon my curiosity of the subject at that point. Within months of commencing my hypnotherapy practise while treating a client for bereavement issues, the energetic world decided to reveal itself to me.

The client had her eyes closed while in the hypnotic state. The visualisation I utilised was allowing the client emotionally connect to their deceased loved one via an emotional chord linking their two hearts. Suddenly the room went completely black and I could see absolutely nothing, not even my hand in front of me. The blackness disappeared and as I looked across at my client, while still trying to hold the session together, I could see an energy 'form' working beside her.

In front of the client was a Guide or Spirit connecting a beam of energy into her heart chakra. She was in a deep trance but I could see her breathing out waves of energy to the Guide. I repeated 'let it go…let all that go now….your loved one is saying…Give IT to me…give IT to me.' The client relaxed and began to smile as the Spirit disappeared while all the time she still remained in trance. The client's appearance suddenly changed as the room went darker. In front of my eyes she transformed into a man, an Indian woman, an African child and then an old woman. I could even see the detail of each particular outfit of clothing, the lines on her face, even the expression of her demeanour. The client returned from her trance and said she felt fine. I could not explain my experience of her session but decided not to tell her about it…..well I was a very serious upstanding psychotherapist and did not wish to be labelled 'MAD' just yet. As I believe there is a logical answer for everything, I did not possess the knowledge to accurately explain my experience to the client. If you lie to a client you will get caught out in that they will realise that your words carry no weight. I later realised that I was given the gift of mediumship and I was being shown her past lives. The Spirit Guide was removing her heart ache with the triggering of her emotions via my visualisation.

I had completed my training analysis in hypnotherapy after which I realised that I received no 'wow' factor of enlightenment from our work. I had learned a lot about therapy from the experience but I knew something was missing. After that particular experience with that client's past lives I knew I had to train in energy psychology. One afternoon on a training course during an Angelic meditation, I fell into a deep healing trance. After I woke up, I saw the bright lights of a persons chakras who was lying on a plinth after receiving a treatment. The chakras were shining, symmetrical and glowing in white energy. All seven of them. It was further confirmation that I was required to study the chakra system and see where it took me. I also knew that I had one foot in the psychology world and another in the energetic world. Being quiet logical this meant that energetic science had to make practical sense to the psychological world as one school of thought had to be in agreement with the other. Little did I realise that this belief would commence the merging of these two worlds into an energetic/ psychological treatment that I would call Astral Trance Healing.

I commenced personal development therapy and study with a gifted Shaman. She was extremely generous with her knowledge and to my surprise; I soon found out that I was a gifted healer in a previous life. That life ended brutally when I suffered sexual trauma and death due to a harsh masculine energy wanting to own my essence. Over the following one and a half years of therapy I healed that past life through energy psychology and proceeded to dismantle the constructs of my present lifetime.

It is from a practical basis of the betterment of my life that I understand and realise the transformational qualities of energy psychology. All treatments and knowledge contained in this book will prove to be accurate time after time. If you find that your traditional psychological therapies are becoming less effective then consider the fact that your development is changing and possibly energy psychology is one way that you are required to develop as both a person and therapist. The more I studied energy healing the less success I enjoyed with my hypnotherapy therapeutic tools. I was put in a position that as I opened up to my own energy, the law of attraction attracted similar clients to me of which energy psychology held the key to the resolution of their problems.

In energetic terms there are three worlds. The Lower world consists of the underworld of Mother Earth. The middle world consists of the physical plane of us living on Earth as physical beings. The third realm is the spiritual world consisting of what we normally describe as Heaven or the higher realms. The astral plane in the spiritual realm is the particular band of frequency of energy that stores the emotionality of all our lifetimes. These emotional experiences are correspondingly held and processed within the energy of our light body on earth. There are many planes of existence within the Spiritual world such as the etheric plane which stores the blueprint of our physical body over all our lifetimes. This book, through astral trance healing, is primarily concerned with removing emotional suffering held within the astral plane as represented within our aura. My gift is to remove emotional suffering from people's lifetimes therefore, my skill set is designed to efficiently remove the negative emotionality within our lives and heal your corresponding light body on earth. I very rarely clairvoyantly see a person's actual experience that caused their emotional suffering therefore success at removing emotions can be achieved by anyone. My interpretation of human behaviour through utilising the spiritual laws of mankind can weave through their emotional painful experiences to determine what emotions can be released at that time. Therefore anyone can learn how to heal emotions on the astral plane that correspondingly heals the light body on earth. As energy flows through our light body creating our future experiences based upon our held emotions we can directly change our future. Being sensitive to energies and emotions will be helpful in transmuting your emotions but after reading this book you should be able to heal on a soul level of our being.

The astral plane is akin to a sea of energy. Everything is floating and merging in unison in that everything is just light. Our thoughts are vibrations of energetic light that flow from one person to another. No barriers exist with regards communication in that you cannot lie to another person in the astral plane. We are always visible and time and space are non existent in terms of our linear concept of reality. The past is alive in the 'now' of this moment of time in that we hold the emotionality of all our experiences within the layers of our light body. The difficulty with human nature is that we can psychologically revert back to the dark times of our past if we are energetically triggered backwards in the present. This means unless we release past emotions, we are in danger of recreating or experiencing those previous emotional experiences in the present through the spiritual laws of mankind. The flow of energy from God through our light body is abundant and is our birthright. If we hold negative emotions then the negative charge of that vibration is picked up by the flowing Spiritual energy running through us and creates those old experiences in our present external world. We have no choice in the matter but simply to become aware of the power that God has given us in the creation of our life.

When Jesus allegedly left Earth he said what ever you decide upon earth you also decide in heaven. He was referring to the spiritual laws and their operation with our emotionality in that we will create our future according to our past experiences. In other words we need to free ourselves from past negative emotions in order to have no emotional charge for the creation of our true life on earth.

Imagine that you are in primary school aged five. You are asked by your teacher to stand up and recite a poem in front of the whole class. The teacher is in a bad humour that day and the atmosphere of the class is one of fear, threat and insecurity. You get tongue tied, the words get caught in your throat and you become speechless. You get embarrassed and internalise that negative experience. Energetically you are now encoding fear, shame, sorrow, despair and guilt into your light body. All these emotions are but a black smudge ebbing and floating for survival around your light body in that they are robbing energetic life force from your normal existence. What keeps these negative imprints in existence is the fact that to transmute these imprints means to re-experience and release the internalised negative emotions through the flame of the heart chakra. But nobody wants to feel that same emotional pain again. We store these imprints and through the spiritual laws governing mankind, we attract more of the same emotions into our lives in order to show us what energy we are holding. When we are best man at a wedding guess what could happen to us? Yes, we energetically revert back to the original experience at age five and reproduce the very same performance as in school. You are, after all, a God in your own right due to you programming the flowing spiritual energy running through your light body.

Worse still is the fact that we will attract similar experiences time and again into our life unless we overcome and deal with the internalised emotion. Each negative emotional experience or black smudge eventually becomes a bunch of energetic black grapes. Each grape will represent a similar emotional experience that must be transmuted even though we will think that we are simply afraid to speak in public. In many ways the previous negative experiences or bunch of grapes are stacked in that our emotions will only release what particular negative emotional experience we are capable of releasing at that time. As everything concerning energy is circular in its creation, the fear of public speaking will cyclically emerge time and time again until we transmute the original sensitising event from age five. The very last particular grape must travel up to the flame of the heart chakra to be destroyed. That particular experience will be the most painful fear of all to release but once transmuted means you cannot attract or create into your life any more of those similar situations. The energy connection is destroyed. You are therefore free.

I describe to people that our previous emotional experiences is like a train leaving the astral plane and arriving to the destination of our light body on earth. Each train carriage of negative energy entering our aura influences the flow of spiritual energy flowing through our light body. This recreates the previous emotional experiences in our life. If a carriage of a train hits our energy then it may be possible to pull that carriage up to the heart for destruction during an energy session. Imagine if that train consisted of ten carriages. Each carriage would carry the same percentage load of emotionality from a previous experience then only ten percent of that particular vein of trauma would have been released during the session. The client would have a further ninety percent of trauma to transmute over the coming weeks. Sometimes a client would jokingly say to me 'I was alright until I met you Gerry' indicating the realisation that the remaining trauma manifests in their life and caused great difficulties once they realise that it is the client that created it.

The astral plane is the final storing facility of the emotionality of all your past and present lives. In cognitive terms these emotions are stored within the subconscious mind which cannot be brought to awareness in the conscious mind. That is why hypnotherapy is a fantastic tool to access the emotionality of the subconscious by bypassing the critical censor or security guard that prevents us from connecting to our true selves within the subconscious. With energy healing we work backwards by triggering those negative experiences by talking to the subconscious mind in the early part of the session to pull in trauma from the astral plane. We can then complete an energetic healing on the 'smudges' within our light body and remove those experiences that correspondingly exist within the astral plane. Talking therapies are but triggers to elicit the negative imprints from within the light body from the astral plane to be released by energetic healing such as astral trance healing. The principle of energetic 'trigger and release' is therefore complete by working backwards from the conscious to subconscious mind and, from subconscious to the imprints within the light body for transmutation.

We on the Earth plane are reliving our energetic emotional experiences that are to the forefront of our light body on the astral plane. It's as if a carbon copy of us exists up in the sky sending out a vibration of emotion based upon what we experienced in our past. Through the seemingly ordinary everyday workings of our life we attract or reflect the emotionality contained within those experiences in order to illuminate our past. Unfortunately the processing of our emotions has a definite pattern of transmutation in that fear uncovers powerlessness which then releases blockages on our male and female aspects. Powerlessness can give way to both sadness and anger. After the emotional swing of both these emotions, despair or heartache can emerge. After heartache, comes an inner strength that is born from the introspection of the person's depression. This inner strength is the rebirth of the new self with a less reliance on the ego for identification. This will show itself in the destruction of what was for them was an old way of life. Many people having reached this stage of therapy describe it as a great silence within their mind. After so much introspection and energetic destruction, the focus slowly turns to the external world whereby the silence brings a clearer awareness to their concept of reality. The person now has a greater control of their life. The spiritual laws governing mankind explains in detail the operation of these laws which simply reflect the emotions we are processing on the astral plane.

Our experiences of the external world are but incoming energetic vibrations that are received and interpreted by our chakras. Chakras are really filters, interpreters and transmitters of energy. The term 'perception is projection' refers to the vibration of energy that we are energetically holding that we project onto the incoming vibrations from the outside world. Therefore we only see what we want to see and reality can be a construct of our past. Our journey in life is influenced by two external forces that trigger the energies we carry – the astrological influences from the changing planetary constellations and the energies entering earth from Spirit to unfold our spiritual journey. In other words, our experiences that are hidden deep within us have an evolutionary path all of their own. When a person's time has come to engage with their inner world then one thing is sure – their physical life will also transform.

As we cannot consciously read what we have emotionally stored as energetic imprints from our past within our light body from the astral plane, we manifest those experiences either through symptom manifestation or ego symptom substitution. The key to good therapy is to map the current energetic/ psychological state and transform those old negative energies through the light body to end the neurosis in the physical world.

The way people evolve energetically through their light body will illuminate the hierarchy of emotions of the human psyche. This means that there is a logical progression to the way we energetically and emotionally dissolve our old experiences. As we progress away from these old attachments of the ego self we release the fear of being ourselves. This standoff will manifest as a tension between the ego and the shadow which will give birth to the true self. The purpose of this journey is to embrace love, acceptance and compassion. This is a bumpy ride but there is no other show in town.

The lies that we live will unfold such neurotic conditions as addictions, compulsions, obsessions, fears and phobias, depression and anger disorders. These emotions dissolve by stealth through the spiritual laws of mankind and the evolution of the light body as represented from the astral plane. Traditional therapies such as cognitive behaviour therapy and other talking therapies will help but may not be deep enough to heal on an energetic basis. It is possible a number of vibrational therapies may be required to help the individual such as Bush and Bach essences, homeopathy, reflexology or Chinese medicines. An example of the differences between traditional cognitive therapy and astral energetic healing is given at the end of this chapter.

When God as Source Energy decided to divide himself in order to re-experience himself as God he faced primordial emotions such as fear, anger, despair, sorrow, rage and grief. As we are part of God, those same emotions are inherent within us as a participant of creation. Through the energetic experiences of our own personality and our incarnational development process we are required to transmute these same emotions as we realise that we are a God in our own right. In many ways we have two mothers; one from the birth from Spirit to being in our mother's womb and our second Mother in the fact that we have a physical mother as her child. Both mother archetypes as per Jungian analysis have to be correctly circumnavigated before we find our own true essence in this world. We will transmute the sins of the father/mother complex as per the chapters on human development and personality development.

That is why we draw from the astral plane emotions that manifest at different energetic levels. Our energy does have a life of its own in that we can be emotionally secure in the morning while we may feel emotionally drained and full of despair in the evening. This is part of the realisation that to find our true nature we must stop controlling who we think we are and let our energy control the direction of our forward movement. This is called alignment. Of course you need a commercial plan to bring your success to fuitition but, if your inner energetic world is out of sync with your physical conscious mind then success will elude you. The danger is that you could be writing energetic cheques from the astral plane that cannot be cashed on the material plane because your astral bank account is empty. It does not contain the reserves of energy to guarantee success in the physical plane. Remember astral plane or inner world governs everything and our life on the earth then follows suit.

Analytical therapy involves talking to the client with no formal induction of hypnosis. As the conversation develops, the astute therapist will turn his attention to the conflict in the subconscious mind of the client rather then their conscious mind. It is the subconscious mind that holds emotion, our long term memory and represents 93% of out brainpower. The words, gestures, intonation and flow of the conversation will illuminate the conflict within the subconscious which is the energy that is waiting to be transmuted at that time in the astral plane. Even if the client talks about his pet cat, the choice of language utilised will be his subconscious telling us the conflict of the integration of his emotions from within the astral plane. The cat and the language utilised is but a metaphor for the required emotionality to be released at that time.

While watching an Irish TV show one night, a young girl talked with her therapist about the detrimental effects to her life of how her compulsion had taken over her life. Cognitive behaviour was the predominant therapy utilised and while some improvement had taken place the girl was now in a position where her life was in danger due to her compulsion. In the twenty minute interview, the girl used a word four times in the course of her ordinary language. This indicated to me that this word was her subconscious way of covertly telling us what happened to her during her childhood. We hear at the front door but listen at the back door. A tin of beans phobia has little or nothing to do with a tin of beans. How many people do you know when as a child was beaten up by a tin of beans?

In energy terms the analysis of the client's subconscious will be the energy imprints stored in the astral plane reflected within their light body. As the client talks, when you are somatically tuned in to their light body, you can feel the energetic imprints emerge when the conversation turns its attention to the causality of their past negative imprints. Somatic healing involves allowing the therapists body be the light body of your client. The particular sensations you feel in your body are but a reflection of the emotionality of your clients past which can be interpreted through the analysis of the emotional light body.

How did you get on with your Father, I ask?
Fine, I had no issues with him, he was great.

On face value this is fine but if his liver somatically flares up I know he is holding intense anger towards his Dad. Anger as an emotion is stored energetically within our liver. Once you start to tune into clients on an energetic level you will pay less attention to what they say as most of it is lies of what they believe is the truth of their world. Our task is to hand back to the client the knowledge of taking control of their life whereby we remove negative imprints that will cease to affect their lives through the operation of the spiritual laws of mankind. If anger presents in a persons liver it may feel hot, burning and intense if their anger is activated. A deep, dull, heavy sensation indicates anger that was internalised from a very long time ago which the client may be unaware of its presence. Unless you bring energy up the body from their feet and start releasing the liver energy into the heart chakra the person will be stuck in an angry state and unable to move forward in their life. As per the spiritual laws governing mankind, the person will attract situations to show him his internalised anger that he has stored within him. He is, after all, a God in his own right.

On the astral plane we have Guides, Angels and Angelic beings to help us on our journey. They are very real but it is easier to feel their energy then to take my word for it. On the lower world or within Mother Earths realm exists Power Animals and Earth energies such as Kundalini energy, Morgan and Serpent energies. The Fairy realm which exists within the Earth, are beautiful helpers of mankind that exist in order to bring beauty into the world. There was a time I was unsure about the existence of all these energies. Trust me, they are very real indeed.

In my therapeutic practise the following occurrences in my client's lives are all indications that the time has come for their Soul to mature into self actualisation in accordance with their energetic development.

> Marie: *Why do I wake up every morning at 4am and cannot sleep for the rest of the morning? Sometimes it's a funny time in the morning like 3.03am.*
>
> Gerry: **The Angels of the Morning have awoken you to commence healing energy on your light body?**
>
> Marie: *I suffer from nightmares, battle scenes, blood and guts everywhere. Sometimes I cannot remember these dreams but I do have weird and scary dreams.*
>
> Gerry: **You have an earth energy healing your light body at this time. Her name is Morgan and is helping you release fear from your light body at this time.**

Angela: I feel there is something in my bedroom. I feel I am being watched. I keep getting cold waves over me. What is that?

Gerry: Did you ever see a ghost or something 'unusual' when you were a child. Do you see blue lights in the grass?

Angela: I did see a face in the wardrobe when I was small, I was afraid to go into that room for a while. Sure everyone see's those lights in the grass...don't they?

Gerry: No, they don't. The blue lights are fairies. The Spirit world is calling you because they know your essence and you can communicate and work within their vibration. You have gifts...spiritual gifts. All that remains now is to see if you want to throw away your childhood fear and embrace all that you are.

Gerry: What brings you here today, Pamela?

Pamela: I was told about you by a friend. I went to a fortune teller and she told me that I could do card readings and the work she does. I was always interested in the psychic world but don't know where to start?

Dennis: My life is in bits. I cannot cope anymore. My job is finished; I was bullied by my area manager and cannot work there any longer. I have no money, no relationship and now no job. I live in rented accommodation. I am at a dead end.

Gerry: We will formulate a plan with regards putting structure back into your life but first things first. Congratulations! You have stopped running. You have drawn a line in the sand and decided

> *to find out why you have created such events in your life. You know Dennis; this is day one of your real life.*

Tommy: *I found out about my wife. She is an alcoholic. Not a public alcoholic but a secret one. She drinks at home in order to be seen to be 'respectable.' She is nice as pie in public but at this stage do you know what my teenage children call her… 'Smurf.' It's after Smirnoff vodka.*

Gerry: **Tell me what has awoken you to finally view your life in this fashion. To finally admit this to yourself is some achievement?**

Tommy: *I feel so ashamed. I have this female colleague at work that is in the same predicament as me. We take our lunch together and go to monthly football outings with the social club. It's just to be together. I didn't plan to tell you this. I feel so guilty, ashamed. I know I should not do this but we only talk, nothing else has happened. Its funny but she can finish the words I am formulating for my sentences. I know you are going to tell me what I am doing is wrong.*

Gerry: **No! I am not going to tell you anything of the sort. Do you know what strikes me about your opening remarks? Its how lonely and isolated you feel. You are not in a relationship at the moment and I don't mean with the woman at work. For so long I bet you have been emasculated by your wife that your perception of reality has become skewed. But there is one part of you hidden deep down there that is being shown to you by God or Spirit. It's what your colleague see's in you. You time has come to rebuild back your essence and to take charge of your life. We achieve this by dealing with your own marriage first. I advise against an** *affair or relationship with this other woman because the danger with affairs is that they serve to muddy the waters and you could fall between two stools if you understand what I mean. You both exist at this time to value and see yourselves for who you really are. How does that sound?*

Clarice: *I work twenty hours a week but my real love is music. I am the lead singer in a band and I am quiet good but I have had enough. I am giving up. I can't do this anymore. I keep getting throat infections. I don't know what to say?*

Gerry: **Feel your throat Clarice. You have a blockage there which tells me there is a situation in which you 'don't know what to say' in relation to a particular aspect in your life?**

Clarice: *Well...My relationship. He never supports me. He is possessive and always argues with me before a performance. It's just a way he has of unsettling me before a performance.*

Gerry: **Lets deal with the real reason as to why you are not in your power with regards your gifts. Your energy is blocked but you must take responsibility for yourself once we remove this blockage. Your throat governs self expression which through the spiritual laws has been shown to you through your relationship. Your time has now come to stand in your own power.**

The following is two approaches to therapy in relation to a client who suffers from obsessive compulsive disorder. John is a bachelor in his forties. He lives alone in his family home as his beloved Mum passed away three years ago. John was his Mothers primary carer but feels guilty about not being present at the time of his mothers passing. They both loved each other dearly with John never having known his Dad as he left the family when John was a baby. John's Mother was a professional who never remarried and was very successful in her career.

John has kept everything within his life in tact since his Mothers passing but has gone overboard. All the rooms of the house are now full to the ceiling with Johns hoarding as even receipts from McDonalds have to be hoarded. John has no time for relationships which makes him sad but he realises that no one would wish to spend their life living in such conditions. John feels powerless to help himself. From the stench emanating from his house, the local council has arranged a therapist to help John overcome what they realise is a psychological condition.

Cognitive therapy was introduced with weekly sessions held for a year in John's home. The therapy consists of examining consciously the need to keep each individual receipt. After one year of therapy and fifty sessions, John had only two rooms within his house clutter free including a passageway to his Mothers room. His Mothers room was still filled to the ceiling with rubbish. John was still single, alone and highly controlling in his own lonely world.

If John attended therapy with an energy healer, the therapy would have progressed differently. John is still suffering from bereavement issues in relation to his Mothers passing. This is masking the fact that his Mother was a strong professional woman who was still the boss in the family home even in her old age. John is dissociated from his Mothers death. The dissociation is mirroring a previous dissociation from a young age due to his damaged inner child who never grew up. John could never develop his masculine side as he became the perpetual 'little boy' to his Mother because his Father left home when he was a baby. To honour his Mother and be complicit in not taking his own power, John is trying to hold together an old way of life. This will allow him control his world which masks his fear and dissociation. In order to protect himself from facing his inner fear of developing his own masculinity he projects his control over his external world. This is the root cause of hoarding his rubbish. John's real issues as stored within his core beliefs in the astral plane have nothing to do with whether to throw out an old receipt; it is concerned with growing up energetically and being his own man.

John requires chakra and ego strengthening which will result in John clearing his house in anger one day. He may require soul retrieval as his masculinity is lost since his childhood hence his paralysis to move forward in his life. John never really knew his father therefore has never had a male role model to mirror in his life. His Mother had a strong personality and was very successful in her own right. John never received or never took the energy to be his own man in his own life and has tremendous rage within his energy. Examining what to do with a particular receipt is simply playing games with the mask of his neurosis. Therapy should ideally have been held outside his internalised world (his home) and allow him emerge from the battleground of his childhood.

I use cognitive behaviour in every client session but it is the principle behind cognitive behaviour that needs to modify with regards therapy. It is time for therapy to realise what we really are – Souls with a Mind.

The Three Worlds of Reality

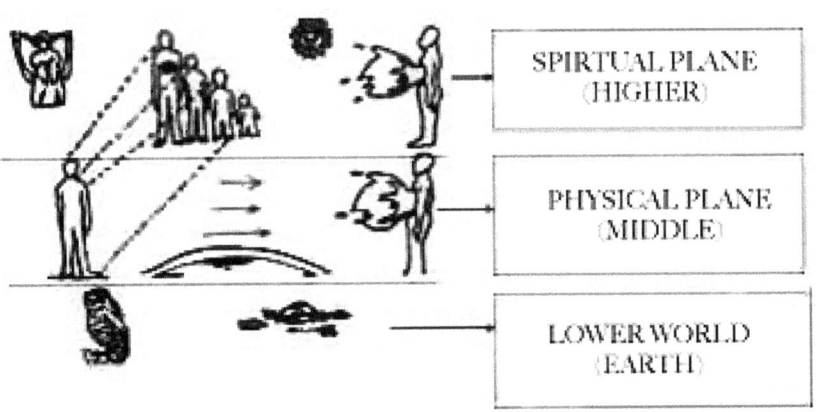

"It is only when we forget all our learning that we begin to know."

Henry David Thoreau

2. Learning your craft as a Therapist Healer.

If you have been called by your soul to transcend the illusion of reality on the Earth plane either by your own direct life experiences or through a therapeutic apprenticeship then you can be said to be learning the craft of your life. This involves you becoming a healer in whatever form it manifests for you in your life. Your greatest protection as a light worker is to invest in the development of your aura. A higher vibration can dissolve negativity and absorb its impact. It provides a greater crust or protection in that you will repel attacks and will allow you illuminate the person administrating the attack. This will involve you keeping your thoughts as pure and loving as possible. If you thoughts are filled with love, light and laughter then the higher celestial beings can resonate, communicate and live to a greater degree within your aura. They can see your light from afar and come to fulfil their work on Earth through you. If you hold negative thoughts then your light will be dim or black. The celestial Angels and beings will be repulsed by the negative vibrations of your aura and therefore will not be able to assist you. One thing is certain; your light body requires protection. Raising the vibration of your aura can be described to climbing a mountain. As you climb that mountain you enjoy the luxury of having a better view of the people living in the low lands due to your increased vibration and the development of your spiritual insight. This will make you vulnerable on two levels:

The first instance being that people you encounter that are operating from a low vibration will want to possess, own or control you due to the insecurities that you will trigger within them. Psychologically this is called 'levelling' in that the other person or group will want you to bring up their vibration in order that you energetically develop them. This is energetically not possible as one person cannot sustain the development of a group of people. As you move vibrationally away from their energy they will feel your rejection. Their old unresolved emotional hurts will be triggered in which you may become under psychic attack due to their negative thinking about your departure from their group. The attacks will eventually stop but you may require a number of specific energetic treatments to remove such energetic items as energetic skewers, knifes or chains from your energy field. This is a very common experience between so called 'light workers' and 'healers.'

The second energetic blind spot will be derived from the fact that your own issues will emerge through the law of attraction and reflection (resonance). The spiritual laws will draw in negative emotional experiences to illuminate the negative emotional energy you are carrying. These are the two main reasons as to why you will be required to protect your light body.

Psychic and entity attack may occur, especially if you are a healer but the rules are still the same. You need protection and become aware of your blind spots within your own psyche. Blind spots are like holes in your armour just waiting to trip you up. Awareness is the key to notice your thoughts, feelings and mood. If you are not aware or, choose to not pay attention to your internal feelings, then you are simply asking for trouble. Responsibility is the key as the inner world will govern the outer world. (See Spiritual Laws of Mankind).

Learning your craft as a healer or energetic person involves feeling your own natural strength inside your being and calling for protection by saying your own prayer for protection.

Your natural strength of Being.

The term I am describing by natural strength of being is whereby you know who you are as a person and are clear about your life's purpose. Doubt creates confusion. Confusion causes weakness and poor defences. A divided house cannot stand as a divided mind will only allow the person to fall between two stools. It is quiet difficult to be training in energy psychology as an energy healer and be a practising therapist at the same time. This is because you will always be at the cutting edge of your energy as the law of attraction/resonance will be attracting your dark side into your life. This will also be reflected in the clients that enter your therapy space. You will be forced to grow and stretch as a therapist but at the same time from the standpoint of the person you once thought you were. That is the purpose of the calling of your soul. Your own therapist/energy healer which you will be required to attend as we cannot complete the journey by ourselves, should understand the difficulties in your challenges that are particular to you. They should be firm and tell you the truth which should be your own yardstick to self judgement. This is not kindergarten. If your therapist is emotive then they are too close to you and the boundaries of the journey are being fudged. It is unlikely that your education will continue in such fashion as often we require different vibrations of therapists to complete a journey. Therapeutic development should not be personal.

Surmounting your individual challenges is the journey of learning the therapeutic treatments within this book. It will involve understanding your individual personality and healing the challenge of your personality to be the spirit that is your birthright.

The Prayer of Protection.

As energetic healing occurs within the astral plane on your light body, you need protection from other energy sources that exist within that plane. You may not be able to see or sense what exists in the astral plane but other energetic entities can see you. The method to utilise for your protection is The Prayer of Protection. There are very little rules with regards what constitute a prayer. Connecting to the external power sources of Mother Earth and Father Sky is imperative otherwise you will be healing by giving away your very own energy. Invoking the help of your Guides and Angels, Teachers and Masters is also necessary. Placing a cross, sword or protective bubble around your aura is also a good idea. Some people like to invoke a power animal. Power animals are energetic representations of the characteristics of that animal and are not the light body of that animal. In a meditation to meet your power animal you may be shown various animals. The way to identify your power animal is because he will come in forcefully to show you his power. A rabbit jumping around your sacred circle within your minds eye is not a power animal but a representation of some of the energy you are holding in your life. A bear that enters the circle that growls and roars would be such a power animal helper.

As energy is controlled by intent, our intention of the prayer of protection is what is important in its utilisation. A trusted prayer will protect your back in the astral plane. Use the protection of the prayer that feels 'right' for you. The following is the prayer of protection I say before I even see a client. I have found it protects me, never lets me down and only fails when I fail in its intention of the prayer or I slip back into 'little child mode.' There is no excuse for sloppiness.

I invoke the powers of the north, south, east and west.

I invoke the powers of the Earth, Wind, Fire and Water.

I call on my Angels, Guides, Teachers and Masters.

I call on Archangel Michael, Gabriel, Uriel and Raphael.

I call on my Power Animals.

I send my roots into the ground to bring Mother Earth into my Body.

I open my crown to the energies of Father Sky.

I place a Cross on my front, back, left, right, above and below.

I surround myself with an energetic ball of Blue energy.

I surround that ball with an energetic ball of Gold Energy.

I surround that ball with an energetic ball of Purple Energy.

And so be it.

Thank you.

As you read my prayer, did you notice a change in your body or light body? Did a weight come over your head, your feet become cold or a heavy energy come down over your body. If not, don't worry. It just means that you are not as sensitive to energies just yet. Meditation through energetic breath work is all that you require to attune to the energetic world in a deeper fashion.

This is probably the most important exercise in the whole book. Please do not ignore this exercise. Take your time and sense what constitutes your prayer of protection.

Write your own Prayer of Protection.

Create Your Own Altar.

I feel that it is imperative that as a Spirit, not to mention practising as an energy healer that you should have an Altar in your therapy room and home. As all healing should be conducted on a soul level, the existence of an Altar is sending out the correct message to the universe that it is your intention to heal on a soul level.

An Altar invokes the power of the universe to be present while the lighting of a candle calls in the Angels of light into the healing space. These are the two basic rules I advise people in their intention in creating an Altar. Personal choices can be exercise in that stones, power animal cards or crystals etc can be used depending upon your own preference.

With the emergence of the Divine Feminine I now include a statue of the Blessed Virgin as representative of the Divine Feminine on my Altar.

My Altar will consist of the following items.

Connecting to your Light Body.

It is important to know what is happening within your own light body. When you connect to your light body you can begin to feel the chakras, emotional imprints, the tree of life sephiroths, Angelic beings and Guides, Earth energies and the energy imprints of other people whether living or dead. There is rarely a short cut in that confidence comes with experience.

Commence with an energetic healing CD or the downloadable CD at the website at the back of this book. You will eventually reach a stage where listening to a CD will only hold you back in that you will be feeling a deeper connection to your energies by connecting directly to Mother Earth. Then your gifts of somatic interpretation can commence in that you can feel you're own or other peoples energetic imprints within your own light body. See chapter 5, the emotional light body.

Connecting to your Guide or Angel.

Some people are lucky in that they can see their Guide or Angel. Other people bemoan the fact that they cannot connect to their guide or Angel. The fact is every person can connect to their Guide through energy vibrations. It is not important that you don't possess mediumship or clairvoyant gifts. We are only a sphere of energy as is our Guides. This book urges people to consider themselves as energetic beings communicating with each other through chords of vibrations. And so it is with our Guides.

Connecting to your Guide (1).

Connect to your energy by saying your prayer of protection.
Ask your Guide to stand in front of you.
Ask them to send a beam of energy into your third eye. Feel the focus of the concentration of energy enter your third eye and flow down your body. Feel the sensation change as the energy flow within your body becomes alive as the negative emotional imprints are being dissolved by the higher healing vibrations of your Guide. Feel the chakras, how they spin, move or develop into a coherent circular mass of energy. Feel your throat, notice if any imprints are gripping your throat. This is the way you read energy as your guide will commence healing on whatever is the greatest imprint that needs dissolving in your life.

Connect to your Guide (2).

The sign of infinity is the sign of God. As God is within all things you can connect to anyone or anything by utilising the power of intent and the sign of infinity. Remember energy follows intent. Each Guide and Angel can be accessed in this manner by building the light body of you Guide. We do this by moving your hand in the energetic shape of the infinity sign as your Guides light body will then form in front of you. The purpose of invoking your Guide within your healing space is to form a relationship with your guide to heal both your client and your own light body. You can actually feel their aura form as you build their light body. You can feel their energy vibrate towards you and commence healing your light body. When you have shown your commitment to working with your Guide in this manner, the power of your thought will be enough to call them in to your space. As you build trust in your Guides, you will raise your vibration and they will be able to communicate and work with you in a more comprehensive manner. As your vibration becomes more loving, accepting and divine then they can be in constant communion with you as two beings in the essence of God.

I advise clients to say 'I ask my Guides to be with me from this moment onwards without having to ask them to be with me, now and forever, Amen.' This does not trap your Guides in this dense earthly vibration but rather gives them permission to come and be with you especially in your hour of need.

How to build your Guides light body in your healing space.

1. *Connect to your energy by saying your prayer of protection.*
2. *Place your sensitive hand (usually left or non dominant hand) within 10" of the ground and make the figure of infinity sign by calling in your oneness connection to your Guide.*
3. *Think within your mind that you are now building your Guides light body within that energetic space as you create the infinity sign upwards, building the light body.*

4. *Notice how your hand may move itself as you connect and create the light body.*
5. *When you reach the head area of the created light body notice how both your hands may be used to outline the shape of your Guides head.*
6. *Repeat the building process utilising the infinity sign if necessary.*
7. *Notice the vibration on your hands as your light body is now immersed with the vibration of your Guide.*
8. *Take a step backwards and connect your third eye to your Guides their eye. Feel your Guides energy enter your light body.*

This is a beautiful exercise and the vibration of your guide will increase as you become more sensitive to their vibration.

Connect to your Guide (3).

Connect to your energy by saying your prayer of protection. Ask your Guide or Angel to position themselves on one shoulder or down along one side of your body. You may notice that you are now tilting your head to one side as you are feeling the energy of your Guide on that shoulder. They may be sending a beautiful beam of energy into your heart or solar plexus. Their energy should be warm and caring. Cold energy is either a Earth energy or a discarnate spirit – the discarnate spirit being colder.

Connecting to your Guide or Angel (4).

Even when meeting clients for the first time I usually ask them to connect to their Guide in the following fashion. As energy follows intent I can tune into their Guide at the same time with them and authenticate what they are vibrationally experiencing.

Imagine that you have a pink ball of energy cupped in your hands. This pink ball represents all the love you have for your Guide.

Throw the pink ball up to heaven and hold your hands outright in a fashion so that your hands do not experience any external source of heat, vibration or energy. I want the person singularly feel the new vibration in their hands.

Ask them to breathe from their solar plexus and wait for their hands to become more accustomed to the developing vibration in their hands.

I usually position my hands 4'' from their hands to join our energies together in order to allow a greater vibrational sense of their Guide.

Sit and meditate energetically in the essence of your Guide.

Record your experience of sitting in the vibration of your Guide.

Connecting to Your Guide/Angel

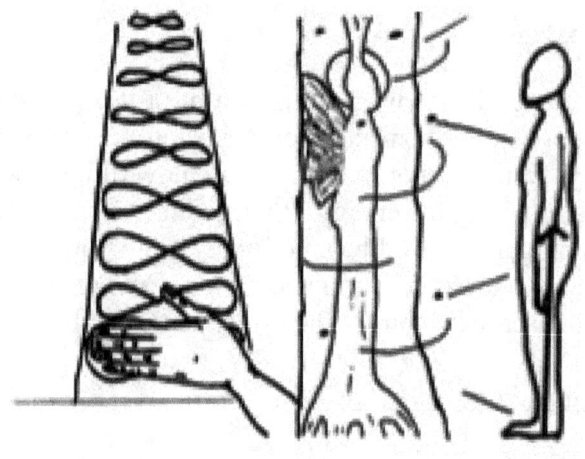

Exercise to build your relationship with your Guide.

Complete the previous exercise on point 4 and draw the vibration of your Guides energy as felt on your hands. Notice the sense of vibration whether warm, cold, still, swirling, pulsy, wavy, strong, weak, prickly or soft etc.

Your Therapy Space.

Think of how an operating theatre in a hospital has to be clean and sterile in order to avoid contamination. As a light worker, even if you do not complete energy treatments to the public, you should treat your home or meditation room in the same fashion. Learning your craft as a therapist healer involves you becoming professional in all manners of your life. Energy work will change you in that you and your work becomes as one. It will eventually mean that you will have created heaven on earth. If you have an unclean therapy space in which clients leave your room in a worse energetic state then when they entered, you will find that you soon will not have a therapeutic practice. The law of attraction will ensure that energetically unclean clients will enter your practice and close your business by not just attacking your space but by attacking you. There is no one to blame but yourself. A master looks inwards for answers whereas a disciple or student points the finger outwards and blames others.

Your therapy space should be clean and tidy. Order and chaos exist in a disorganised world. Negative energies and entities love chaos. A window should be opened when you feel the air is stuffy or unclean to let new fresh air enter your therapy space. A candle should be lit to call in the Angels of light to be in your space. Pictures that carry a high vibration should adorn the walls of your rooms. This is a matter of choice that energetically suits your practice. Sage should regularly be utilised to cleanse your room. Sage is an energy healer's best friend that can lift off external energies from your therapy space or client. Salt can be placed in the four corners of the room for protection. Crystals can be used if desired. Amethyst absorbs negative energies while rose quartz emits the vibration of love.

Exercise to Increase the protection of your therapy space.

This exercise was given to me by Kieran Henson, a healer's healer based in Moate, co. Westmeath.

Connect to your energy; call in your Guides, Angels, Teachers and Masters.

Ask Archangel Michael to place a blue mesh of protection over each wall of your therapy room. Hold up the palms of your hands and feel the shield come into place as you energetically position the protection shield over each wall.

Place the Infinity sign over the floor of your space and over the roof of your therapy space. Say or think the following prayer:

'Thank you, Archangel Michael for placing your shield of protection over my therapy space. No one can now enter this therapy space unless they are of the light and send love and light to all that is in this room.'

It is important to have a calm, relaxed environment. This will come with the mastery and intention of the person's energy as some of the most relaxing therapy rooms I have had the pleasure to visit have been in busy city centre locations. Relaxing music should be utilised if you find it helpful. The mood of your energetic evolution will be mirrored in your choice of music.

Care for the Healer.

Imagine your light body as an electric cable. Electricity flows through that cable from Mother Earth or Father Sky. If you think 'I am great, I am a healer,' then that is the manner by what you will be channelling healing energy i.e. from your own essence. Your ego is influencing your attitude which will control your energy. Energy follows intent. Depleting your energy from your light body rather then being a conduit for spiritual energy is a sure method to approach burnout. Burnout occurs when a healer is not channelling energy from original source or an incomplete exchange between the client and therapist is present. The therapist does not value their work and receives no exchange for their services and will be left depleted.

In energy terms if you conduct a treatment energetically worth 'x' value then you must receive 'x' value in an energy exchange from that client. If you only receive a lesser value then you are saying to the universe that it's not alright to receive and that your self worth is inadequate. That is what the world will present to you. Life will get very difficult all because you don't value yourself. If that client has abundance issues (which they possess as like goes with like) they will find that there will be no flow in their life and life will become stagnant.

Some healers make the mistake of taking as many clients per day as possible. Working somatically takes a lot of physical energy from the therapists light body. Unless you spread your appointments, clients and energy work evenly over the week then you can become drained or even physically sick. As we transmute old negative patterns through our light body, the negative beliefs and attitudes of those patterns will be expressed through our client base. At times, this may mean no clients as it may be deemed more appropriate to deal with our inner world rather then with our client's problems. I know of one therapist who books eight clients per day for hourly sessions on two days per week, a Monday and a Tuesday. She takes the rest of the week off having earned a very decent wage from her two days work. She is probably very good at what she does but I cannot help imagine what it would be like to be the sixteenth client on the Tuesday evening. This imbalance of energy will surely be returned in the future for this therapist.

Here are some tips for care for the healer/therapist.

Remove from your room geopathic stress and lay lines.
Spread your client base evenly over the week. Ideally have a day off midweek.
Nurture your body and eat a well balanced diet. If you eat meat know if the emotion from the deceased animal is affecting your light body and emotional state.

Try not having appointments back to back. This gives your energy time to rest, your room to cleanse if necessary and your clients the dignity of privacy as they leave that they deserve.

Learn how to spot and remove discarnate spirits that will rob your energy. Know the characteristics of entity possession.

Regularly use sage or ventilation to cleanse your therapy space.

Have a uniform or work clothes that are not used in your private life. This sends the message that you can leave the problems and responsibilities of therapy at work.

If a client is bothering you, then emotionally they are too close to you. Seek supervision or consult your therapist who will help you analyse what energy they are carrying that is resonating with you.

Set appointments like airplane terminals in an airport. Clients slot into your schedule as you are in charge of your appointment book not your clients.

Walk in nature and connect to the land.

Get to know and trust your protection and spiritual team.

Eat a healthy and variable diet.

Develop a personal life including a good intimacy life. Do not bring your personal life into the therapy room.

Watch out for needy clients. Earth energies can be raw and be mistaken for desire.

Do not fight your energy on any level. Accept it and work with that energy.

Be aware of your energy levels. Be cognisant of the need for fair exchange.

Know the spiritual laws governing mankind and how they operate.

Life is not meant to be a burden. Enjoy your life as it is meant to be lived.

Have a back up team consisting of your own energy therapist/healer and/or a healer's healer to repair damage to your light body.

Learn to laugh and have friends who honour, nurture and value you.

Engage a healer's healer who has specialised knowledge of psychic protection and clairvoyance that can repair your light body when you require specialised treatment.

How to end a session correctly.

Both for yourself and your clients it is important to end the session correctly. This enables the light body and mental functioning to return to normal. If the third eye is not closed down correctly then it will be taking in too much light and information which can result in the person being unable to sleep due to their overactive mind. Other people can literally rob the person of their energy if they are too open especially if they are in contact with sick people. Sick people have a depleted energy system and will behave like sponges absorbing energy from everyone foolish enough to not protect themselves. If the person has their crown open they may find themselves spaced out and not present in the real physical world.

If a person's roots are unattached to their light body then they will be flighty and unfocused in the real world. Personality types one and two (schizoid and oral) have not got their physical and light bodies integrated for various reasons which is why they both will find it difficult to attain success in their life. This is because they cannot integrate the spiritual energy flowing into their body and their chakras (life) due to their disconnection between physical and spiritual aspects. Always ensure a person reconnects their light body to their physical body by gently yanking their ankles or telling them firmly to reconnect all parts of themselves together.

Always check that a person does not leave their light body behind them on your plinth or in your home. With practise you will be able to see and sense external energies in your room. Create your own formal closing down ceremony with the intention that the client will be closed down properly and safe upon leaving. If this is your intention then your Guides will ensure the task is completed correctly. I use the following system:

1. Start with the crown chakra. Place your hand over the chakra and spin your hand clockwise. Imagine that a rose in full bloom is closing into the shape of a rose bud, develops into a ball of light with a gold cross on top of the ball of light. Remember a cross is simply a seal and denotes more then the Christian connotations of the cross. I think the words 'fully closed and protected.' Spinning the chakra clockwise ensures my protection will psychologically influence the functioning of that chakra positively.
2. Proceed downwards closing all the chakras in the same manner.

3. It is possible to leave the base chakra half open in order to receive Earth energy from Mother Earth.
4. I wave my hands in the infinity sign over the light body of the client placing the symbol on the front, rear, left and right side, above and below the body of the client.
5. I then wrap a wave of protection around the client as if they were encased within a cocoon.
6. Place your hands on the ankles of the client and gently yank then back into the physical world. Say out loud 'Completely back in the physical world now.'

The client is now safe to leave your therapy space and your therapy space is left safe and protected.

Energetic Healing Sequence Process.

As emotions are held within the frequency of the astral plane, the client will only be feeling the emotions of what energies are alive within their light body at that time. The client may attend in inner child mode being stuck as a little sad five year old child or may be angry from the time his ex girlfriend who dumped him when he was eighteen. The law of attraction will illuminate what emotions we are projecting but rarely will we stop to think what programmes we are energetically running because we flow easily between state to state. Lack of self love is ultimately behind all heartache in our lives.

The sequence of healing in an energy practice is trigger and release. We must first trigger as much emotional energy from the astral plane into the light body of your client usually through chatting to them about the emotionality, chance occurrences and interactions in their life over the previous weeks. Your preferred method of energetic healing will then alleviate or release the associated energetic imprints and thus end the negative influence of that emotional charge being created within the person's life.

Explain this method of healing/psychotherapy to clients at the first session. Use examples such as 'Your light on the right side of your car breaking down may have nothing to do with your light bulb. It is as a consequence of the spiritual laws illuminating their operation of an aspect of your life that requires addressing in your life.' Link in somatically to the imprints that emerge within the clients light body and release the imprint as you both engage in therapy. Also explain how essence is affecting their life i.e. financial problems or attracting the wrong type of partner into their life.

If a client requires much energetic development to complete their journey then tell them so. Some people expect to be better in a few sessions. The psyche of the client must first constellate by building its foundation upon which it will form the bedrock of the emerging self. The true self will then be born out of the conflict between the ego and the shadow self. This conflict will be akin to a crucifixion in that the client will eventually realise the old way of life is strangling their life force. The emerging self will be born from the resurrection from the crucifixion which will be the salvation of their Soul. The shadow aspect will turn the man into a bitchy woman and the woman into a cold, illogical man. Resurrection can be explained as if the person is at the edge of the cliff ready to jump off into the air. Their trust in Spirit or their own energy will be what will keep them airborne, supported and safe once they jump. But here is the catch? You don't know if you will be supported unless you first jump off the cliff.

Build a foundation by advising them to start developing their roots/base chakra through energetic homework. Advise them to address major issues in their life that they have overlooked i.e. there is no point in healing a lost childhood if the person is days away from being evicted from their one bedroom bed-sit due to being unable to pay their rent.

Advise the client to notice their feelings, emotion and thought patterns as they progress in therapy. This will start to give them emotional freedom in that they will notice when they have control over their emotions as opposed to when they powerlessly reacted with anger or fear due to the emotional imprints being triggered within their system.

Advise the client to notice when they will start to feel secure, connected and content with who they are and their position in life. Tell them life will come to them as the energy starts to flow through their open heart chakra. They probably won't believe you after the first session but by the end of session three, they will. It is through the spiritual laws governing mankind that they have no choice but to see its operation in action within their life. This will be their physical life ending its belief of being consciously controlled by their thoughts and their life developing into alignment with their energetic Soul.

If you are challenged by a client by such a statement as 'I was worse ten days after a treatment then before I attended you,' the answer is simple. The negative emotional energy being fed from the astral plane into their light body on earth varies in strength and intensity. Today we may be dealing with five percent of our trauma of the emotionality of our childhood in sixth class. When that five percent has been transmuted i.e. in the treatment you administered to your client, their light body is now stronger to pull in a greater amount of that particular trauma. On day ten they may have accessed thirty percent of their trauma that their light body is now capable to transmute. That is why the person is feeling so bad. Complete the treatment on the client, explain what energies they are now transmuting and explain how energy enters the body from the astral plane if necessary. It is progress but may not feel as such. Treatments generally are effective for five or eleven days after the session. If energy has been pulled in from the astral plane then possibly the client is ready to re-integrate the lost soul fragment behind the trauma of that part of their life. The trauma experienced after the treatment was the storm before the calm because they released more of their emotionality by integrating their lost soul fragments.

If you complete a treatment on a loved one, be mindful that they may require another treatment soon after their first session due to the normal pattern of energetic release of negativity. It would be unethical to conduct a singular treatment and send them home unaware of the developmental door that you may have just opened. If a treatment does take place then try and check in with them a few days later to see how their energy is developing. This is not for the benefit to say 'didn't I do a great treatment on you last week' but simply a matter at determining how controlled and centred they are in their mindfulness. This will show you if their new energetic state has been properly grounded. It is best to avoid treating your own family and loved ones as your energetic chords will leave you biased in your diagnostics. This is unprofessional and unfair to your relative.

After the energetic treatment on the plinth, tell the client the emotions that were released through the somatic reading of their emotional light body. Explain the emotions that will emerge over the following thirty days and the physical occurrences that will be created to energetically create the vibration of such events. Explain for example as we energetically transmute imprints upwards towards the heart chakra, a release of a band around the solar plexus during a session will mean that the light body is now free to transmute their liver/anger energy. The anger energy will interchange with the spleen/resentment energy within the next thirty days. Tell the client they will feel angry and sad at times as they attract situations into their life to reflect the projection of this energy from their light body. Explain to them that they are a God in the creation of their life.

Expect the unexpected.

During treatments expect the unexpected but be prepared. When you embark on what David Ashworth describes as 'the calling' of your soul to evolve then realise that life will never be the same again. You may change employment, your relationship dissolve, old friends that you have enjoyed for years you suddenly realise that you now have little or nothing in common are all signs of a rebirth of your soul. Its not easy, can at times be lonely but the rewards are wonderful. The journey is about creating heaven on earth and letting go of the fear based ego.

As your vibration increases so does your abilities. Your career may continually change in unison to your soul's choice in its expression of your life's purpose. Life has a way of unfolding itself so that you realign yourself continually into your soul's desire. This will be difficult as your energetic work will change year after year. This means that a new type of client will enter your practice or old treatments perfected over the years will now not prove successful for your 'new' clients. It may mean at times that your client base may dwindle in order to force you to commence group work as your skills may be required to reach many people. At any rate, your Guides will communicate your energy to you through the law of attraction. The following is some stories to show you different aspects of energy psychology which were beyond my control and were a gift in my education by my Guides.

Angel conducting a treatment on my light body.

As I commence training in energy psychology the notion of Guides and Angels were always presented to me but on another level this was not real to me. I could feel heat and vibrations coming towards me but one vibration were the same as the next. I meditated through energy almost on a daily basis for many months but the only noticeable change was the emotional swings from my hidden emotions emerging from my subconscious. One day as I lay on a plinth, I felt a strong heat enter my feet. This heat travelled up the meridian channels of my body and I started to feel my chakras spin vigorously. With my eyes closed I could see a golden haired Angel smile and sit on my left hand side and direct the treatment. She eventually faded into a bright light when the treatment was finished. The lesson behind my experience that day is that we don't need to see Angels or Guides to know they are there or conducting treatments upon us. My task involves introducing the worlds of traditional psychology and energy psychology to each other in a complementary fashion. Therefore this function does not require the gifts of being able to travel to the astral plane to actually see the middle world (us on Earth) function as energy beings (the spiritual world). Such a gift would bring the danger of serving as a distraction to the practical application of my life's purpose. (That's not to say I am at times envious of people who have the gift of clairvoyance even though I have the gift of mediumship through clairvoyance).

The time I spent meditating during the first few months was simply the Spirit work determining my resolve in the application of my goal to learn energetic science.

Beam of Light into Clients Heart.

After completing an energy treatment on a client, I paused to close down and protect her light body. The client opened her eyes to chat while she rested on the plinth. After a few moments, we both gasped as we saw a beam of light, approximately 2 ft long, enter her heart and continue to work around her heart like a laser. We saw how the beam of light moved on its own accord, circumnavigating her heart and work into the centre in a circular fashion. After two minutes the treatment finished as we both chatted about the experience. This was a wonderful gift by my Guides to show me physically what they were doing through me as an energy healer.

Karma Killer. (Not the song by Robbie Williams).

Sabrina made an appointment for hypnotherapy but after 20 minutes it was evident that hypnotherapy would not work for Sabrina. I advised Sabrina to reschedule another appointment to determine how successful the hypnotherapy had been in the interval between the sessions. I asked Sabrina to undergo energy healing to fill in the remaining time of the session.

During that treatment as I placed my hands over her third eye and solar plexus. Sabrina went into a seizure. She rocked, chocked, grabbed the quilt and squirmed on the plinth. I continued what I was doing as I knew the energy had changed and we both were being shown something for our education. After a few minutes Sabrina relaxed indicating the session was over and I waited for Sabrina to get up from the plinth.

> Sabrina: You won't believe what just happened to me, Gerry!
>
> **Gerry: Yes, Sabrina, I would. Do you wish to share it with me?**
>
> Sabrina: No. You or anyone won't believe me?
>
> **Gerry: Sabrina, I feel that what happened to you was in a funny way, for both of us. It is part of our education as evolving spirits. The choice is yours but what ever you say is private.**
>
> Sabrina: Alright. I saw myself as a medieval torturer in a dungeon in a castle. I was torturing someone to death. While on that plinth, as I tortured that person with horrible instruments, I felt every pain I inflicted on that poor persons body until he died.

Incorrect Energy Attunement.

I met a friend of mine in public where I noticed that he had a rash on his nose, forehead and around his eyes. As we talked I realised I kept looking away from her and had to blink my eyes every time she looked directly towards me. I asked her if he experienced anything new or exciting in the last few weeks checking in with the law of attraction. She replied that during a three day course she recently became an 'Energy Master' of a particular healing frequency. This involved receiving three different attunements over the three days of the workshop. Attunements involve sending a very powerful energy vibration down into all his chakras via the crown chakra. Each attunement takes time to filter through and develop its charge of vibrational knowledge into the chakra system. Many months should be left between each attunement to allow the light body correctly and safely develop before acquiring the next attunement. To receive three separate attunements over three days would be akin to connecting the national electricity grid to a watch battery.

The reason why I could not look directly at my friend was the second attunement received on the second day was too powerful for her chakra system to contain. Instead of the charge of energy travelling down through the chakra channel it burst out his third eye and burnt her face. As a result of these attunements she was transferring a huge amount of spiritual light going from his crown charka and projecting out through her third eye. We repaired her third eye and I advised her that she should realise that the second attunement did not pass down through her chakra system and that she had only received the first attunement. His system was incapable of handling the power of the second and third attunement of energy. Working with energy requires responsibility both by the therapist and the client.

Concert in Krakow.

As your vibration increases so does your ability to help people. While on a short trip to Krakow in Poland, we decided to attend a church concert. I decided to energetically listen to the vibration of the church music by placing my protection in place and tuning into my energy. Eventually a soprano singer entered the stage and scanned the audience. Immediately I knew my energy had changed whereby my solar plexus became nervous and dishevelled due my light body reading the singers nervousness. I knew it was safe to proceed as my protection had held and my Guides wished to use me for an energy session.

As she sang her solar plexus vibrated with the force of her singing. This indicated to me that she was not holding her power but trying to force the song from her body rather then let the song gently flow from her body. My Guides used my third eye to connect chords from various statues of Saints adorning the church to the singers light body. My friends asked me why she was looking at me. Maybe 'flattery will get you everywhere' but on some level she knew what my Guides were doing through me. At the end of the concert her solar plexus was strong, concrete and flowing with the natural pulsation of flowing energy. She played an encore of the song Alleluia. It was really beautiful as the glory of the vibration of the song entered the church. She bowed in my direction as she left the stage. It is nice to leave the energy world behind at times and just be an ordinary bloke doing ordinary things but this was one occasion that again proved to me the value of my Guides educating me in the use of energy psychology.

"And forget not that the earth delights to feel your bare feet and the winds long to play with your hair."

Khalil Gibran

3. Utilising Spiritual & Earth Energies.

My first encounter with energy healing was with the ancient healing energy of Reiki. I really enjoyed the concept and feel of this energy but was content to leave my studies of Reiki after I completed a level 1 workshop. I continued my practise as a hypnotherapist until one day when treating a client while they were hypnotised, the room went completely dark and after the fog had lifted, the young client was now an 'old woman or hag.' I was intrigued and knew I wanted to learn more about energy healing or what I now describe as the science of energy psychology. I discovered over time that different energies are utilised to help the individual heal, release or rebuild aspects of their lives. Through various personal encounters with these energies I now know that they have a consciousness of their own that can be really beneficial in the therapeutic treatment of our psyche. I classify energies into the categories of Angelic, Guides or Spiritual energies, Earth energies and psychological energies.

Angelic or Guide Energies.

It is very beneficial to know the vibration of your Guide. In times of danger your Guide will come in very strongly to warn and protect you. You will be required to work with new Guides from time to time according to your energetic development. As you increase your light bodies' ability to channel healing energies more advanced Guides will come to work with you. They impart information through your thoughts, ideas, brainwaves, feelings etc in their communication to us. It's not as if they have email and can send us a mail with an idea from time to time but is simply a matter of trusting your intuition as you listen to yourself. Get to know the energies around you and you will feel the energy of your Angel or Guide come to you. Its very comforting to realise that we are never alone and that help is always at hand. Once you learn that you can hand over your treatments to your Guides then the power of your treatments are greatly enhanced. This is called trance healing. Listening to a famous international medium answer a question one day as to how long it took him to develop his trance healing he replied 'twenty five years.' That may be so on one level but he forgot to add that you can learn the art of trance healing from the outset of your energetic education. It's the fact of trusting yourself to let your hands channel the energies and actions for the purposes of healing that is what is important. It is strange but the more you surrender and let go, the more power you will be given to help heal the client. This is the art of trance healing. It is the same with all spiritual gifts in that the more you personally 'get off the stage' and let your Guides take over, the more they will put you back on stage through the utilisation of their power.

When we commence healing we usually try and get everything correct, copy our teacher and play it by the book. That is not strictly correct. During a healing session the sooner you give control over the movements of your hands, actions and breath to your Guides, the better. Your actions will become more graceful, flowing and deliberate. Even at your first practical workshop with me I will advise you (sometimes torment you) to be different then me. Its better to be a second rate healer in your own right rather then a first rate me.

Angels and Archangels.

There are four Archangels - Michael, Gabriel, Uriel and Raphael. Each has a specific function e.g. Michael for protection and getting the task completed, Gabriel for communication, skill and trust, Uriel for Divine wisdom, family issues and transformation and Raphael for healing and releasing guilt.

Angel Daniel is given the responsibility for marriage and releasing anger and resentment. His energy is cold and is therefore very easy to mistake for an earth energy or discarnate spirit. Strange how anger, resentment and marriage go together. It probably concerns the past life Karmic contracts in operation in current relationships.
Angel Sarah has responsibility for helping release powerlessness. Sarah is therefore especially good at repairing the solar plexus which governs our mental processing.

Saint Germaine governs the transmutation of karma, cutting chords and releasing us from the past or the patterns of past life issues.

You may also be given the privilege of Saints or Egyptian energies working with you. If a Saint enters your healing space working with you they will from that time onwards continue to work with you. They are very powerful. They will gradually enter your aura until eventually you can feel their energetic physical appearance cover your own body. It is possible to feel their hands, face, beard and clothes energetically cover your body. It is very comforting. Once you accept them into your life then they will help with trance healing etc.

The Blessed Virgin or Divine Feminine.

As at 2012 the purpose of the energetic evolution of Earth is the emergence of the Divine Feminine. This is an energy that no one on Earth has previously experienced and the turmoil experienced by the world at this time is representative of the development of this energy on the inner planes of existence. Many cultures and spiritual sciences have different words to describe this energy but to Roman Catholics the nearest concept we have to understanding this phenomenon is the Blessed Virgin. The purpose of this emergence is that males and females will embrace their feminine qualities that have eluded them for so long in their expression on Earth. She is our true Mother in that she is soft, nurturing, gentle and accepting. She is in direct contrast to the harsh, cruel, unforgiving power of the Old Hag aspect of Morgan energy. Quiet often you will feel or see both energies working with a client either through encounters with people in their physical life or through energies on the astral plane.

Earth Energies.

As we are a ball of spiritual energetic light in energetic terms, we require an energy source while living on Earth. We have two major sources of energy, Spiritual energy from the spiritual realm and Earth energies from the lower worlds. The nurturance from Mother Earth gives us energy for our physical life. Our roots channel energy into the three lower chakras that relate to our experience of physical life here on Earth. If the lower three chakras spin anti-clockwise then the persons life is out of control and will possibly have suicidal thoughts. As these chakras mature in chronological order, Mother Earth healing provides the opportunity to re-experience our natural maturing process that was possibly dysfunctional in our younger years. This is why we always connect the person to earth energy in order to build the person from the base chakra upwards that provides a foundation for the emerging self. The lower three chakras can be said to be connected with the lower self while the higher chakras correspond with the higher self.

When a person meditates over a considerable period of time they will have their crown chakra open which allows greater spiritual energy into their light body. If this energy is not grounded through earth connection then the person can be flighty or airy fairy. Their 'feet may not be on the ground' and their physical life may become stagnant. I advise such people to abstain from Father Sky connection for a few weeks and instead to connect to Mother Earth and utilise Oak energy. Oak energy will help ground them and allow they hold their position in life. Many times I encounter people who practise Yoga in this condition. They usually have brilliant flowing light bodies but not living in the real world. If they are stuck in a psychological complex such as the Father of Mother complex they can find life quiet difficult as they usually relate their spiritual practise as being on the right track in their psychological development. Unfortunately as complexes are subconsciously blind they will be travelling up the incorrect road in the execution of their life.

The deeper you breathe down into Mother Earth, the colder and denser the energy will feel. This is the deep healing that will uncover and dislodge the negative emotional imprints within the light body. It is best to lie down flat on the ground. Connect to your Guides and Spiritual Team to oversee the treatment and breathe from the Earth up into your solar plexus. This will pull the healing energy directly into the solar plexus and light body in a very powerful fashion. Always remain breathing with your Earth connection until the energy enters your heart chakra. The energy must pass upwards through the imprints within the lower section of the body and therefore carry the imprints for transmutation into the heart chakra for transmutation within the astral plane.

Fairy Energy.

Fairies exist and are very real. Fairies are the Angels of the Earth. Many of my psychic friends would tell me that there was a fairy at my back but I was never able to see or even feel their energy. A spiritual friend that I trust told me that I was advised to erect a shrine to the Earth Elementals in my garden. A shrine does not have to be big but you will recognise what constitutes your shrine when you see it. The week before I got that message, I kept noticing Goblins, Elves and Fairies as little garden ornaments when out shopping. Over the following two weeks I completed my collection of ornaments consisting of Two Goblins, a Robin and a Windmill for playfulness for my shrine. I had no contact or communication from the Fairy realm for many months knowing that any contact to be made was in their good hands. Still, I only half believed that they existed.

One week I noticed a pattern was emerging in my life. My computer went on the blink in that it would work when it felt like working. My diary for appointments went missing. I saw blue flash's of light around my room. I noticed an unusual connection of energy between a female colleague and me. It was not a sexual chemistry which can sometimes happen with the rawness of Morgan Energy but had a cold temperature yet felt like champaign. The connections between us made us giggle and laugh but were left in no doubt as to its effect of the energy between us.

I went to my energy teacher who told me that I had the Fairy realm working with me. Then the coincidences made sense. Fairy energy can be mischievous at times in a funny, harmless type of way. Since the time I honoured the Fairy realm by creating a shrine to them in my garden they came to determine if I was worthy to work with them. I passed the test. The length of time that nothing happened with the Fairy energy was the duration of the test. I noticed the coldness of the energy around me. I was given spiritual tools that allowed me to complete a healing of a light body in minutes. When I rechecked the energetic treatment on the various systems with the astral healing imprints on the crown chakra I realised that there was no trauma in their system. The Fairy energy was working through my light body.

There are two types of Fairy energy that predominately work through people. One type, for want of a better word is the feminine aspect of Fairy energy. This was the connection of the other woman's energy with my fairy energy. It is feminine, soft, giggly and bubbly. The other type of energy is the male aspect which is somewhat of an awkward energy to understand. The person holding this energy will not be in tune with the subtleties of etiquette or 'bringing people with them.' They will be somewhat insensitive and will say things without thinking. They will be usually of a big build with big hands, feet and possess a small head with a long lanky body. The purpose of the Fairy Realm is:

    1. To remind us of our connection to Mother Earth and

2. To get us to contemplate on the sacredness of the essence of our Soul.

We need Mother Earth's connection to live, develop and prosper into the manifestation of God as Souls within a human body. We need to think of our lives in terms of 'Soul essence.' Our Soul is sacred and requires protection, care and attention. We carry it with us from lifetime to lifetime. Think of a woman who is physically and emotionally abused in her family home. She may decide to take the abuse due to her own insecurity or for the sake of her family. But what about that part of her that is her Soul deep inside her that she is letting die? She is letting the light ebb away from her spirit. Ask such a client to contemplate on the word 'ugliness.'

The Fairies will not tolerate ugliness. That is why they spent many months examining my modus operandi to see if I utilised ugliness in the conduct of my affairs. Many people I see are undecided with regard the continuance of their relationship or staying in a job etc. All you have to do is ask them to contemplate upon the respect the other person is providing to their soul essence and they will find their answer. It is a great honour to have the Fairies work with me. I certainly do not take them for granted even though my computer goes on the blink from time to time.

With the development of a persons energy comes the ability to see Fairies. They can be quiet large in energy terms i.e. as tall as a person but in the actual traditional Fairy shape I can see them as large as 6 inches tall. While walking a student to my front gate one winter's night I saw an amazing white Fairy about six inches tall fly bye and float into my Fairy shrine in my back garden. My student replied 'I see the fairies are visiting tonight Gerry.' It was wonderful to see her light body mature in order to be able to see Fairies after being a student for less then six months. Even to this day I laugh at myself at the thought of seeing Fairies but they are real.

<u>The Green Man/ Woman Energy.</u>

The green man/woman meditation is the accessing of the blueprint of our development of human essence and human sexuality. Our true selves as the mature essence of who we really are is contained in the earth energy called the green man/woman energy. This energy will come from deep within the Earth and will feel quiet cold and earthy. This energy is useful to programme your future when you are approaching the final stage of your energetic journey. It is advisable when connecting to this energy to visualise exactly what you wish to achieve in your life. This is because the green man/woman energy will appear at an energetic seeding time in your life. The green/man woman energy is representative of the free, unencumbered person who lives according to his own dictates within the freedom of his world.

Morgan. (Crone or Crow energy).

This energy is present in many cultures but in Celtic spirituality can be referred to as Morgan, Crone or Crow energy as in the power animal. Traditionally in Irish folklore she is the 'Old Hag or banshee.' Her official title is Morgan. There are three aspects to this female energy – the young innocent little girl, the adult mature sexually voluptuous female and the venomous blood thirsty old hag. Morgan's function is to 'integrate the opposites' in energy terms within the psyche of the individual. This means that if a person is holding fear, your Guides may allow Morgan come and work with you to remove that fear. Traditionally Morgan would strike such terror into people that they would cause harm to themselves running away from the intensity of their own fears. Morgan can remove fear through dream work in which you could be dreaming of battle scenes or being chased by wild animals etc. If a person conducts night vigils in the woods she will probably visit and show you the construct of reality with regards the three energetic worlds. It is at night time the veils between the worlds are lifted and travel between the worlds becomes easier.

The fear administered to further your development will naturally be administered by the 'old hag' element of Morgan. This aspect is ferocious in that it can be unmerciful. Morgan can be extremely helpful and supportive in your life but at this stage she can energetically leave you for dead. In my early days learning energy healing she would visit me and literally have me on the floor due to the way she would bombard me with her old hag energy to demand that I face my fears.

Morgan will give you dreams of a sexual nature when developing your intimate life through removing your fear and integrating you back into your true essence. This can be a bemusing time in your energetic development as the dreams will naturally reflect your deepest desires with a far grater production team then any Hollywood film set. If you have fear in your system you will naturally be bashful in expressing your intimate life. Intimacy in reality means 'into-me-see' which will be administrated energetically by the middle voluptuous sexually mature aspect of Morgan.

Many of my clients have Morgan working with them. If you do your best and make an effort in developing yourself she will support you. If you stop developing she may give you some leeway for a time but expect a reminder that your fears are controlling you with a communication from her 'old hag' aspect.

I use Morgan in many of my healings and at times she comes into the sessions very strongly to help and support the client. She is like my bank manager, a good friend but a bad enemy.

Stag Energy.

A young stag leaves the family home, wanders in the woods and calls out for his own herd of belonging. As he wanders aimlessly calling for his female, herd or new family he realises that this searching is necessary to throw away the past in preparation for his future. His future will be that he can be sovereign onto himself and his own family. A young stag also represents a youth searching for his own self, sexuality and position in life. It is Earth energy so is therefore cold. When a person is transmuting the baggage of their youth, recovering their essence or developing their sexuality then stag energy is recommended to help the transformation. Stag energy is usually utilised in conjunction with the cauldron system of human development, intermediate stages of treating sexual abuse victims and inner child healing methodologies. The stag is representative of the journey of the fool in tarot cards.

Oak Energy

As a person starts to find their essence they will become aware of the times that the world will throw a curved ball at them to test their newfound abilities. It will occur in such situations as paying for an item in a shop, your solicitor taking your opponents side in a legal argument or an argument with a waitress over who should be served first with only two people queuing in an quiet restaurant. The situation will not reflect the logic of reality in that the other person will be a channel for darkness or their darkness will be projected on you. The trick is to firmly stand your ground with your roots intact and feel your energetic power circle clockwise in your abdomen. Oak energy can be called during such situations in helping to ground the person energetically in their body. Feeling the fear of the conflict coming towards you from the physical world will require that you remain strong physically and energetically in your body. The first two personalities in energy terms, the schizoid and oral will leave their body during conflict and so will require stag and oak energy at some stage during their spiritual energetic development.

Wild Boar.

In American Indian culture, if you were caught telling a lie you had a choice to make in terms of being accepted back into the tribe. As men were braves, their honour and strength was sacrosanct. A lie represented weakness thereby being fearful of having someone not like you if you spoke your truth. To overcome this deep rooted fear, your choice was to fight a wild boar or be banished from the tribe. The fight against the wild boar would energetically match the fear behind telling the lie. Boars are carnivorous therefore to win the battle of life and death against the wild boar you had to overcome your own fear. Call on wild boar when your fears are holding you back in your life and this energy will help you transmute and acknowledge your inner fear.

Cow Energy.

My clients and I always laugh when they find out they have to work with Cow energy over the following weeks. Cow energy is very sacred in Celtic Druid traditions in that the cow as an animal represented fertility, abundance and wealth. The cow reproduced animals for food, fed those animals and provided milk as nourishment to its owners. In energy terms the Cow represents all these qualities. Symbolically, the Cows horns represent fallopian tubes along with a chord to channel spiritual energy from the heavens. Any time a person is undergoing huge change in their personality they should be advised to meditate with this female creative essence that is cow energy. If the bull energy represents masculinity then its counterpart is the cow energy. This is the Ying and the Yang. If the masculine aspect would be a car then the feminine aspect is the petrol that fuels the car and propels it forward. Forward movement without the creative force driving the propulsion will eventually burn out the masculine essence. With the emergence of the Divine essence, the world is now only beginning to come to terms with its feminine aspect. That is why the old masculine organisations are being undermined as they do not resonate with the cow energy of the Divine Feminine.

Bull energy.

Bull energy is the masculine force or the Yang essence. Did you ever hear of the expression 'bull in a china shop? That is the force of the bull essence. A bull has anger, force and uncontrollable rage which is focused solely on what its own goals. It is rough and uncultured. This force can be dangerous which is why I only advise clients to work with bull energy for a short time (usually a week) until they commence working with both bull and cow energy. With this combination they will find balance. When someone commences working with bull energy they will find that they will be curt, sharp and bullish about their attitude to people and their life. This may be necessary for someone with an extremely female essence but again, only for a short period of time.

Spider Energy.

Spider energy is a sister energy to Morgan (Crow energy). Whereas Morgan energy has three aspects, Spider energy has two aspects. These two aspects are one being supportive and benevolent (positive aspect) and one being mischievous and crafty (negative aspect). Any time that spider energy is active in your energy field you will find that large spiders will be everywhere in your life. Often you will see large spider webs in your garden or it's as if a nest of spiders matured in your house. Spider energy at its worst can be bothersome. You can loose items, have a flat tyre or have delays in processing your wages into your bank account. When helpful, life will flow and obstacles will simply dissolve in front of your path. As I write this paragraph, I notice that Spiderman, the musical on Broadway had to close due to the number of freak accidents that occurred on set. Is it a coincidence or am I mad?

Spider energy is great to utilise in sealing cracks in peoples head/crown chakra. Think of the strength of a spider's web, how versatile the fabric is and how useful it could be in your healing practise. In terms of a phobia of spiders examine the person's fear of their spiritual gifts or being afraid of their persons in childhood.

"And remember, no matter where you go, there you are."

Confucius

4. The Chakra System: Human Development in a Physical Body.

We are spiritual beings in a human physical body. Earth is a free will zone in that our creator allows free expression for everyone and everything on this planet. Good and evil are but a continuum on the same expression of consciousness in that darkness serves to illuminate the light and visa versa. It is impossible to have one force without the other. Be aware that both forces exist because Spirit wills it so. Much of the events on planet earth are but an energetic battle for control of our free will. External forces from all over the galaxy battle for control of the expression of the people on Earth. The human race is not free in its expression but is like puppets on a string being controlled by different vibrations for particular purposes. If a particular set of beings desires control over Earth or its people, it will use particular people on earth to manifest its wishes. Think of swine flue with the extremely effective images of shopping centres in a foreign country with people cleaning stairs, floors and shop fronts. All the TV stations in the western world had to do was to show these pictures and let the vibration of fear take over the people. Notice how the Earth moves from one major event to another. We are not free to enjoy our expression as Gods and masters of energies in our own right. This book is designed to show you how to gain freedom by taking back ownership of your light body and therefore your very life. By ownership of your light body you are free to enjoy the abundance of the universe's energy flowing through you in a positive manner for the enjoyment of the expression of your life.

Imagine the world as a ball of energy. On that ball of energy are smaller balls of energy called life forms. These life forms have an aura or light body that pulsates at different frequencies. An aura expressing itself in its own essence emitting its own vibration could be said to be in charge of its own life force. As the energy of the universe flows through all light auras, its function is to propel the energy of the aura out into the universe. Through the spiritual laws governing mankind we then attract in or reflect back the corresponding vibration of energy that the light body is emitting. Therefore the happiness of our life depends upon the purity of the vibration that the person is holding and emitting to the world. The greatest threat to us emitting our improper vibration is such negative emotional vibrations as guilt, fear, resentment, anger, sorrow and despair. These negative emotions will attract in situations where these emotions will be experienced by us. This is where the gospel of St. John reminds us that 'we are Gods' but of course in the evolution of mankind this knowledge has been deliberately withheld from us.

We as humans decide to incarnate on Earth. Entities and other life forms also decide to incarnate on Earth. As we are created to live in this particular free will world called Earth, we create God's expression through our lives here on Earth. The way that God knows he is God is through the expression of our essence through our lives. Some Souls decide to incarnate on Earth to help other souls evolve, to finish contracts from previous lives or simply be a bystander to watch others evolve in their time on Earth. Very little is left to chance in that our Guides decide with us as to what family, country and social standing will provide the greatest opportunity for growth in the education of our soul. We decide before entering Earth:

1. Our personal tasks.
2. Our world tasks.

The development of our true self or the therapy of our lives allows us transmute the negative emotions of the ego. Negative emotions can originate from experiences in our present life, a past life issue or the collective unconscious. The collective unconscious is simply a Karmic pattern i.e. as a member of a race, family or energetic archetype. The history between Ireland and England is but a karmic relationship that needs to be evolved. It does not serve to hold on to the past and thankfully that collective imprint is dissolving.

From lifetime to lifetime we incarnate our individual essence within us. This means that the type of core being that we are within our Soul essence is hidden within our psyche at the start of each lifetime. I use the word hidden in that our personality is formed due to the circumstances that we experience in the formative years of each lifetime. Once we transcend our issues of personality then our true individual essence is free to emerge. We may choose a nervous, shy or anxious personality or determine that brash, arrogant or bullish personalities will greater serve us in our time here on Earth. Once we transcend the personal issues of our lives then we find that the true individual essence plays a greater role in influencing our lives. Our higher self is freed from the chains of the lower self. The lower self will integrate into the higher self in that its negative beliefs and attitudes will surrender their falsehoods from previous negative programming. Our inner world and our outer world can then be said to be as one. We will naturally be in alignment with our soul's expression.

The lower self of our personality is concerned with the bottom three chakras of our light body i.e. base, sacral and solar plexus. A person transmuting energy from the abdomen area of their light body can be said to be in the 'destroying' phase of therapy while transmuting energy in the top chakras can be said to be developing the creative aspect to their life. The upward chronological maturing of the light body develops with the emergence of base chakra by age one, the sacral chakra by age six and the solar plexus by age fourteen. This is as per the normal developmental process of childhood. If a trauma is experienced, it is held energetically both within the corresponding chronological developing chakra and the chakra responsible for that particular psychological functioning. So we hold our negative experiences from both a chronological and emotional viewpoint. Therefore our past experiences must be therapeutically healed through energetic means via both time and emotionality. This is achieved through visualisation such as inner child healing which reconnects to the past and the energetic healing of the damaged chakra which releases the emotionality of the stored experience.

From the moment of experiencing a trauma, the shock usually stops or distorts any further maturing of the developing chakra. The negative trauma may shatter, stop or dissociate the soul of that individual through the experiencing of that trauma being lodged vibrationally within the light body. This is why many people are stuck at an energetic inner child development stage of growth even though chronologically they may be thirty of forty years of age. Being stuck as an inner child stage of development will mean that you will at times act and think as a child and possibly relate to the opposite sex as a child e.g. as in a child/ parent fashion. They will experience hidden anger and sadness, often referred to as depression through the insufficient resolution of your normal development. Energetic healing is one key to releasing such a past.

We may choose to develop specific qualities in each lifetime. If we need to learn to be powerful then we may choose domineering parents or we may chose to be born into a family where they have a long ancestral lineage of leaders. If we need to learn to express our sexuality we may choose a country or family where sexuality is suppressed or where sexual expression is deemed natural and healthy. The possibilities are endless.

I am often asked at what stage of development a spirit enters its body. Is it at conception, twelve weeks or at birth? I have experienced many spirits that have died in the womb through miscarriage, abortion or stillbirth. They have a light body and Spirit that needs to go to the light. One should never berate yourself for the past as everyone does their best at any given moment of time. What is important is that we all go back home to the light. Even if we fail to make any spiritual progress in this lifetime, the golden rule is to remember to go back home.

During our time in the womb we commence integrating into our physical body. This is our second birth as we previously have made the decision to incarnate to Mother Earth from Spirit. This is one of our first major developmental tasks to be circumnavigated. If a pregnant mother experienced a fright or something untoward then their baby in the womb experienced the same vibration of that event. Integration from spirit to physicality may be halted or stunted. The difficulty associated with the process of birth is that suffocation, fear, blocked nasal passages or the umbilical chord wrapped around the baby's neck can also cause a cessation of the light body merging correctly with the physical body. Rebirthing is the process by which the person energetically rebirths into their physical body as an adult. The time of our birth up to age one corresponds to the development of the base chakra. Incomplete integration up to age one will result in the schizoid personality which is the predominant fear and suicidal personality. The person is energetically stuck between the physical and spiritual planes with the danger of death by suicide being a relative easy process in order to return back home.

Chakra, a Sanskrit word for wheel, is simply energetic power points that channel energy from the world into our light bodies. Each chakra is a receiver, interpreter and channel for external energies that is interpreted psychologically according to each chakras particular function. We therefore make sense of the external world through the intake of the energetic vibration from the world that enters each chakra. How we interpret and act upon the energy we receive from the world will be relevant to the degree of accurate functioning of each chakra. This will directly correspond to the psychological and emotional functioning in that person's life. Therefore, we can only interpret, act and manifest in our lives relevant to the functioning of our chakras. If our filters or chakras are damaged then our perception of the world will be damaged in that it will distort our perception of reality.

Chakras should spin clockwise as you look at the person as clockwise corresponds to the psychological function of that chakra being express positively in the persons life. An anti- clockwise spinning chakra means the function of that chakra is being felt negatively in that person's life. A still or dormant spin means the chakra is blocked and so is its corresponding functioning in that person's life. As our chakras are a living, breathing entity their functioning changes according to our thoughts which filter backwards from our subconscious mind to be read by our energy. Loving thoughts creates a strong light body whereas negative thought simply depletes our light body. The degree to which a chakra is spinning in a particular manner can be determined by the development of your somatic ability or with the use of a pendulum.

The protective filters over our chakras are not fully formed until age nine. We are like a sponge absorbing the energies of our world and have no choice but to take the interpretation of those energies as our own truth. This anomaly of nature is aided by the fact that mature adult cognitive functioning does not commence development until the age of nine. When working with people I ask them 'what type of woman was your Mum and what type of man was your Dad? I imagine the younger person as a ball of light absorbing the vibration of their family and home they describe. If the family environment was congruent to their vibration they would probably not be with me for self development. I describe it to people as follows:

'When you were small and if you were a car, you would be a Toyota. The trouble being, from what you described to me over the last hour, your family would be Honda's. Honda's and Toyotas unfortunately don't talk the same language if you get what I mean.' That is no one's fault but simply a way you choose to develop your life's purpose here on Earth before you incarnated in this lifetime.

The layers of the aura correspond to the different position of the chakras. When you clear a chakra, its energy channel permeates through out all the levels of the aura. It is then that you know that the corresponding layer within the aura is free from negative emotional imprints. The base chakra corresponds to the physical layer of the aura which is the layer of the aura closest to the physical body. Our base chakra when functioning normally express's positively in our life:

> The foundation and security of our life.
>
> Our right to exist.
>
> Our will and drive in our life.
>
> The maintenance of our physical power.
>
> To hold our position and attitude in time of adversity.
>
> Trust in life, creativity and sense of self.

The base chakra therefore is our anchor. It is our rock upon which to build our life unfortunately formed by age one and influenced by how secure we felt as a baby.

If the base chakra is spinning negatively or is blocked then:

> Life is a struggle.
>
> Attitude that everything will be difficult.
>
> Problems with poverty consciousness.
>
> Will not be solid or have a foundation with anything in their life.
>
> Fear, anxiety, stress and disorder will permeate their life.

The base chakra actually travels from the trunk of our body downwards into Mother Earth. It does not run from front to back in our bodies like the other chakras. If you are somatically linking into another person then you may feel the base chakra 'roll out like a red carpet' down from the trunk of their body as far as their feet. Asking the person to connect to Mother Earth via the roots of the earth wrapping around their feet and legs will usually be enough to reconnect their roots. If a persons roots have been dislodged it is important to know what vibration or event that may have caused their roots to become dislodged. This can help prevent re-experiencing the problem when the person encounters the same vibration or event in the future. Through the spiritual laws this event will energetically remerge so the originating sensitising event must be uncovered. If the person is extremely sensitive then it may be a matter of the person learning to adequately protect their energy.

From the base chakra two energy chords run up through the body alternating their flow in a twisting fashion around each chakra. They are called in Hindu, Ida and Pingala. There is also the centre column of the energy chord running up the body linking together all the chakras which is called Sushumna. Energy chords also flow up the light body linking the emotional light body imprintation system and the tree of life system but these are explained in detail in their respective chapters.

The energy flows upwards to the next chakra - the sacral chakra. The next five chakras have a front and rear aspect to their physiology. The psychological functioning of the chakras will now be divided into two distinct aspects – the front of the chakras represents the feeling aspect of our lives whereas the rear of the chakras represents the action aspect of our lives. It is possible to have a chakra spinning positively on one side of the body and spin negatively on the other side of the body. This will lead to great frustration for the person as their will either be all action with no feeling or all feeling with no action in their life. Balance is the key.

The sacral chakra is formed by age six and governs our emotions, sensuality and sexuality. It allows us to express feelings and love. If open and spinning positively at the front of the body we will feel:

> Good about our sexuality,
>
> Like the opposite sex in a caring and loving manner and
>
> Will be able to share sensuality and pleasure with the world.

If expressed negatively we block emotions, pleasure and sensuality from our life.

The sacral chakra at the back of the body governs action in relation to the expression of our intimacy. If spinning negatively it means that we may be impotent or inorgasmic. We may be afraid of sex or at best have sex for its expression and view the emotionality of love as something separate from lovemaking. If the front chakra is spinning correctly and the rear sacral spinning negatively then we will have lots of loving feelings but will have the frustration of not being able to put those feelings into action. It is something of a trick of nature to find that our adult intimate life is formed by age six. Remember a trauma experienced at age five will affect our sacral chakra and therefore our adult emotional sexual life. A trauma held in a lower chakra will impede the energy flowing from Mother Earth up our body therefore all higher chakras will be negatively affected in respect of their functioning and maturity. Lower back pain, which is quiet common, can indicate a blocked sacral chakra.

Energy travels up the light body from Mother Earth developing or healing the chakras. Energy flows from the base chakra upwards and correspondingly heals the person's childhood and presenting imprints as per the chronological development of our light body. When developing a person's light body the healing energy will move up first through the front of the body (feeling centres) as opposed to the back chakras of the person. When the energy reaches the heart chakra, it is only then that the energy will proceed upwards from the base chakra up the back (will or action centre) of the light body. This is simply a protection measure of our light body to provide us with responsibility for our actions in that new power will not be given to us until we have learned the emotional responsibility of that power. This can be very frustrating for a man who wishes to make love to his partner but is unable to achieve an adequate erection. Since it may take many months for the energy to firstly travel up the front of the body before it enters the back of the sacral chakra, he may drop out of therapy due to his impatience. The difficulty with this scenario is that the emotional baggage from his childhood held in the front sacral chakra is what is causing the dysfunction in the back or action aspect of the sacral chakra. You have to work with the nature of a person's energy and the natural evolution of our light body which has its own blueprint. I explain to people that another word for sex is intimacy. Intimacy is spelt 'into – me-see.' Unless you are comfortable in your emotions then no action at the rear of the chakra can take place. It is poor comfort being able to make love but possess little or no emotional feeling with your partner.

Children place energetic chords around objects. They take ownership of objects whereby they become one with their external object via an energetic chord. The pain of taking a toy from a child with their expression of their temper tantrum is the severing of the link of that energetic chord. I think of an adult utilising obsessive compulsive disorders and how the person projects their thought process onto external activities as a defence mechanism or a symptom substitution. This is exactly what we do as children with our energetic chords.

As we progress into our toddler stage our wonderment with our world increases. We need the freedom to explore. The eldest child is usually curtailed more then his younger siblings due to the fact that his parents are more insecure and protective of their roles as new parents. Middle children are more relaxed while younger children get can away with murder. If we come from a large family but are the youngest child by many years we can grow up in the same vibration as that of an only child. By age nine we learn that we are different from others. We begin to appreciate that we need to accommodate others in our lives. We start to comprehend the 'I-THOU' aspect to relationships.

Approximately three inches above the belly button is the position of the solar plexus. The solar plexus governs our power and our decision making concepts therefore our thought patterns in our mind is governed by the solar plexus. The front of the solar plexus governs:

> Our self worth,
>
> Boundaries,
>
> Our command of life and the ending of dependency from
>
> others in our relationships.

If spinning positively we will find little need to prove ourselves in the world, negatively spinning will mean that we will feel powerless in our life. The rear of the solar plexus governs one important aspect of our life – our attitude towards self care and our health. As our self esteem increases so does our self care which will be a necessary factor in the opening of our heart chakra for love to enter our life. It is always a good sign to see a person attend therapy and say' I was at the dentist this morning for my first visit in years.' This means that the rear of the solar plexus is receiving Mother Earth energy, positively spinning and maturing.

Around our solar plexus will usually be imprints of powerlessness. These imprints swamp our power and stop us moving forward in our life. It always marks a big change in a person's journey when these imprints dissolve and so the solar plexus is free to connect upwards to the heart chakra. Greater emotional transmutation can take place and the person becomes more sure of who they are and their position in the world. They can then start to put power into what they love in life.

Issues in relation to power emerge during adolescence. We are in the unfortunate position of not being an adult but yet not being a child. This swaying of energies results in what is termed 'the terrible teens' years of development. Patience is required as the parents must extend their children's boundaries and responsibilities to match their newfound abilities. When talking to teenagers who are battling for control with their parents I explain to them how you get control is to give control and responsibility to your parents. This builds trust and as per the spiritual law of attraction, your parents will trust you. What you send out you get back. You will then gradually receive the freedom you desire.

By the teenage years the influence of our parental figures will be evident for all to see. The degree by which the child will be in their own essence will be in direct contrast to the influence of the parental energies overshadowing the child's essence. A person may dress in old style clothes i.e. tweeds etc or may have rounded shoulders from the imprints of their parental energetic weight on their back. It is always interesting to view family photographs as you can clearly see the child that is energetically burdened by their parental influence. They may have older friends or feel that the level of responsibility in their life is stopping them enjoying their life. This is the projection of the spiritual law 'as within so without' expressing their internal energies externally. Attachment theory states that the key maternal quality to allow a child develop securely is for the child to experience sensitivity. If the child can 'breathe' energetically then the child will grow in confidence and self respect. The maternal aspect is an archetype and is therefore not sex sensitive in that the dad may provide the feminine maternal aspect in a child's development.

The heart chakra is positioned in the breast bone between our lungs. The heart chakra governs:

> The flow into our lives,
>
> Love for mankind,
>
> Accepting who we are,
>
> Liking oneself and the joy of just being.

An energetically flowing heart chakra pouring energy into our energy field usually brings abundance which means that we begin to be successful in our financial dealings. The back or will centre of the heart chakra is where our ego is energetically held. Spinning negatively means that you will try and force your ego will on the world. This will create such feelings as resentment, bitterness, fear, force and suspicion.

All chakras, emotional imprints and sephiroths are connected to the heart chakra which is the gateway of the astral plane. This means that the heart chakra is the gateway from the light body in the physical realm to the heart chakra that exists on the astral plane. It is on the astral plane that we hold and release emotions. Therefore we cannot release emotions from within our light body until they pass through the transmutation flame of the heart chakra. For instance fear is held energetically in the kidneys. The imprint of that fear needs to pass upwards through the light body probably via the solar plexus (giving back power) and from there being dissolved in the heart chakra. It is easy to see how behind that particular fear was powerlessness which is why holding or releasing emotions follows a pattern according to the effects of the emotionality of the stored vibration. This is where the origin of the concept of the hierarchy of emotions as explained via the serpent path. The heart chakra from time to time will become blocked due the quantity of negative imprints entering the heart chakra to be released. If clients consult you monthly for a therapeutic treatment then many times you will find that traumatic imprints via the spiritual laws has emerged during the previous week in order to be released during their monthly session. A particular vibration requires a higher vibrational energy to move and transmute that old negative energy. Remember the spiritual law 'you cannot complete this work on your own' and a vibration requires a higher vibration to transmute the old vibration.

Fire does not put out other fires. The high vibration of love, forgiveness of self and others can move most negative energies.

The years of our twenties should be spent enjoying the expression of our essence in building a career and the formation of relationships. Unfortunately, if we do not correctly energetically mature then stagnation can occur at any stage. This is where the saying 'youth is wasted on the young' is derived from. By our thirties it is desirable to know what type of person we are and what concerns the meaning of your life. Many people find that between the age of thirty eight and forty two that life completely changes for them. This is more then the proverbial mid life crisis. This is the time that our soul calls us to find our true essence with the fallout being the destruction of our old way of life.

The business of life should hopefully subside to a quieter mature second half life of acceptance and ease. That is what is meant by the saying 'life begins at forty.' We should, at this stage, be coming home to ourselves. We should have built a happy home and family life. People use the term mid life crisis to describe the effects of the realisation that they are getting old and have to deal with their mortality. Some men (also women at this stage with the advent of the concept of cougar women) decide to deal with their existence by having an affair, leaving home or starting a relationship with a much younger partner. If a person decides to leave his relationship then fine; as long as he is doing it for the right reasons. The traditional concept of a mid life crisis is steeped in the underlying insecurity of growing old. Their old way of life is simply too hard to contemplate but the prospect of a younger companion offers the promise of eternal youth. The older person is energetically seeking to partake of the youth and vitality of the younger person. As with all relationships you cannot define yourself from your relationship. Two broken wings never made a complete wing in order to fly. Successful relationships are formed by first having a successful relationship with yourself. It is only when you have found yourself that you can successfully relate to another. This is the law of attraction and the mechanics of the formation of soul mate relationships.

The throat chakra is positioned at the base of the throat. The front (feeling centre) governs the expression of our professional gifts. Functioning positively we will not be afraid to speak the professionalism and creativity in our chosen career. The throat also holds hidden tears and suppressed anger. You will often find that a deep energy treatment releasing imprints and clearing chakras will finish with the unblocking of the throat area. It may feel to the person that a lagging or coating of the physical windpipe has been removed. The person may also feel a chord of energy going from the throat up to the eyes where tears can be released. The back of the throat chakra governs communication with our guides and the action of speaking the professionalism of our career. The strength within our voice comes from the power centre of the solar plexus. If we talk from within our throat we generally have a high pitched voice. If we are positioned in our power we generally speak slowly with a resonance from deep within our tummy. Children are great at picking up on this. They can tell in an instant the adult who is centred and in charge as opposed to who is telling fibs about being angry.

The third eye is located slightly above your eyes in the centre of your forehead. The third eye is part of the mental functioning centre of our body. The front of the chakra governs the ability to see the larger concepts of life, the big picture, the ability to trust our insight and intuition. The back of the chakra governs the minute detail of plans and procedures in a practical fashion to bring our plan to fuitition. Balance in the operating of both aspects of these chakras is necessary or otherwise the person may be brilliant at the conceptual aspects of plans but may be unable to turn those plans into reality. A client may talk for ages about a new business they are creating. Have you even got a stapler Mr. Client? No…not yet. The Crown chakra concerns the spiritual mergence of our life with the ideas and ideology of the universe.

Being able to feel the chakras and to feel them transmuting energy is a real bonus completing this work. Knowing the emotional imprints of the body will also illuminate how these imprints directly affect the chakras and therefore the psychological and emotional functioning of our life.

Eriksson's developmental personality theory and the energetic light body developmental process is now explained in the following chart. Notice the similarities between both aspects of human maturity.

Chakra	Position	Colour	Function expressed Positively	Exp. Negatively	Age Developed	Erikson's Personality Development Theory	Expressed Positively Erickson Emotional development	Expressed Negatively Erickson's Emotional Development.
Base	End of Trunk of body	Red	Foundation of life security creativity maternal feelings protection	"Top heavy with energy" Insomnia fear/ Scarcity/ Poverty Excessive Masculinity	0-1 years	Early infancy 0-1	Trust	Mistrust
Sacral	3 inches below belly button	Orange	Sexual expression self esteem power/ passion, removes negative emotions, intimacy, emotional boundaries, love is not sex	Fear, fighting sexual/ emotional abuse, holds negative emotions, "sex is love"	1-6 years	Later infancy 1-3 Early childhood 3-6	Self Reliance Initiative	Self doubt/ Shame Guilt and indecision
Solar plexus	3 inches above belly button	Yellow	Positive thoughts, clear thinking, high energy, power to influence life, possess own voice	Stress/ Anxiety, Low energy, power ego-mania	6-14 years	Middle childhood 6-12	Industry	Inferiority and inadequacy
Heart Chakra	Centre of chest	Green	Love, career, life expression, narcissism	Selfishness, Resentment love egotism Lack of self love	14-21 years	Adolescence 12-18	Personal Identity	Role Confusion
Throat Chakra	Throat	Blue	voice of heart, receiving from life	Toxicity	21-28 years	Young Adulthood 19-35	Intimacy Commitment	Isolation
Third Eye	Forehead	Indigo	Spiritual Insight, knowledge	Spiritual egotism		Middle adulthood 36-65	Family Interest	Stagnation
Seventh Crown	Top of Head	Violet	Wisdom			Late adulthood 66+	Personal Integrity	Despair

74

Five days before death our light bodies begin to shut down. This commences with the dissolving of the bottom three chakras. Each day a charka is dissolved as our connection to Mother Earth diminishes. Our skin tone changes colour. Our life is flashed in three d right in front of our eyes which is where the origination of the term 'my life flashed in front of my eyes.' Our Guides replay all the experiences of our life to our essence. As we literally 'hop' out of our physical body we are left with the same cognitions as when alive. If we didn't have much wisdom when alive do not expect that person to have much wisdom when dead. Our emotions at that time will be concerned with how ready we were to pass over to Spirit rather then how attached we still were to our physical earth life. If we had a particularly difficult passing then we may require a length of time recuperating in spirit before we evaluate our most recent life on earth.

As we exist on many different planes of existence, the word incarnate correctly describes the evolution of our spirit while on earth. We transmute the negative emotions of past lives in our present life on earth but luckily bank the positive aspects and lessons of that previous life to aid our evolution. All lives, past and present are one in that patterns re-emerge until we release them. The spiritual laws therefore operate on a micro and macro scale for our education. The outer layers of our aura are the level on which we hold these imprints which can be course to the touch. These issues can also be felt in the past life bands that can emerge for transmutation around the chakras.

Diagram of a Baby's Aura.

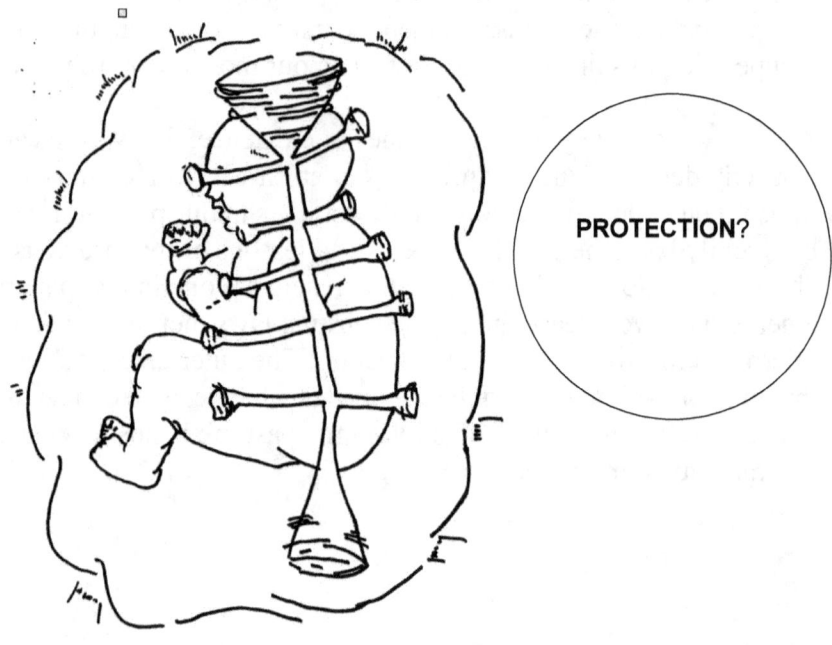

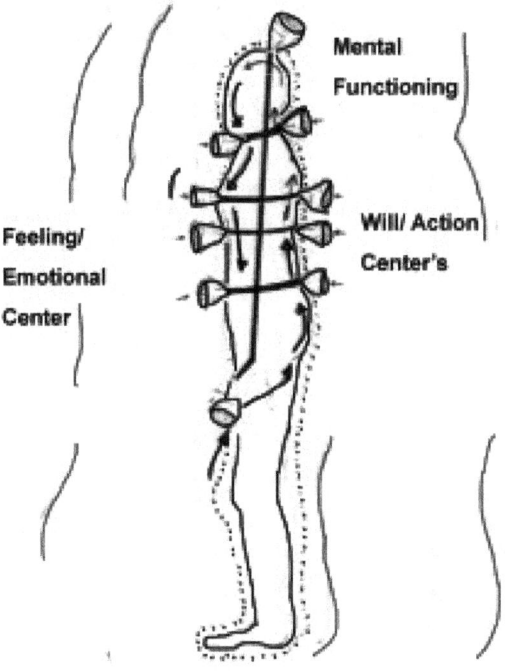

The Chakra System

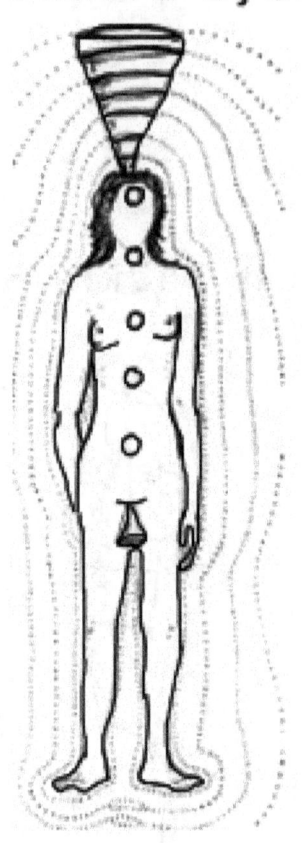

Crown Chakra	Top of Head
Third Eye	Centre of Forehead
Throat	Centre of Throat
Heart Chakra	Breast Bone
Solar Plexus	Stomach
Sacral Chakra	Below Belly Button
Base Chakra	Groin

Secondary Knowledge Chakra above solar plexus and Soul Chakra concerning life's purpose at base of neck. (See Tree of life and Sexuality chapters).

Caduceus as a Symbol of HEALING

The Three Main Channels of Energy.

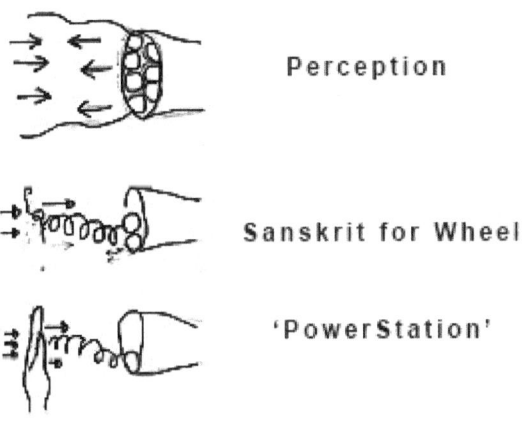

Perception

Sanskrit for Wheel

'PowerStation'

"A clear understanding of negative emotions dismisses them."
Vernon Howard

5. The Emotional Light Body.

We are energetic beings in a physical body. As viewed by our Guides we are simply light and everything is a vibration of energy. Vibrations can be classified as to the level of frequency of light that they carry. As per the hierarchy of emotions, gratitude carries the greatest level of light, even greater then love itself. Giving thanks for the abundance of the universe is acknowledging what is already there whereas asking for wealth signifies wanting. We do not require anything in that everything we need is given to us through the spiritual laws and therefore all we have to do is to remove obstacles in order that we receive.

Emotional, physical, mental and sexual trauma affects us on different levels of our being. To be released from our past involves healing the trauma that is stored within our light body. Our conscious mind channels the memories of our experiences complete with its emotional charge into the subconscious mind so that we protect ourselves from our history. We do not have direct cognitive access to our past within the subconscious because a chain of molecules or censor acts as a security guard to withhold the past from conscious awareness. That is why hypnotherapy is so good at bypassing the censor in order to directly access the trauma of our past. The difficulty with the operation of our subconscious, which governs 93% of our brain power, is that it develops defence mechanisms or symptom manifestation to illuminate the trauma of our past. Neurosis within the psyche of the client is an attempt of the subconscious mind to fool you that everything is controllable. We develop fears and phobias, depression, obsessions, compulsions, nightmares and dreams, blushing, nail biting, teeth grinding, anger, guilt and shame disorders, thrush, knee and hip replacements as energetic distortions in order to fool ourselves so that we do not look at what is really wrong with us. Some talking therapies utilise exposure therapy to desensitise the client in order to allow the client live with their particular anxiety or disorder. That is not good enough in this day and age because fear of a tin of beans has little or nothing to do with a tin of beans. It is likely that the person when as a child was in a room where there was a tin of beans present when something traumatic occurred. The subconscious, as a defence mechanism through dissociation, projected the fear onto the beans in order not to connect to the emotion of the sensitising event. Any therapy focusing predominately on the beans is a cop out. How many people do you know when as a child was beaten up by a tin of beans in the playground? Deal with the sensitising event and the beans will look after itself.

With regards energetic science, negative imprints require an energy source in order to exist within the light body. Energy is directed to feed the existence of these imprints rather then be utilised by the true expression of the life force of that person in the enjoyment of their life. For example obsessive compulsive disorders are simply an energetic traumatic mass that requires an energy source in order to sustain its existence. Think of a person who may say 'I am so tired of my compulsion to wash my hands or my fear of public spaces is wearing me out.' What they are describing is that their true essence is competing for a limited amount of energy of which the neurosis is at odds with the true expression of their essence. The ebbing and flowing of the energy imprint determines the intensity of the strength of the obsession psychologically expressed in the person's life at that time. When the traumatic imprints are removed then the expression of the behaviour of the imprint will not be projected and the person will not attract similar people or experiences into their life. Behind obsessions are always trust, love and acceptance issues. These issues can be expressed in a variety of disorders but the core beliefs can originate from the same source. What sustains the life of the traumatic imprint within the light body is the fear of re-experiencing the originating sensitising event in order to release the trauma of the event. That is the reason through energetic therapy why we always develop a persons roots in session one which is the foundation for removing more serious trauma in subsequent sessions.

Emotional trauma has a pattern of storage within the light body that corresponds to physical organs within the physical body. Once you can either feel energy within a persons light body or feel somatically their imprints within your own body then you know what emotional issues they are transmuting at that time. This system can be very accurate. A person's light body is constantly changing as per their energetic experiences and the vibrations they are pulling in from the astral plane where we store our emotional imprints. One minute their energy is calm and fine, the next minute they are a blaze of burning hot pulsating energy in their liver once you mention a trigger word such as 'mother, father or school.' You cannot lie in energy terms. At this stage you can project words towards people telepathically as an energetic vibration which is then read by their light body. Their language, tone and body language will change as they react to what you are vibrationally communicating to them. Their body language and language utilised is the answer to what you asked of their energy in the astral plane.

The following is a list of the physical organs, chakras and their associated emotional imprints. The imprints are mapped from the base of the body upwards as per the healing methodology of the Astral healing technique. This matures the person to grow up energetically to match their chronological age as per natural maturing of the light body.

Organ/Imprint of Energy	**Emotional Imprint**
Left side of Body	Female/Creativity/Yin energy
Right side of Body	Male/Masculinity/Yang energy
Left Leg (Knee to Foot)	Past life Issues
Left hip	Female Support
Right Hip	Male Support
Base Chakra	Fear/Right to exist
Sacral Chakra Front	Feelings of Sexual/emotional nature
Sacral Chakra Back	Action of Sexual/emotional nature
Left Kidney	Fear of Females/Femininity/Creativity
Right Kidney	Fear of Males/Masculinity/Action
Solar Plexus	Powerlessness

Solar Plexus Back	Power in Action/Attitude to Health
Left Adrenal	Stress/Anxiety on Female aspect
Right Adrenal	Stress/Anxiety on Male Aspect
Left Base of Ribcage	Sadness/Female aspect blockage
Right Base of Ribcage	Force/Male aspect blockage
Extreme left rib cage point	Resentment/Sadness leading to heartache
Extreme right rib cage point	Anger leading to sadness
Liver	Anger
Gallbladder	Rage
Spleen	Resentment/Sadness leading to Heartache
Knowledge Chakra	Spiritual Knowledge/ Releasing the past
Heart Chakra	Heartache
Throat Chakra	Shame/Suppressed anger & sadness
Third Eye	Distrust/Lack of future vision
Top of Head	Guilt/Identity confusion
Right Shoulder	Lack of expression of masculinity

Left Shoulder   Lack of expression of
                                 femininity

This comprehensive list of emotional imprints will be the blueprint of the somatic reading of the emotional imprints within the human light body. The heart chakra is the energetic spiritual flame made from the energy of love that exists on all levels of our aura. The love within the heart chakra can transmute all emotions that emerge from other layers of our aura once they are fed into the heart chakra. The pattern of the dissolving of each emotional imprint is the hierarchy of emotions as to the releasing of that particular imprint on the astral plane. The progression of the releasing of the energetic imprints up through the bodies meridians usually follows the same patterns every time. This means that you can predict what emotion the client will be feeling over the coming month once you know what imprint has just been transmuted. I advise therapists that they have a responsibility to advise clients on what imprints they are transmuting, what emotional imprints they have just released and what imprints are likely to emerge within the next thirty days. They can be felt somatically within the light body. If you somatically feel anger in the liver then you know that the client will attract anger and confrontation over the following month with occasional sadness from the spleen emerging. The client will not move forward until they open the energetic channel from the liver to the heart and empty the liver energy for transmutation into the heart. Advise the client through earth connection and working with your Guides how to complete this work.

Kundalini energy or the sexual life force energy will be activated through moving the kundalini energy serpent from the base to the sacral chakra. A person's sexuality will develop if they are in Kundalini energy mode. If the person has encoded negative imprints from their past concerning their sexuality then the hurt/anger, fear or force of that traumatic imprint will also be enacted within their sexuality. As their sexuality (sacral chakra) develops with the new Kundalini energy, the stored negative emotions will likewise be channelled up through their body to the heart chakra for transmutation. This person must be advised of the awakening of these energies which means those negative emotions may be acted out in their life due to those imprints influencing the whole chakra system. This is why many spiritual teachers advise against the awakening of the Kundalini energy and call it 'the serpent.' There is nothing to be afraid when a person's Kundalini energetic channel is activated as long as you unravel the energy back into its new home in the sacral chakra. Also advise the client that their cognitions may be skewed for a time during the releasing of the trauma within the sacral chakra.

As you somatically feel another persons energy imprints within your own body you can determine the intensity of the emotion behind the imprints due to its level of burning, pulsation, fluidness, movement, waviness or hardness of the sensation. Trust your intuition. If an imprint somatically feels like a brick then the person will possibly require a herb remedy to help break through that imprint. Batch or Bush flower remedies allow with ease the dissolving of the imprints within the light body. Remember the spiritual laws. You can not complete this work alone and this concerns energetic vibrations from time to time.

A list of Spiritual Essences to help remove imprints are as follows

Heartache	Rose
Fear	Dandelion
Anxiety/Stress	Passiflora (Vogel)
Sexual Abuse	Holly
Remembering the past	Spinaflex
Protection/release with ease	Fringed Violet

The base chakra concerns our right to exist and our security. If a person's roots are out of place then you know some vibration, external or internal, knocked them from their position. This vibration will also develop emotional imprints in other parts of the light body in particular fear in kidneys and powerlessness in solar plexus.

The sacral chakra, if somatically felt as if it is stretched across the abdomen usually indicates sexual abuse. The trauma is akin to taking a hammer to a beautiful stained glass window and smashing it into little pieces. Bringing energy into the sacral chakra will knit the damaged parts back together. Soul retrieval will possibly be required but as always with retrieving lost soul fragments they will only return when the sensitising trauma is partially released and the foundation of the new personality is in place.

As we progress energetically up through the energy channels we come to the kidneys which allow us release fear. As fear paralyses the solar plexus, both organs will be transmuting their energy in tandem because fear and power are the opposite scales of the same continuum. The more fear you release, the more strengthened your solar plexus will become which will directly generate more positive cognitions. This is because our mental processing is governed by our solar plexus. As the solar plexus opens and becomes circular the energy progressing upwards will ignite the negative imprints to the sides of the solar plexus. These are the adrenal glands which hold powerlessness, anxiety and stress, the right side being the male aspect and the left side being the female aspect. At this stage of development any 'impurities of negative experiences' held within the sacral chakra will directly influence the solar plexus and thoughts of the person. The client will be in danger of projecting or attracting any sexual issues they experienced from their past.

To the extreme side of your ribcage lies force or a blockage on your masculine aspect on the right hand side and mercy or a feminine blockage on the left. When we balance force and mercy you achieve power in the solar plexus. The force imprint comes into play when the person starts to feel their own power coming into their life but more importantly will realise the limits of their power. This is the stage when we try and force issues i.e. anger, a new job, standing up for oneself for the first time etc. This usually only achieves mixed results because the channel of energy through their body is still coming from an insecure base i.e. force and not power. Success can only be guaranteed when our desires and the flow of the energy of the universe is channelled through the heart chakra. The anger imprints in the liver are very close to the force imprint and influence each other. As the left and right sides of force and mercy intermittently become clear emotional turmoil is guaranteed. Mercy is the imprint of sorrow, resentment, sadness and doubt. As the person becomes excessively masculine from force through their developing masculine side they will swing to being too weak or introspective on their left feminine side. Doubts about the therapeutic process will appear at this stage due to insecurity arising within the body. The client will ask 'Why is this happening to me. I was doing so well. I though I was moving forward. I cannot even get this process correct.' This is simply a peeling away of the layers that are necessary to uncover the real self. Situations will appear in the person's life to trigger anger and sadness such as road rage, a row with the placid postman or your dog dieing. Reality as the person used to perceive reality will be turned on its head.

The cycles of the spiritual laws will become painfully clear to the person as they will realise that the development of their life will be in unison with Spirit. The person's dog or family member may die to release further sadness but also to illuminate the cyclical nature of the operation of the world. Where there is death, there is also rebirth. The physical death will also replicate a death and rebirth within the evolving person.

While dealing with the energy around the tummy area, past life energetic bands may appear around the functioning of a particular chakra. Energetic fear in the kidneys will appear from time to time as will emotional turmoil in the sacral chakra. At this stage of development all the energy points are connected to each other and one imprint uncovers a deeper level of emotion within an associated imprint. When a person enters into significant trauma of the past, great changes develop within the solar plexus. The solar plexus usually changes positions by moving four inches upwards which causes great sensitivity in the person's emotions. Even the smallest emotional encounter will regress the person back to the sadness of their childhood. This can show itself in the person crying in floods of tears. I advise such people to protect themselves emotionally by keeping very much to themselves at this time. Watching an emotional film such as 'Lassie come home' could have you crying in tears for half an hour. This situation will only last a few days or at least less then two weeks. It only happens when a person transmutes severe trauma very quickly.

When I find a client who has attained this development within their light body I jokingly water down my comments to them by saying 'be careful now Sandra as you could become emotional or start crying as you are handed your chips in McDonalds.' Even though I laugh, I have been in that position?

Imagine a young child who suffered emotional abuse through a lack of sensitivity due to their parents parental functioning. They would have a myriad of emotional imprints to transmute such as, the base chakra experiencing the right to not exist or being acknowledged, the sacral chakra where emotional neglect would be stored, the kidneys would hold the fear to be themselves and be powerful, the solar plexus fear of life and utilising their power, the force and anger imprints on their right side will be blocked which will alternate with their sadness on the left side ending with extreme heartache in their heart chakra. Guilt will emerge as will their true voice travelling downwards from their throat to their solar plexus as shame, repressed anger and sadness leaves their throat area. Tears are also stored in the sinus and throat area.

Above the solar plexus lies a secondary chakra, the knowledge chakra. This is an extremely important chakra as this is the energetic point where a person sees through their life when the knowledge chakra starts to receive energy. When a person consults in session one with such anxiety as 'what if he leaves me….I don't know what to do, I will kill myself, becomes 'I can't believe I went out with that looser' after the energy enters the knowledge chakra. This is also the area where energetic chords to the past can be severed. Hypnotic cutting the ties that bind is a great exercise but useless when the person has energetic ties to a past relationship or situation. These chords have to be severed before forward movement can be achieved and usually they can only be severed through increasing the person's true vibration of their own essence. Achieving a purer vibration of their essence through energy healing will repel an old external energy from their life through the law of attraction. With the severing of the past also brings the cognitions of the childhood issues that suppressed their energy in the first place. They will then identify their behaviour in adult life when they slip back into those old energetic patterns. This will bring anger and the challenge to become their own adult person. Anger will give way to sadness and projected bitterness will become resentment and later heartache. Heartache will be internalised and will bring depression and a silence within the clients mind.

During an energetic treatment, when a huge amount of trauma has been processed by the heart chakra, the heart may require an energetic spark to ignite itself back to normality from transmuting such trauma. The client may cough, splutter or choke but it will be the indication of the total release of that old imprint that flowed into the heart chakra from the astral plane that was being transmuted at that time. In reality, the trauma was released and you provided an energetic spark to the heart chakra in the astral plane to re-ignite its functioning. It is always a nice story to tell the client at the end of the session.

At this stage of energetic development the person's pattern of handling of the processing of their emotions will reveal itself. Their energetic process of emotionality may alternate from anger to sadness, from fear to sadness or from fear to anger. The schizoid and oral personalities are not very good at anger while the masochist and psychopath personalities will generally show frustration and anger. It will all depend how the individual person channels their particular emotions. At times it will feel as if their life is closing in on them due to the level of trauma that will arise internally and externally as indicated through the spiritual laws. Deep depression may come over the person as if a bottomless well of sadness has been uncovered in the person's life. These feelings will alternate to fear, anger and powerlessness which will tear at the very fabric of their life. The person may start to regret that they commenced their journey as they may now be loosing friends, relationships cease or may be required to change job. They will be painfully aware of how their mind wants them to live their old way of life while their soul demands that they change to the programme of their soul's desire. The soul will always win.

The person's voice will start to break as their throat charka develops. They will be able to feel the energy from their voice going down from their throat, through their heart chakra which will be opening into their solar plexus which holds their true voice. The expression of our voice lies in our throat chakra while the power in our voice originates deep within our solar plexus. A development in a persons light body will always be reflected in the clarity and strength of their voice.

The person may experience sinus problems, chest or throat infections due to their light body expressing tears and withheld sadness. When a person has a lot of repressed sadness, this will show as fluid retention within the body. At times you can see this sadness emerge during energy treatments as a chocking sensation in their throat. Often you can somatically feel little tears in your eyes while talking to a client as you then know their light body is crying in the astral plane. Many times when you energetically connect to a client you can feel as if a fire is burning under their feet as energetic tears stream down their face. This is the mystery of fire and water which is the spiritual fire burning away the tears of sadness within the cellular body of the person.

All the time their past will be shown to them via the spiritual laws of mankind but correspondingly greater peace will reign at times within their lives. The three aspects of the maiden/youth, old hag/tyrant and mother/father energy will energetically enter their life if the client has to sexually mature.

At times the person will start to feel their liver pump with energetic anger as their cheeks will go red and feel a hot flush come over their body. They will be aware of when they hold their position as opposed to when they energetically retreat or give up. They will realise when they stop using anger to hide their fear as they will begin to trust their own individual essence. If the person is passive aggressive then spiritual progress will become stunted as the person is not operating truthfully within their own voice. This will eventually close the heart chakra as the person is still operating their life through fear as opposed to the truth of an open heart chakra. Their finances will stop flowing as the person will be creating such difficulties in their life in order to show themselves how to operate as a co-creator with God. If this person has children they may find their children become fearful and hide under a table or bed because their children are scared that their parents internalised anger will explode. A parent's fear of self expression will create fearful children.

If the person has spiritual gifts encoded within their light body then this is the time their gifts will start to emerge as energy will be entering the third eye and fear leaving their light body. The strength needed to anchor the gifts in the third eye will be the strengthening of the base of the light body. Spiritual gifts such as psychic and mediumistic development will originate from the feminine aspect but requires the masculine aspect to anchor it in the light body. The true developmental course of spiritual gifts therefore lies in meditation to merge the male and female aspects of your light body once fear is removed from the body.

Abundance will still not be flowing freely at this stage of their lives. The throat chakra which governs withholding money will develop by going into spasm as old beliefs of self worth will emerge to illuminate the opening of the throat chakra. As these beliefs are transmuted the throat chakra can eventually fully open and abundance enters the person's life. As always energy moves in cycles until you fully adjust to the complete new chakra.

A client telephoned me angrily one day as they said they lost five thousand euros in a business transaction. They were angry at the promises of self realisation yet this misfortune had entered their life. I listened quietly until they finished speaking. 'How have you created this' was my reply. They stopped and paused. The next sentence stated was the fact that they didn't listen to their gut feeling about the business venture. There is no hiding place from your true essence once you become an expression of God in your own right.

A greater joy and lightness will enter the person's life as their vibration increases. They are able to qualify people and situations because of the amount of energy they are channelling. Their lives become more peaceful, quieter but not necessarily lonely. Jesus went into the towns and preached but later left as he had his base in the countryside. He entered the madness but did not wait there. And so it is with people who find their souls expression through such therapy as astral healing.

During their dreamtime, energetic healings may be conducted on their light bodies through the workings of Morgan, their Guides or Master Guides. This will remove fear and bring the back side of their light bodies (action aspect) into alignment with the front of their light body. The person will be torn from their old sense of reality as they will trust Spirit and their spiritual gifts. They will then know the meaning of the term 'Soul with a Mind.' This is the phase in sand play therapy when the Divine of God enters the influence of life in the tray.

A person's relationship may strengthen or disintegrate. The client may attend complaining about the noise their partner makes while eating; 'He scratches his plate, he eats with his mouth full, he always has dirty hands etc' may be the issues on the surface. The truth is that your client is finding fault with the essence of their partner and is using such complaints as a projection of the ties being broken within their relationship. The person could go to dinner with someone completely new who has the exact same culinary habits but not even notice such behaviour. This relationship is unlikely to last. If such issues are raised by a client, at some stage of therapy expect the client's imagination to be taken by a completely new prospective suitor. This is the spiritual laws in action showing them the lack of expression of intimacy in their old relationship.

Energy will at first transmute the front feeling aspects of the chakras at in order to give balance to the action centres developing at a further stage.

The energies the person will be holding will show itself in the fact that they will become painfully aware if the woman is in mother energy, perpetual daughter energy, inner child, male energy or old hag energy. The man will start to realise if he is in inner child mode, wild/caveman energy, tyrant, mother energy or father energy. Conflict between the shadow, which needs expression and the ego, which is fear based will ensue as the pressure to maintain such a dysfunctional energetic stance will be brought to awareness in the everyday workings of their life. This pressure will build which eventually will be the energetic cross on the clients back i.e. the crucifixion. As the ego and shadow dig deeper for survival, the true self will start to show itself in such areas as the client taking a new boyfriend who is completely different from anyone else they previously dated or the person taking a leading role in a new play 'just by chance.' Doors will open as doors from the past will close.

Their inner rage will be the last emotion to be reached as their aura will become heavy, thick and more masculine based. This is their real inner strength emerging. This will be a difficult time for the client in that they are not yet a child but not completely a mature woman/man. I describe it as if the person has come to the edge of the cliff but needs to jump off the cliff to be supported by Spirit. The conflict being that you don't know if you will be supported in mid air unless you first jump off the cliff. You will be given the nod as to when to jump off the cliff. Wonderful opportunities will cross your path; all you have to do is say 'YES.'

The client's cognitions will be illuminated whereby the negativity or positivity of their thoughts will directly influence the functioning of their chakra system. Often I see clients who get weary of their journey which energetically swamps their heart chakra in sadness. They will realise the importance of positive reinforcement which filters back from the conscious to subconscious mind and from there to the light body. The person may be required to take a break from light work or spirituality and learn to engage with the physicality of life on the physical plane. Promoting their new work or taking a part time job may be required to reengage with humanity as will be the emergence of their 'soul mate.' Where the person would have thought of themselves as ugly, ordinary and uninspiring they will be shocked to find that they are lovable, cute, funny, warm, caring and desirable. The client will have to feel what means to have someone touch them, hug them and laugh with them just because they are who they are. At first their heart chakra may close becoming fearful of accepting love but once it opens they will find an enchanting partner who is the coinage of their dreams. They will be shocked to find a partner who will want to built, support and add to their life just because they are who they are. This will create a circuit of energy based upon giving which allows receiving to continue through the spiritual laws of mankind.

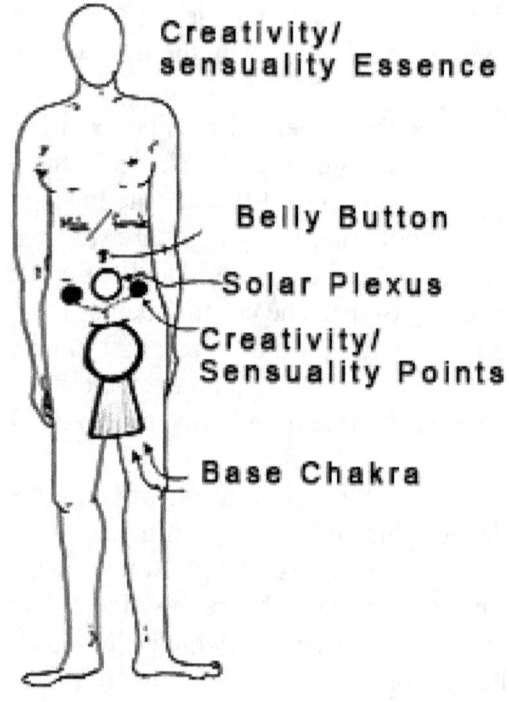

Emotional Light Body

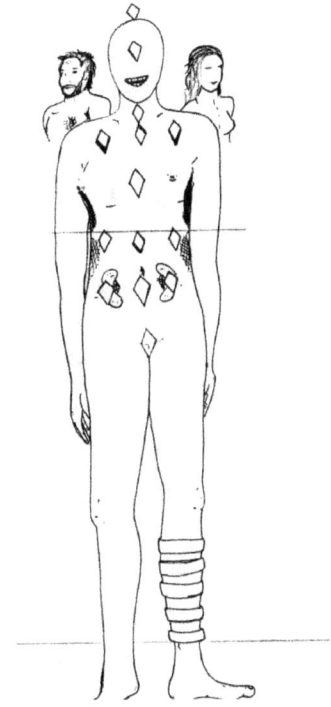

Imprints on the light body which usually transmute upwards towards the heart chakra.

Energetic connections of the emotional light body on the crown chakra

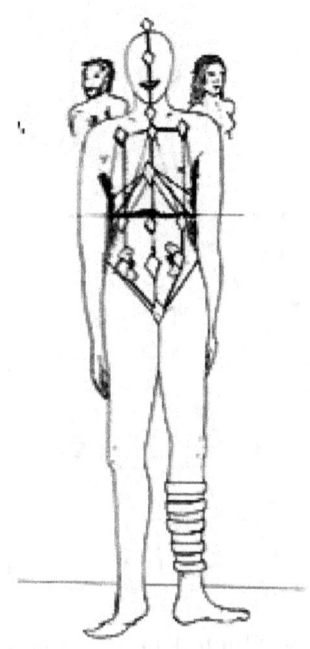

Energetic connections of the emotional light body on the crown chakra

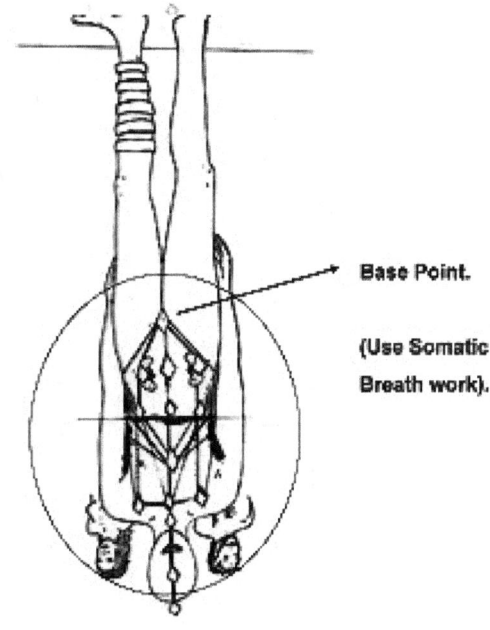

Astral Sparks.

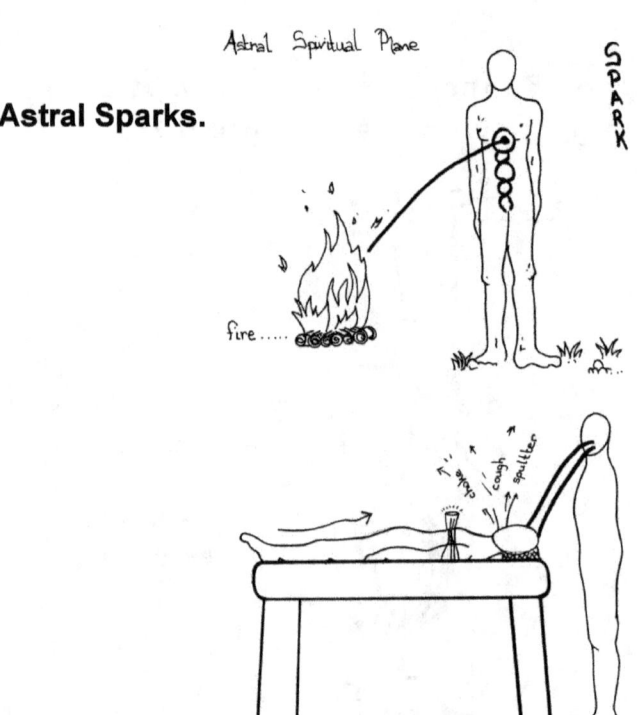

Energetic Spark Igniting the Heart Chakra.

Developing emotionality of the solar plexus

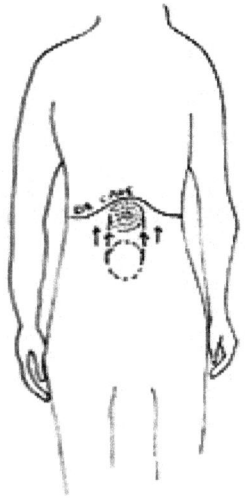

The upward movement of the solar plexus will bring forth much emotion.

Abundance is not something we acquire. It is something we tune into."

Wayne Dyer

6. The Cauldron System of Human Development.

In Celtic Shamanism, the development of the individual is concerned with the activation of three cauldrons. Cauldrons are power points that operate in a similar fashion to chakras. Each cauldron has a specific function that governs a particular aspect of our life. Their functions and position are as follows:

Name	Position	Function
Base Cauldron	Abdomen	Governs our life/position/security
Heart Cauldron	Heart Chakra	Governs our career/what we love
Crown Cauldron	Crown Chakra	Governs our knowledge

The cauldrons need to be activated which should occur during normal psychological or energetic development. When activated the functionality of the cauldrons should successfully influence life and therefore the experience of life can proceed in a balanced and harmonious fashion. A dysfunctional cauldron will compromise that function in the life of the person. If a lower cauldron is damaged then no energy can flow upwards to the higher cauldron and therefore its functionality will be severely limited. The channels of energy from Mother Earth flow upwards to nurture and connect the cauldrons so the base cauldron must flow energy upwards to the higher cauldrons.

I imagine the cauldrons as a fire. The essence of the universe is channelled trough these cauldrons and utilised in the life of the person. Remember the spiritual laws state that we look for answers on the inner world first and then secondly in the physical outer world. If a person has a damaged base cauldron then they will be ungrounded to such an extent that their essence will be floating outside their body. If you ask them to look into the energetic radar of their closed eyes you will find small white dots floating around the energy map of their closed eyes. This is the map of their aura showing their essence floating in limbo in the eye radar system of their light body. This is typical of the oral and schizoid personality whose light body and physical body are not integrated with each other. Life will be barren and unemotional if we are not connected to ourselves. A common consulting neurotic complaint of clients whose cauldrons are not physically functioning within their light body would be:

How do I know I am me?

What's the difference between me and my pet dog?

What's the meaning of life? What does it matter?

Why am I obsessive about cleaning my kitchen i.e. external projection of their essence?

This person, only after reconnection to their essence can successfully proceed with inner child work and ego strengthening. They are projecting their energy on to external objects rather then being centred within their own being. I explain to people that the light body is like a car. The chassis of the car is the cauldron system while the emotional body is akin to the body of the car that is built on the chassis. If you don't have any backbone in place there is no point in proceeding to build an emotional structure. Often I see clients who have really worked hard on their emotional health with their therapist but have not achieved the desired fruits of their labour. The therapist may have conducted brilliant inner child work, ego strengthening and cognitive behaviour modifications but because the foundation was not in place the work could not be anchored within the psyche.

A person's base cauldron is concerned with their inner strength and being living as their own person. Think of a person you know who is solid and centred, see how grounded they are in their body language and life. If a person is solid and mature, people will trust your inner security and so will be comfortable with trusting you with their affairs. Money can therefore only be attracted to inner security. We cannot attract financial security unless we are secure within our being. Success is concerned with being rather then doing.

The heart cauldron governs our career. When this cauldron opens its channels to the other cauldrons it supports our career in our life. This may mean that our line of work will gradually change; we attract a different type of clientele or employment we conducted for the last five years no longer bears results for us. Success may come from a different avenue of work or new insights will definitely appear. The knowledge cauldron provides the knowledge to complete our employment for our life's purpose.

After reconnection of the three cauldrons the person will become centred and more solid in stature. They will find that people will stop and listen to their opinion. No longer will people jump ahead of them in a queue. They will start to see through different situations and realise when they revert to 'inner child mode.' They will begin to see their relationship in reality which may bring forth the hidden inner child emotional baggage. This will illuminate such hidden emotion as anger, despair, fear and guilt which was the driving force behind their life via the law of resonance. Members of the opposite sex will start to notice them and they will react differently in a new and exciting manner. This is the foundation upon which you build the emotional security of the person.

The schizoid and oral personality will require the formation of their base cauldron as they will usually not have this cauldron functioning in their light body.

How to energise and connect the three cauldrons in your light body.

1. It is best to connect with Mother Earth via sitting on the ground for this exercise. As you sit on the ground you will begin to feel the coldness of the earth around your legs that gently rise upwards. This is your light body connecting to the energy of Mother Earth.
2. Connect to your Guides, place your protection in place and send your roots down deep into Mother Earth.
3. Place both your hands on your abdomen just below your belly button. This is the position of the base cauldron.

4. Send down your breath deep into your body to the centre of your base cauldron. Breathing deeply into the cauldron will draw the energy from Mother Earth into the cauldron and so igniting its function.
5. Repeat this breathing exercise at least once a day for up to a half hour for the next 10 days. The person will experience lower back pain due to the reopening of their energetic chords and the ignition of the base cauldron.
6. Within the ten days the energy from the earth will form a tidal wave rising up through the body. The above exercise should be repeated but breathe firstly to the base cauldron and from there up to the heart cauldron. This is the method we use to connect the two lower cauldrons. This exercise is conducted between day ten and day twenty.
7. From day twenty to day thirty the energy should be brought from the base cauldron up to the heart cauldron and, from there to the crown cauldron. This is the reconnection of the three cauldrons. The energy from the crown cauldron will then flow downwards completing the circuit.

The anchor is then in place to build the emotional body of the person. It is then important to ask the person to be aware when they energetically leave their body. They will notice at times of stress or boredom that they simply tune out or become vacant in their thinking. A friend could be talking to them but they may not be taking in what is being said to them. It is then that the person will have to be consciously aware to stay grounded and focused by pulling themselves back into their own body.

No therapy will succeed if a person does not wait in their body to release the past and so build a new future. This is one of the most common problems that clients attend my therapy if they have spent months in other forms of therapy.

Case Example: Therapy not working.

John came to see me because he felt his work with his therapist was not working as he attended monthly sessions for over a year. John felt that great work had been completed but felt their relationship had disintegrated. John was turning up late for appointments and was questioning his homework that he was completing. The big sign of conflict was that his therapist was getting frustrated with him. John knew that this was wrong and unprofessional. Worst of all was the fact that no real benefit was experienced by John in his physical life. The law of attraction was showing him that the energy of his light body was all wrong. John's car broke down requiring thousands of pounds of repairs. His heating system constantly broke indicating the lack of warmth in his own relationship. At times he described his therapist as cold, cutting and frosty. I knew that these were all issues of energetic imprints that John was carrying but first things first – John was not in his energetic body.

John had little or no self esteem. He disliked himself and constantly gave his power away. Success always eluded John in that he had bad luck financially. His could daydream his life away and was running out of options with regards his work.

I explained to John the cauldron system of energetic development and advised John to attend in four weeks. John was to utilise stag energy to compliment Earth energy.

Session two.

John attended and was astonished to find the effects of the energy entering his body. He experienced lower back pain and felt the energetic chords open up through his body. After day seven the energy could not be contained in the base cauldron and had made its way up to the heart cauldron. After day fifteen, the energy entered and opened the heart cauldron. The crown cauldron was ignited within twenty days of commencing this energetic work. John began to settle in his life. He started to see patterns develop in his life for the first time. One such pattern was the way he was bullied by other people. This was caused by the fact that John was not present in his body so was therefore thought of being a pushover by other people. John was now being grounded and was given the power to take responsibility for his life. John continued his journey building his emotional intelligence after his energetic structure was in place.

Case Study: How do I know I am not my pet dog?

Amy came to see me because she had tried traditional psychotherapy and cognitive behaviour therapy but had only found a moderate decrease in her anxiety. Amy talked for one hour but nothing significant was emerging to indicate the anxiety in her life. At last Amy said 'Gerry, I think I am mad. I thought yesterday how do I know I am me rather then my pet dog. I mean what's the difference or what does it matter?

It was with this statement that I knew that Amy's energetic body and physical body were disconnected. This explained how the work completed on Amy by other therapists was the correct work but at the wrong time. Therapy would only be successful if Amy's essence came back into her body and later rebuild her emotional body.

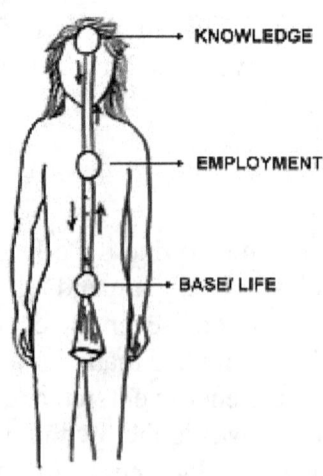

Druid Caluldron
System of Develpment

Astral Healing
The Cauldron System

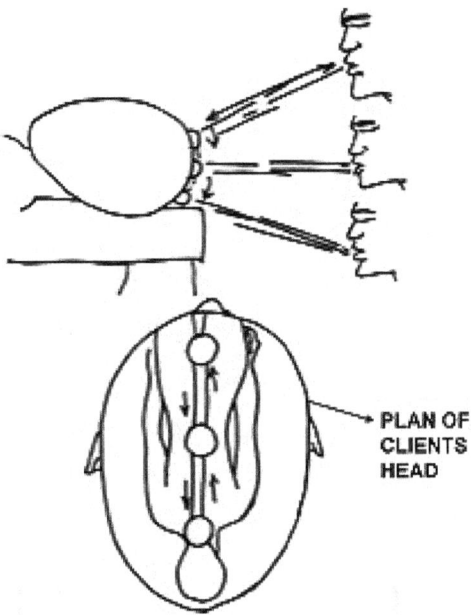

PLAN OF CLIENTS HEAD

"A tree growing out of the ground is as wonderful today as it ever was. It does not need to adopt new and startling methods."

Robert Henri

7. The Tree of Life Human Energetic System.

The Tree of Life Human energetic system, represented by the Sephirotic tree, is esoteric wisdom that has roots in ancient Jewish mysticism. The central work originates from the Cabbala, or more precisely, the book of splendour (Zohar). Cabbala itself is a Hebrew word meaning oral tradition which explains that much of the teaching of Cabbala was taught through the spoken word. I feel that this concept could be expanded to encompass the fact that healing, psychotherapy and the concept of the tree of life is best learned through the direct experience of life itself. Thus, even by reading this book you will realise that there is a unique personal self development course within this body of work. That course will be experienced through meeting your postman, going shopping and interacting with the world in general. The sooner you realise that 'you are a God' within your own right the better. This mystical manifestation between our Creator, the universe and all of us existing as one is adequately expressed through the science that is the Tree of Life. This is the origination of the words 'God created man in his own image.'

The Cabbalistic tradition believes that Adam was the first to receive this body of knowledge from God. The loss of this knowledge can be described as the descent of man into darkness. Darkness, in reality is ignorance of truth and light. When Adam and Eve were in the Garden of Eden, the Serpent came and presented the choice to eat the fruit from the tree of knowledge of good and evil. The serpent represents matter or our physical life here on earth. It is also interesting to know that Kundalini energy or the human sexual energy is sometimes called serpent energy. This is not to be confused with many religious undertones that sexuality is bad or evil but simply the fact that an awakening of our sexual energy will bring forth any impurities lodged within the lower self of our light body. We have choices presented to us. Those choices, the ones that represent a descent into the depths of our humanness will result in pain, suffering and a disconnection from the very nature of our being – God. But look closely and see that help is at hand. This help comes in the form of another tree – The tree of Life. The tree of life is the system of esoteric knowledge that can deliver us to the realisation that we are one with God and remove ignorance that is burdening mankind.

It is now easy to see that meditation, contemplation and inner study of the very fabric of our life is the ultimate learning course to self actalise. Any learned knowledge will take second stage to the fact that you will energetically develop in accordance within the time frame of your own energy and the effort your attribute to transmuting your own emotional imprints. The transmuting of negative energy within the ten sephiroth, or energy points will lead to the merging of your nature with the true nature of God. The energising of these energetic points which can be felt akin to the chakra system in our energy field is what will convince you of your true nature. The object of transforming your tree of life is the purpose of creating heaven on earth.

The top three sephiroth or energy points represents the part of us that is in heaven – the crown, emanation, which is divided into two columns representing our male and female aspect. On the left we have wisdom and on the right we have understanding. One aspect is useless without the other therefore a balance will be required to bring equilibrium to the person's life. How will this balance be achieved? By having a row with the postman, telling your friend that you feel their friendship is based upon functionality rather then mutual respect or realising that you have a marriage in name only. Yes, the Divine Spiritual Laws will not let you off the hook with regards self actualising. The centre of the chest represents the sephiroth 'Knowledge.' This is not always represented in all presentations of the tree of life knowledge. I know from working with people that a great change occurs within a person's cognitions when this area is energised within their light body. This sephiroth also corresponds with the knowledge chakra, the secondary chakra positioned between the heart and solar plexus. This makes sense because what destroys relationships is one persons increasing vibration moving adequately away from the other persons vibration. A row over who 'scratched their plate at dinner' is not about our table manners. Sadness is usually released with energising the knowledge sephiroth as past regrets, lost time of aspects of our lives and fear at having to change direction gets intertwined in the confusion of our new life.

On either side of the lower ribcage, we find the balancing of our power i.e. the solar plexus. On the right (liver) we find 'strength/force while on the left (spleen) we find mercy/ sadness. If we balance force and mercy we get balanced power. The energetic line linking force and mercy is 'the line of Karma.' This can be felt within each light body system which also represents the merging of our identity (base cauldron) with our emotions (heart cauldron) of Celtic shamanic tradition. In the tree of life, the solar plexus is represented by beauty. It is a beautiful way of presenting the centeredness of our essence with beauty in all our being.

We can see how force and anger is a male energy in essence while resentment and bitterness is a female based energy. The contra expression of these emotions by the opposite sex is the anima/animus complex being emotionally expressed by the hidden shadow aspect of the man or woman.

At the hips we find Glory on the right and victory on the left. There is no point having glory without victory in our life especially when the lower aspect to the tree corresponds to our humanness on earth. The balancing of these aspects will provide the sephiroth 'foundation' to our life. We need to be solid and strong in who and what we are in our life. This culminates in the 'kingdom' (of God) sephiroth manifesting on earth through our light body and life. The kingdom sephiroths is positioned in our left leg/foot while the foundation is positioned at the genitals or base chakra point.

The tree of life system emerges on the crown chakra for energetic development. It sometimes emerges along with the emotional light body on the crown but as can be seen, similarities exist between each system.

The following is the psychological and energetic understanding of the true nature of our soul – the tree of life.

Sephiroths	Position	Function
Crown	Crown Chakra	Emanation/potential
Wisdom	Left shoulder	Duality/opposites
Understanding	Right Shoulder	Womb of Becoming
Knowledge	Heart Chakra	Moving Forward
Mercy	Spleen	Unconditional kindness
Force	Liver	Anger
Beauty	Solar Plexus	Power
Victory	Left Hip	Progress
Glory	Right Hip	Becoming/Manifesting
Foundation	Genitals	Base
Kingdom	Existence	Left Foot

The Tree of Life

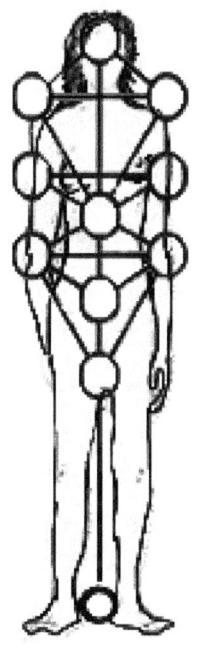

"There is no sexuality that is greater or lesser than another."

Jasmine Guy

8. The Creation of Human Essence and Human Sexuality.

The most common problem I find with people attending my therapeutic practise is that the person's essence is suppressed within their psyche. Personality refers to the development of self in relation to this lifetime whereas individuality refers to the essence of the person that lies behind the personality. Individuality resides within the person and is part of the inner being of the person that is unchanging from lifetime to lifetime. Our individuality can be considered to be that part of us that is God and knows its Divine nature. It is deeper then the concept of the archetypical 'self' in that individuality combines the uniqueness of the person with the oneness with God. The trouble with life on earth is that our human development and its association with the personality hinder the connection to the riches of our individuality.

The term I refer to as essence, transcends the concept of male and female sexuality. The degree of balance within our essence in accordance to our individuality is the key to what life is all about. We are required to ask of ourselves 'What type of Man/ Woman I AM. (I AM being God in its expression within us). The key to the expression of our life is that we find our true essence that lies within our inner being. Our inner world is concerned with our true thoughts and feelings about ourselves and our position in the world. This inner belief controls our life that is our light body within the astral plane. We may become trapped by negative imprints and conditioning that filter through to our lives in the physical plane. Through the spiritual laws of mankind we are not in control of our lives but simply are a pawn to our negative emotions until such time as we develop our essence and find our individuality. In reality, we are Gods in our own right. For instance, how can a person achieve abundance if they believe deep within their heart that they are worthless through low self esteem?

The flow of the energy from Spirit is abundant. Spirit never asks what you are going to do with this energy. It just gives spiritual energy unceasingly. The energy flows through us, picks up the software programme from within our self concept in the astral plane and launches that programme into our physical world on Earth. Our self concept can change. It is fluid. The trick is to merge our inner (astral plane or essence) and outer world (physical life on Earth) by attaining congruence of the unification of our essence into our psyche.

Dissociation from a persons own essence can be caused by the trauma of becoming a spirit in a human body in other words nature, or our upbringing i.e. nurturing. There is the problem of trauma stopping the evolution or flow of energy within our light body. This usually results in a situation where the person's essence or light body is energetically left behind in some other time and space. Inner child work or soul retrieval is necessary to take back those lost soul fragments. This person will be experiencing a lot of emotional pain in their life because the flow of energy from the universe will be utilised by their light body but not through their physical body due to dissociation of physical and light body. We are energetic beings in a physical body and we live in a physical world. The dissociation will allow no success into the heart or throat charka therefore all our actions will be tainted with failure. As per the five energetic personalities, the first two personality types (oral and schizoid) experienced this problem acutely as their early trauma caused dissociation before the solar plexus was formed by age fourteen. The solar plexus governs power and our career; therefore these aspects are usually not developed to maturity in these personality subtypes. As the bottom two chakras are formed by age six and are concerned with our emotional life, dissociation before this age results in a bumpy life of failure and depression on earth.

Our essence is our core inner being that is unique to us. It can be hard or soft. It can be gentle or gruff. It can be primarily masculine or feminine and is closely related to the mask of the anima/ animus complex. Our concern should be to achieve the expression of our own individual essence which will allow us attract a similar essence in our relationships that will be a suitable match for us. This will be the spiritual laws in action in our life. It is not the case to bring the harsh man in touch with his female side or to show the gruff female how to act like a lady but simply a strengthening of the ego to allow the inner being merge with the outer personality. This is achieved through Earth connection which will rebalance the psyche.

Homosexuality should be viewed in the same fashion in that the person's individual essence ideally should match their outer world. I describe this concept to homosexuals with regards to viewing their sexual gender and then ask them 'are you usually the male or the female within your relationships.' I then ask them to describe the essence of their past relationships. This is to build a pattern of their history of the emitting of their energy to date to view it with regards the spiritual laws of mankind. If you are the female homosexual essence, there is no point in attracting in the same kind of similar essence within your relationships. There is no point in bringing snow to the North Pole.

When we decide to incarnate for a particular lifetime, we have choices to make with regards the education of the emergence of our essence. If we need to learn humility we can decide to be born in a poor third world country or we can achieve this task by agreeing with our brother that he becomes brain dead in a car accident at age thirty. If we need to learn responsibility with regards finances then we can decide to be born into a wealthy generational family with old money or decide to be born into an unemployed, unskilled and uneducated family. The choices are endless with regards to the influences of our essence.

The effects of your essence being dormant within your light body are as follows:

1. Will have a damaged inner child.
2. Will have a poor self concept.
3. Will have a weak presence and will not be able to hold their energetic space.
4. Will possess bad luck i.e. be at the wrong place at the wrong time.
5. Will be unsuccessful in the expression of their sexuality.
6. Will not get the equivalent return in energy terms from a project in relation to the results they deserve.
7. Will have no central thought pattern as to who they are i.e. can be a different person to suit the particular situation.

8. Can be influenced easily.
9. Can have displaced thinking patterns i.e. thoughts such as 'how do I know I am me and not my pet dog' will cross their mind.
10. They will not be in control of their life due to the conflicting energies emanating from their light body. They can possess many other people's energy and so will not have a true bearing on their own individual energy.
11. The person may be inarticulate in that their relationships may be poor or non existent. They may be controlling or manipulative to others under the guise of self righteousness.

People not in their own essence will have many disappointments in life. They can marry a partner that matches the harsh energy imposed on their weak self if their dissociation occurred in childhood. A man in energy terms can marry their father. If the child felt unsafe to be themselves with their father's brash personality then the adult child is likely to marry a brash bully of a woman. This couple will have a parent /child relationship.

Abundance flows from the merging of the inner and outer self resulting in the heart and throat chakra being anchored in your body. As this is impossible to achieve for the dissociated person, they will have financial problems. For a time they will be successful at work but eventually their lack of foundation will be unearthed as they progress up the corporate ladder. This is the Peter Principle at work. This states that a person rises to a position in which they will be unable to fulfil the required task. At first everything will go fine for the person but sooner or later they will realise that success stems from an energetic bank account on the astral plane. If that bank account is empty and they attempt to cash a cheque in the physical world, they will find there is only one outcome – bankruptcy. I know of many young therapists who spend large amounts of money advertising their new practise only to find that many appointments end up as cancellations. Success lies within as they are finding that their own fear to stand on their own feet is blocking their financial rewards.

Being energetically vacant from your body will result in such occurrences as people invading your space or jumping ahead of you in a queue. They may find that others talk over them when they attempt to express themselves as their voice does not carry any depth or weight. At times, they may overcompensate by leaning forward and attacking another person's space. This will be short-lived as they eventually realise that on some level they are inadequate and fade into the background.

Energy vampires are people who crave other people's energy. They expand their auras to engulf the whole room sucking energy from every person within the room. It is common to find that the person is either quiet insecure and was never seen as a child by their parents or has a contract in place with a dark entity to rob others of their energetic power. The intent behind their energy projections as an adult is 'please see me now; I have a right to be seen at last.' In a self development group this person will try and hold the limelight as their energy will invade the energy of all other participants. Constant protection is needed to defend chords or energetic hooks emerging from this person not to mention the interference of the work of the group. Your belief in your own protection is vital dealing with such forces.

Think of an animal in the jungle. Imagine how it lives i.e. the food it eats and the animals that pray on it. See the defence mechanisms that it has adapted over the centuries in order to survive or compensate for its inadequacies in being weak, powerless or defenceless. And so it is with us. We live in our world in accordance to how we can best achieve our desired results depending upon our own individual psychology. The best result is when you merge the inner and out worlds to allow life become into alignment. You will then be in the flow of life.

A person not in their essence tends to look upon the world through rose tinted glass's which in other words is to tell white lies. These white lies are not malicious but are a way of avoiding the truth. Most people live their lives as a lie but the best lies are the ones we tell ourselves. The aim of therapy is to set a person free by being true to themselves. Psychoanalysis over an extended period runs the risk of paralysing the person into inaction. The individual needs to realise that regaining their essence is one task while rebuilding their life is another. This is the rebalancing of the self and the emergence of a strong masculine and feminine self from the inner to outer world.

Children are like sponges absorbing the atmosphere of their environment. The chakras have no protective cover until age seven therefore no filter exists to protect the child from absorbing external negative vibrations.

> Think of a person that irritates you…..That gets on your nerves?
>
> If that person was an animal, what animal would they be?
>
> Describe the characteristics of that animal…..they would be…….?
>
> Now blank your mind.
> I am going to describe someone from your youth/childhood,
> They would be……..(repeat the characteristics as from above).
>
> Who has just popped into your mind?

More then likely it is a significant person that was in your life from your younger years. Every time you come into contact with another person carrying the same energy as that person from your past, you will go into what I call 'little child mode.' Feel like a temper tantrum now? Be my guest but this time as you rage give yourself permission to feel from your younger self. If you breathe deeply down into your sacral chakra you may be able to bring that stored emotion up to your heart charka and release it forever from your psyche. With projections of our energy Whitmont in his book, 'The Symbolic Quest' describes it as 'every hook needs a hanger.' The hook is the energy from the other person that hangs onto the emotionality of what experiences we have stored within the astral plane. What personality faults we usually describe in others is the same energetic faults we contain within our own psyche. This usually stems from our energetic development in childhood.

Past life issues of a dramatic nature that are reincarnated into the present life is not that common e.g. a man living his current life from the energetic viewpoint of a previous reincarnated female life. While all patterns in existence in our current life were previously experienced in a past life those patterns will cease once you have learned a sense of self from the lessons of the experience. However, some people have past life issues that have to be experienced with traumas that occur in their present incarnation on Earth. There is a reason behind this emergence in that their soul has now decided to deal with those past issues in the present lifetime. With the transmutation of this particular trauma the person's spiritual gifts can become anchored in their light body with the emergence of their individuality. The removal of the trauma will mean that the spiritual gifts learned in that previous life will emerge in the current lifetime. A sign of past life trauma is when the clients presenting neurosis is disproportionate to the effects of their experienced trauma. Their case history in other words will be out of sync as per their symptomology. As it more accurate to view people as essence rather then either male or female, the past life trauma could be related to a female lifetime while their present incarnation could be experienced as male. In this instance, the trauma of the past female incarnation would have to be healed, their present life sexual essence found and developed and then their masculinity/femininity rebalanced. This would be a long road to travel in order to spiritually progress but certainly the person would know about individual essences.

Before a person's essence can be developed you must ensure that no soul retrieval is necessary. If there is no fragmentation of the soul then you proceed to build the person via energetic breath work of the cauldron system of development. The base chakra will also develop, healing trauma before age one and issues relating to survival and identity. The sacral chakra will then develop healing life's experiences up to age six and emerging the sensual, sexual and emotional aspect of the individual. The development of the light body involves energy flowing up the front (emotional) aspect of the body over the first few months of therapy. This will later progress to opening the back (action aspect) chakras and channels of the body. Therapy through energy healing can be one step forward and two steps backwards at times as this process will take months to achieve. The sacral chakra emerging to a new deeper level of maturity may need to transmute a corresponding level of sexual trauma. This usually uncovers fear in the kidneys, powerlessness in the solar plexus, anger and sadness in the liver and spleen followed by heartache in the heart chakra. Everything is emotionally connected even for seemingly one traumatic experience from your past.

Intimacy should be spelt 'into-me-see.' To be able to freely express yourself in your own essence means that you are comfortable in your own skin. Being in your own skin involves liking yourself. You may have a flabby tummy, a big bum or a little less hair on your head but how does that concern essence. Your perception of yourself may not reflect the reality of your essence. Looking inwards usually involves being self conscious and self critical through the illusion of the lower self. The internal focus of the conscious mind will always paralyse us into inaction. After mankind lived for thousands of years in the forest we naturally developed a fear of change as 'eating the new red berries that looks delicious' could be fatal. Too much rumination and we naturally revert back to our history as a protective mechanism. Looking outwards knowing that we are all one or that it's alright not to be at one with yourself will eventually be acceptable. You stop judging and accept your position that you have attained on your souls journey. This means that you stop putting down negative karmic imprints that will require transmutation in the future. You are becoming free from the chains of the emotions of this world.

If the man is to be the male of the relationship it means that he has to be more then the proverbial caveman. He will be successful at nurturing, providing and protecting his family. He will give space for the woman to be the cavewoman. This will mean that she will control the feminine aspects of the home and will not be required to conduct masculine chores/tasks within the relationship. Respect will be given for each others function and individuality. They will support and give to each other with generosity so that they ask what they can contribute to each other and their family. This is the driving force that underlines the relationship. Insecurity is banished in that no entrenched positions exist and the 'grabbing' mentality of a closed heart is non existent. One way to spot a closed heart chakra is to be aware of how often a person utilises the words 'no but…' during a conversation. In reality the person is not accepting what you are saying to them in that they cannot receive your higher vibration into their heart. Their heart is closed and they are afraid to open communication with you in a heart felt manner so they block off the receiving of the vibration of your energy. This person is trapped, lonely, scared and will definitely push people away from them. They cannot receive or express love. They will withhold intimacy from their marriage.

Examining a person's clothes and expressions can illuminate ones essence. Some people do 'walk their talk' in that their colours and style of clothing is a suitable match to their essence. They will be natural with everyone and will not try to impress others with their showmanship of their ego. They will be relaxed and will emanate a glow that will be warm, gracious and loving. A person who is not in their essence can walk funny, have airs and graces, be demanding and will project their insecurity through projections of anger, backbiting or levelling. Nothing will ever be good enough for them. All you have to do is look at their friends and they will reflect back the same ethos of dysfunction in their psyche. People who are not in their essence will look heavy and sigh quiet a lot. The weight of their emotional baggage will be uncomfortable to bear in their dissociate state. Their shoulders may be hunched from carrying the weight of the world on their shoulders. They may over compensate their sexuality by overdressing for occasions e.g. a female student may wear an elaborate silk evening dress to an evening class. Just sit back and let the men come and chat her up. As like attracts like, water will find its own level. The guys that wait around will the ones needing the greatest amount of therapy.

The old saying 'tell me your friends and I will tell you who you are' is true. The masculine female will be attracted to homosexual 'males.' This is the cross reference of the insecure female essence expressing their sexual essence with males who will not be sexually attracted to her. She will be both astonished and captivated by her friends who possess in essence the feminine qualities that she craves. The beauty about possessing such friends is that her sexuality will not be on show in having to be intimate with her 'male' friends.

If the male is predominately feminine, he will probably attract a more masculine partner in his relationships. This will mean that both parties will be living in their head as their sacral chakra will not be connected to their heart chakra. This relationship will work well as long as the woman wears the trousers and the man cleans the dishes. There is nothing wrong with that energetic arrangement but, if one party decides to develop themselves through therapy then the relationship will become crowded. Energetically the relationship will consist of two men or two women. The developing partner's essence will become suffocated by the competing essence of their dysfunctional partner. As a result of the developing partner's true essence being caged for so long due to fear and self love issues, conflict will definitely ensue. The relationship is doomed energetically unless the new partner decides to live a lonely crowded life or the other partner enters therapy. The facts are that both parties may come together after therapy and agree that they should separate but as friends. Even if one partner enters therapy and decides to leave the relationship, I advise them not to rush matters. You cannot successfully leave a relationship unless you have fully anchored your true essence and have no issues with your old partner. They must develop a friendship and not be a former lover. The chords of the relationship and the energy of the parent from their childhood who originated the energy of their marriage needs to destroyed. This will probably take a time frame of one to two years. It will be difficult for the developing person to remain in the marriage but is necessary.

A weak male may channel his sexuality into porn or prostitutes. His buying of the expression of his sexuality will mask his insecurity and provide him with a false sense of dominance. The female may channel her sexuality into fantasy or work. If sexual relations break down in her relationship it may further entrance her position back to what she knows best i.e. the expression of her masculine essence. The defence mechanism that both parties will justify to themselves is that he will feel hard done by marrying an uncaring hard masculine female which gives emotional justification to his porn. The female distrusts her partner's masculinity which mirrors her distrust of her own femininity. This alienates her from her partner in that they are in competition with each other and she is now a mother to a male teenager. No woman desires to be intimate with a minor. Remember a woman makes love for closeness while a man makes love for acceptance. The developing male will have to fight for the expression of his masculinity with his 'male' wife.

To bridge the gap in the relationship both parties need to stop pointing the finger at the other and start taking responsibility for their own essence. This involves open and honest communication. Listening to each other involves letting the words sink in and be felt by the other listener so an emotional connection is established. As the couple examines their lives, frustrations will emerge that were present all along but were never previously communicated. Issues such as 'Jane' having to remember to put out the rubbish bin on a Tuesday night at 11.30pm will surface. The issue is not 'who put out the bin' but rather that 'Tarzan' didn't take responsibility for his caveman activity. There is a big difference in saying 'Darling, the bin men are coming to collect the bin in the morning' rather then 'I bet you forgot to put out the bin just like last week.' The first statement is coming from a support and loving essence while the second statement is not a statement but an energetic attack.

If Tarzan's male side starts to develop he will be amazed to find that he will start to attract the admiration of women. Where he previously got nervous around women he now finds that he is emitting a different signal that is getting attention. This is the time that the opposite sex will show the person their sexuality. It is a fun time in the development of the person with the full promise that youth can bring. If 'Jane' is not developing her sexuality and feminine essence then she stands the risk of loosing her sexual partner because she has failed to raise her corresponding sexual vibration. The male needs to become comfortable in taking the lead sexually, especially with a masculine essence partner. His partner needs to develop her femminity by investing in her lingerie or the sensual aspects of sexual expression. This is what both parties truly desire. There can naturally be an energetic standoff in that bother parties do not trust their partner's core essence. The woman feels if she reverts to being the woman, who will earn the money or pay the bills on time. The man feels I am too crowded to be a man and I am afraid of my partner's angry male aspect. Someone will have to be the hero and learn to trust their partner if the relationship is to survive.

Both parties need to realise that they are not competing for the same energy in the relationship. They must learn how to be themselves in order to grow. Each partner will be rewarded with the wonderment of the inner feeling of their own essence. It is then that they will find the inner strength to communicate their requirements and offer support to their developing partner. This is the true meaning of the open heart chakra which gives with love. The couple form a reciprocal energetic bond of giving that is unceasing.

Once a person starts recalibrating their essence they will notice that its results will be evident for all to see. Their clothes may change in terms of style and colours. Their body language will become more confident. They will find that the world will start to revolve around them rather then the way they previously ran around everyone else like a headless chicken. The male may find that he now gives simple 'yes or no' answers where previously the answer would involve an apology and a gestalt discussion of the proceedings for five minutes. He will become more concise in his body language and movement. He may stop wearing his prise possession – his designer pink shirt. Ordinary blue/black/navy will be the order of the day with little jewellery, boring plain shoes and understated accessories is what I advise men to wear at this stage of their development. This helps anchor the internal switch of their emerging masculinity in the physical world. They can of course go back to wearing the colour pink after they have found their essence but that may be unlikely due to the fact that they are starting to enjoy their new masculine blue/black essence.

The male will find that tensions will emerge with their mother or mother figure. Where previously he may have communicated with his mother or mother figure once a day, he will find that the conversations will become shorter in duration and less frequent. He will be detaching himself energetically from being his mother's son/husband to being his own man in his own essence who has a mother. I sometimes ask a man 'if making love to a woman while drunk, would thoughts of their previous ……girlfriends…or mother…enter their mind? If they respond yes, it means that an energetic chord exists to their mother and they have a mother/son relationship with their mother and therefore all women. They will not be an adult male in their own right but the eternal archetypical youth/son figure.

This tension may manifest itself as an argument over something very silly such as why were you ten minutes late for dinner and you didn't even ring me? This is the reality of the pain of the chords disintegrating between mother and husband (I mean son of course). His mother's psychology will be evident for him to see in that her insecurity will be base upon the premise that 'I only deserve love if I am useful to you.' It probably won't have dawned on his Mother that she is loved for who she is rather then the function she provides. His mother will have to then look at her own relationship with her essence but her diagnosis will not be channelled in the direction of her son. He is becoming his own man so he will not be privy to this information any longer from his Mother as communication will practically cease for a time. This is the destruction of the Oedipus complex in action.

The female will change her relationship with her parents in a similar fashion. She may have arguments with her parents. Her hobbies may change. She may look upon her father differently. She may realise that he was never there when she was young or that his brooding is simply insecurity and lack of expression rather then the power of the masculine. Her shopping habits will change in that she will start to make decisions in terms of what food is for dinner and will invest in her wardrobe to illuminate her sexuality. She will start to support rather then challenge her husband in his life which will be evident in her newfound choice of language.

The energetic development from being a male child to adult male in relation to his mother is as follows:

> Mother figure and male baby
>
> Mother figure to male child
>
> Mother figure to young male child
>
> Mother figure to male adolescent
>
> Mother figure to male teenager
>
> Mother figure to male teenager with girlfriends
>
> Mother figure to young male adult with intimate girlfriends
>
> Mother figure to adult male with wife
>
> Mother figure to adult male with wife and children.

Unless a male child develops his relationship with his mother in this fashion he will find that he will become the eternal child to all females. No female wants to go to bed with a child therefore his sexual conquests will be few and far between. As the maternal complex is designed to be continually destroyed by the mother being pushed aside, the vacuum must be filled by another energetic archetype. That archetype is the paternal or male complex.

Sadness will emerge for the developing person. The female may realise that she always rejected men before their relationship entered the intimacy stage or that she rejected them before they had a chance to reject her. This will uncover the way she was treated as a child and the way fear and rejection of her essence was subconsciously felt by her as a developing child. There is no way a person will allow them be rejected a second time so the trick is to get there first. The conflict exists in that to feel with her heart is to surrender to her inner hurt whereas to push a partner away is to remain trapped in this lonely isolated state. The woman may possess gay male friends to hide her secret that she is deeply insecure about her sexuality. She deludes herself by the fact that her intimate expression is under no threat with her gay friends but still has 'male' friendships. She may describe herself as being flirty and other men craving her attention but cannot fathom why that is so. Yet a deep relationship eludes her because she is 'the maiden' in Jungian energetic terms. She goes to the ball, dances all night but does not kiss. You can look but not touch. The issue is whether she wants to mature and become the adult female in her own expression. This involves maturing her energetic age up to her chronological age. This involves healing her inner child and finding the true expression of her essence. It is only then that through the law of attraction she will attract a mature male in his own essence.

Both energetically damaged people can be healed through rebalancing of their energies through astral trance healing of their light body. The children of a developing person will reflect the internal transformation of their parent. The parents who previously were weak and were a pushover will find that their children will at first become frustrated. This is due to the fact that they can no longer bully the parent and perceive their loss of position with regards their diminished boundary. After the initial shock with their developing parent, the children will become calmer and secure. This will be reflected in the games the children play in that they will express their essence easily and may cease outbursts of frustration and anger. They will sense the firm boundary of their father and feel his inner strength protecting their developing self. The way the child's playtime will change will reflect this internal security developing within the psyche of the child. It can possibly show itself where previously they put clothes/makeup on their father they now want to play football or wrestle on the ground with their dad. They will confide their problems more easily with their dad and want to be with him going to the shops etc. This is the time where a balance needs to be struck in the developing children. The emerging Dad needs to nurture both male and female aspects in their children. The emerging security of the masculine side of the child must not be sacrificed at the expense of the child's creative female side. The young child needs to feel supported in his music talents, acting/ drama skills or interest in cooking rather then being coerced into traditional masculine activities of football and sports. This is the real task of the dad to promote and nurture the essence of their child in letting their child be their own child.

The female child needs to realise that she can be powerful in a feminine manner and to see that her mother nurtures her femininity. To be a woman means to value your inner beauty by physical action in the real world. It also means that her partner allow her exist as the female and that her position is not being undermined by her partner. If a man complains or withholds money from his wife, is he not insecure in himself to let his partner be herself? The games we play with our loved ones are endless.

If no intimacy exists between husband and wife the danger exists that the individuals will project their own sensual needs onto the opposite sex child. The parent can become seductive or the child may require recognition from their opposite sex parent due to the same sex parent rejecting their own natural sexual expression. This burden is too much for any child to carry and will result in conflict such as the masochist or psychopathic personality.

As people develop over the months, they become sensitive to the laws of resonance, reflection and cause and effect in their life. These are but nudges along their sacred path that illuminate the energies they are processing and to where their soul's energy is progressing. They can be helped by Earth energies such as Morgan, Cow or Bull energies, Stag for development and Oak for strength. It can be desirable for the person to feel the presence of their Guide or Angel beside them in times of insecurity.

As the person matures they will attract into their life different experiences to challenge them in their growth process. By experiences I mean vibrations that will test them to be more mature, to stand up for themselves in order that they hold their ground. At this stage the person will be so accustomed to reading external energy that they will intuit such events in real time. For instance, at the check out in a department store the sales clerk has doubled the price of the socks by accident which has presented the opportunity to refuse the purchase. Previously they would have remained silent in order for a quiet life. It is then the person knows that the flow of life is about energy and nothing to do with our conditioning as to what we describe as reality.

What will comprehensively show the person that they are arriving as an adult is the attraction of three different energies. Remember energies are not gender specific but for clarity purposes I categorise the three energies into male and female expressions.

For the Developing Male	**For the Developing Female**
The Old Hag	The Tyrant
The Mother	The Father
The Maiden	The Youth

The developing person will attract in experiences of the following three energies as per Jungian psychology.

The Old Hag/The Tyrant.

The old Hag/Tyrant is the third essence of energy within each person. The other two essences are the innocent young child and a sexually mature confident adult. This energy is vicious, cutting, demanding and venomous. They take no prisoners and will back down from nothing. Sorry is a word they do not understand. They suit themselves and once they sense fear they focus immediately on the kill. The purpose of these energies is to ask you 'are you sure you are mature and able for the big bad world out there? These energies will illuminate any fear within your light body which is held within the kidneys and base chakra. As the Old Hag is also associated with Morgan (Crow energy), which has an independent consciousness as an Earth energy, she can come and treat your light body after energetic fear has been triggered.

As the old Hag is within every woman, this expression of energy will definitely be attracted into the person's life if they had a strong, curt, masculine mother. The purpose of the attraction is to get the developing person to stand up for themselves against the backdrop of their childhood fear of this energy. If they energetically retreat backwards and crumble against this energy, then the person will literally be annihilated.

For the developing male, if he is to be sexually in his own power he needs to have any fear removed from his psyche to the fact of taking his woman and having a good night of passion. This description is a bit crude but facts are facts. You will not be a good lover reliving a fearful energetic imprint stemming from your mother or primary school teacher. What's more you have little control over when those imprints will kick in and spoil the expression of your essence. That is the reason why male porn stars are so difficult to find. Psychosexual neurosis is very common and directly affects male performance. With men and these matters there is no hiding place. At least that's what I have been told!

The old Hag/Tyrant energy will bring forth anger. He/she will illuminate depression and heartache from the imprints of the developing person's childhood as per the hierarchy of emotions. Lastly, rage will emerge as the person tries to recalibrate their inner power. The person will only find a greater sense of self after the release of the tears of their sadness. The old Hag/Tyrant may show its face a number of times to the person over the months of therapy but will finally be appeased from the developing persons energy field when they stand up to both this internal and external energy and becomes an adult.

The Maiden/ The Youth.

As per Jungian psychology, the maiden is the young carefree girl, not a woman but yet not a child. A teenager is more apt to describe the psyche of this femme fatale. She will epitomise the 'look but don't touch' aspect of human sexuality. She is the young woman in a mini skirt, stilettos, black sequence top, bright red lipstick and adorned in jewellery. She knows how to get attention and adores the feeling of power she enjoys of being in the spotlight. The youth would be carefree, funny and possibly irresponsible even if he was a fifty year old man. These two aspects of energy connect the developing person with the maturing maiden/youth energy through the law of attraction. The maiden/youth can be full of the trickery that youth brings in that she/he may not want to consummate the relationship, if there is a relationship there at all. The question remains does the maiden (youth) want to become a woman (man)? If the developing person is older and meets a maiden that is actually quiet young i.e. 18-30 year old, the chances are that the relationship will not be a long term success. It is best to wait and see what develops as both parties' energy develops. The developing person will now be confident about himself as to attract the interest of such an alluring and intoxicating partner.

The Mother/Father.

The Mother/Father energy is the third energy archetype that will enter the developing person's life. Being quiet opposite to the Old Hag, this person is carrying the ideal energy of what constitutes an archetypical Mother/Father. The woman for instance will be warm, homely, caring, considerate, soft and affectionate. The trouble with operating from Mother Archetype is that eventually no man will rush home, grab his mother (I mean wife in reality) and make love to her on the kitchen table. The relationship is based on the caring aspect of 'what might have been' from the developing person's childhood and will probably develop into a parent / child co dependent relationship. The Mother/Father energy will trigger sadness within the developing person's heart chakra. The mother/father energy will help ground the person after the commotion of the old Hag and maiden energy.

The developing person will swing from sadness to anger and then from excitement to depression. After three such partners entering the developing persons life they may get disillusioned with the idea of romantic love when they understand the complexities of relationships. It is common that they fall head over heels in love with someone but to find after day three they are gone from their life. This is because they will realise that deep rooted insecurity was illuminated by their new perspective partner. If they endured rejection from their Mother and reverted back to grabbing the love from this new prospective partner, their neediness will push their beloved away. Discussing this encounter in therapy hopefully brings the realisation that the sadness and loss of this person was similar in vibration to the loss of their parental love when they were young. After analysing this attraction they will realise that they have to transmute the sadness of their little child at this very deep level. It's not about the loss of this special person at this stage; it's about opening the heart chakra to a greater degree of self. Great sadness will be felt by the person even though after one to three years of therapy may have elapsed and the person will have protected their heart from opening to others during this time. Therein lies the problem in that to remain closed will not be tolerated by your Soul as with such deep rooted sadness will not be allowed reside within your heart. The answer lies in the creation of such a magic bullet that will rock the person to their core.

What the person will learn is that true love involves creating a concrete relationship within you. This is something the developing person possibly never experienced previously in their life. If the child was never held in their parents arms then that person as an adult will either crave affectionate love or be repelled by physical touch. Occasionally I meet clients who consult with a physical nervous reaction of repelling an embrace from another person. The karmic imprints of not being held as a child are being reactivated when embraced as an adult. This is the time when those imprints of rejection will emerge where the developing person will look deeper into their childhood. As they have completed a lot of energetic therapy to date they will take responsibility for the rejection as it's the law of attraction operating from the astral plane. The person will start to realise that their childhood was not any particular persons fault in that it was just the way it existed.

It is best the developing person remain celibate at this time as sex can muddy the water with regards their perception of affection and sexuality. Their energy system will be developing quiet rapidly and a quiet time within their own essence will help them examine who they really are as a person. Eventually the emergence of the developing person's sexuality will be intoxicating. They will start to notice people staring at them from across the street. While doing their shopping in a supermarket a male may follow them from aisle to aisle only to ask them a stupid question about 'bread soda.' They may get a flat tyre and the men vying to change the tyre will develop into a frenzy. The forty five year old mother will be asked out on a date by a twenty five year old single male. This is quiet amazing when you see it in action.

If a person is insecure, needy and craves a relationship then their essence is not developed and may be energetically sending out a signal 'please love me, rescue me and see me for who I am.' Their neediness will swamp the energy of the relationship and will not give their prospective partner the space to live and breathe as a person in their own right. The person will start to realise when they energetically slip back and seek a relationship for their own self approval. Strength to exist as your own person will be reflected and created in a secure loving partner.

The person may be sending out a dual signal at this stage. One is the new confident signal of the real self while the remnants of the old self will still be receding. This can result in a double anima/animus for the individual in terms of expression and laws of attraction. The male may be between two minds with regards who is more alluring, the soft gentle, caring woman in a pink dress or the black leather clad woman in high heels, fishnets and studded chain. Great confusion will exist within the mind of this person as to how one could be attracted to two diametrically different women. This is not the time to think in terms of concrete relationships. If a relationship does enter the person's life, by all means have some fun, just don't get married. And take precautions!

Doors will start to open for the developing person at this stage of their life as their career flows through the heart chakra. The opening and transmutation of that chakra will bring opportunities for growth in terms of expression of who they really are as a person. Their inner strength will be illuminated by the fact that some old friends will be left behind in that their vibration will not be mature enough to sustain the friendship of a higher evolving person. This is simply the law of resonance at work. The developing person may be told intimate details of their friend's life as their vibration opens up their friend's energy system.

Their children may now become frustrated at the fact that their personal boundary has got smaller. The child may use language as 'lock you in or tie you up' which in reality is describing the energetic changing position of their parent. A child needs boundaries so they can feel the safety of the protection of that boundary from their parents. It is from this same place of having a secure strong open heart that the parent can love their children from their true essence. This will not be a lie in energy terms to the child after which the parent child relationship will develop. If you love your children from your heart then the presents you give them will be imbued with that true love. The child will be amazed with their presents because they were given with the true love of an open heart. Some children break their toys within the first hour of receiving their toys which indicates that the toys were given with the incorrect energy. If a child had a parent that was unable to play with their child then that child will internalise that imprint as an energetic programme. That child when they become an adult will have to learn how to play with their children. One of the factors I examine with adults unable to play with their children is to ask how 'safe' they are in their own essence. If one is self conscious then they are unable to go to that silly place of being a big child with their kids. As the person develops, those old imprints will resurface and later be removed which will free the adult. The mergence of their male and female aspects will find the adult wanting to play with their children. The children will respond with more affection to their parent and will 'laugh' from the bottom of their belly because the play is now coming from a secure energetic standpoint rather then from a forced insecure standpoint.

The developing person will dream from an energetic and psychological standpoint. Their normal psychological dreams will illuminate the conflict within the psyche at this time. Their energetic dreams will be Morgan conducting energetic treatments on their light thus body releasing fear and powerlessness. The emotional releasing of fear is necessary if a person is to stand in their own power rather then fear blocking the emitting of their true vibration. Fear within their light body can be triggered by such external vibrations as a self employed person not receiving adequate business for a month. This is how we develop focus and trust. Where once a person had a damaged inner child with the commonplace grandiose swings of a spending spree to cover their emotional pain usually counteracts with an energetic wipe out of business to focus the person on their inner world. This is how the universe will show you how to value money and that money will not buy you happiness. The astrological planet Saturn is the educator and taskmaster for such karmic lessons.

The developing person will enjoy days if not weeks of stability where life will be spent in an unemotional state of detachment. Often I hear people describe their life as uneventful or even boring. This is the ending of the cycle of attachment to the so called real world. Detachment means that you stop laying down karmic imprints that are required to be transmuted before the cycle of incarnations is ceased. Developing people that are in relationships may decide to end the relationship because their vibration has 'left behind' their partner. That does not mean that the couple does not love each other but their relationship was formed out of insecurity in the first place. Insecure relationships cannot survive as the new energies entering Earth at this time is intended to maximise personal development. Little things such as their conversation, their hobbies and their fascination with their insecurities become unbearable as the developing person realises that their partner is trapped in a world of their own making. The choice to remain in such a relationship is feasible but the aware person will feel lonely and misunderstood. There are no easy answers at this stage and great care must be taken with clients to give them the space to make up their minds with regards their own future. A great concern of the aware person is that as per their parent's relationship they will not wish to project their dysfunctional relationship onto their children as per the law of resonance.

Occasional imprints of deep despair, sadness and introvertness may emerge. This is to teach the developing person that their life is controlled by their energy. A master looks within always while a student looks outward. The person's base chakra may become dislodged from time to time as their sensitivity increases to external influences. They will require an energy treatment to put their roots in place after such an event. Once the mask of the lower self is uncovered then their emotions will swing to illuminate their defence mechanisms. A person will hold fear which can be channelled into anger (projected onto others by being expressed externally) or withheld internally as sadness/resentment (depression). I find that these are the two usual methods employed when coming to the final phase of the integration of the self. The brain may come first in commencing the fearful thoughts such as self sabotage, guilt or blame which will then be transformed into the negative functioning of the solar plexus. Then the person will retreat, blame themselves or possibly get angry as they blame others for their inability to employ their masculine side to protect their essence. This is the flow as per the path of the serpent in the hierarchy of emotions. The person must be aware of their thought patterns and channel those negative thoughts into their solar plexus to be transmuted as positive cognitions in their life. Some people are very good at turning emotions such as fear into sadness. The oral and schizoid personalities who internalise emotions are experts at this process, while the psychopathic and masochistic personalities (type 3 and 4) usually channel their emotions externally from fear to projected anger. Type five personality, the rigid personality usually channels their fear into industry and money making schemes.

The Alchemists spent their life trying to turn base metals into gold. The last stages of therapy will see the energetic mystery of alchemy being performed on the clients light body. Alchemy is conducted trough the mystery of fire and water. The fire is the Earth energy which enters the very cells of the light body from both the crown and base chakra. This energy will be burning hot and will scorch the channels Ida, pingala and sushumna within the light body. This will squeeze out the 'water' within the cellular body which is their suppressed emotional tears. The client may get a cold, lung infection, sinus or flu at this time as a lot of sadness will be released. Sadness will emerge from the opening of their female side which will put their spleen under energetic pressure. The spleen governs our immune system. It's interesting to note the people that get colds at this time as opposed to those that 'decide' to deal with their emotions through their light body. This will bypass the need for a manifestation of a cold.

The object of the therapy is to grow up energetically. This also means that the person will be sovereign onto themselves. They will be free and self sufficient in that their gifts will sustain them in providing abundance in every area of their life. Their essence will match their expression of their outer world. Their clothes and style will match their inner world. They will find success at work whether it be healing, trance, mediumship or simply remain in their old career. Their friends will be true friends. Their lives will be uncomplicated. They will avoid unnecessary aspects to life such as big loans or anything that takes from their freedom. They can become rich if it's in their essence but not just in a metaphysical sense, also on a financial sense. They will drive a car that is in touch with their essence and it will be 'just a car.' The car will be for their benefit and not for your benefit. They will live the life of the Wild Green Man.

Many times clients tell me how strange it feels that a new partner wants to touch them, hold their hand in a queue, walk up to them in a supermarket and give them a kiss on the side of their head and walk off without saying anything. For so many years sensitive people dissociated from themselves will be stunned to find that they are desirable, valued, good looking and even sexy. You can read this concept and imagine that it is true but it is totally different when you feel it occur in your new relationship.

By wild green man I also mean women of course. He is the real you that exists deep within the earth as an earth energy. It is the embodiment of all that you are that is the life you came here to live. Connecting to that earth energy will be cold and strengthening to your aura. It will rebalance your essence and bring forth your gifts that are your heritage. The meditation in The Wild Green Man is the exercise to connect to your essence within the earth.

Once you open the door to such a degree of healing, turmoil is guaranteed to visit the person's life. Life will never be the same. It is impossible to describe to someone how their life in their new world will feel. It can take as little from one year to three years work of monthly sessions. Above all it involves determination and a vision that this development is what you desire with regards the evolution of your soul. Soul essence to be fully understood will need to be cross referenced with energetic personality development, anima / animus complex, the cauldron system of human development, the Cabala tree of life energetic system and its astral trance healing energetic healing methodology on the emotional light body imprintation system.

The person who feels that they are bisexual will have a lot of confusion in their mind. Bisexuality is fine as long as you realise the orientation of the essence of a partner that best matches your essence. I have yet to meet a client that is homoosexual that had a strong role model in the opposite sex parent. Some people naturally like sex which you can see in some children being curious about boys and kissing etc even from age six. If a young girl is not seen in their father's eyes with regards being a young girl then their sexuality may be introverted to their own sexuality. As with all gender issues, determine if a power or soul retrieval is necessary. Strengthen the light body through earth connection thereby developing the essence within the light body. Notice how the imprints from their mother and father are shed which results in the development of their male and female essence. After the building phase of their therapy, their essence should settle in that they should know what orientation is best suited to their individuality.

The dream of finding a loving relationship and career does come true. It involves taking responsibility for our part in the development of our essence and, forgiving and accepting our past. This means examining the lessons we learned from our childhood and accepting responsibility for the implementation of the fruits of those lessons.

As intimacy, sex and essence is closely related we need to focus on examining sex addiction. The addiction to sex can be every bit as destructive as an addiction to alcohol or drugs. One of the over riding aspects to sex addiction is the hidden guilt and shame that exists within the psyche of the sex addict. Contrary to many people's belief, a sex addict may not have been exposed to sexual abuse as a child. The sex addict, as a child, was exposed to very severe emotional abuse that caused dissociation between their emotional body and their physical body. Love and acceptance was not present for the young child or possibly the type of love that the child required was not forthcoming for the developing child. This either caused or contributed to the dissociation which alienated the child from their external world. An underlying theme of their emotional state comes with the caveat 'what's wrong with me that I was so unlovable.' To a child, love, sex and emotions are one and the same in that the sacral chakra is formed by age six. A stagnant, blocked, distorted or lost sacral chakra will stunt emotional growth and maturity which will distort their adult sexuality.

For many addicts, the sexual act is but a mask to cover the dissociation of their light and physical body. The act of sex energetically pulsates kundalini energy up through the chakras thereby healing and nourishing all the chakras. If a person is energetically out of their body i.e. dissociated energetically, then they can crave sex in order to try and feel their essence within their physical body. Success is not achieved because they are dissociated from the emotionality of the intimacy of their love making. This energetically brings up great feelings of despair, disgust, dissociation, confusion and guilt. The person's thinking becomes even more distorted in that they don't know how to feel emotionally in the sharing of their essence. If you cannot share, that invariably means that you cannot receive. When true loves come to the sex addict, they push it away in that the pain of the received vibration of love will open their childhood pain that is hidden behind the locked doors of their closed heart chakra. Thus love making and the opposite sex becomes objectified in that it is a means to an end, not the emotional intimacy of the sharing of their essence with an accepting loving partner. Their fear of love is great. In adult relationships they usually project onto people that genuinely love them the rejection they received from a parent during their childhood. Likewise they will constantly attract partners that will reject them as per their emotional experiences in their childhood or they will suffocate a lover and force them to leave the relationship.

Sex addicts usually end relationships shortly after commencing the relationship. With all this hidden shame and guilt, the sex addict will, on many levels, be emotionally closed. They are scared to share their secret with another human being 'in case they will be caught out.' Many husbands or wife's have affairs, masturbate many times a day or engage in computer porn as a release to their destructive emotional state. To compensate for their loneliness, many addicts become workaholics or specialists in another field. This task is easy for them in that many sex addicts are type one, schizoids or type two personalities, the oral. When one is so connected to the astral plane they retreat in times of stress by leaving their body and entering energetically the astral plane.

Within the astral plane, everything is possible. We can see and think information without the limits of time or space. We can study and bring unearthly knowledge back with us to the physical plane. These gifts can result in a person being a brilliant song writer, drummer or electrician etc but from a spellbinding effortless standpoint that leaves others in awe. Success will be difficult to find in that the heart chakra is dissociated outside the physical body. Therefore success, which lies within the heart chakra, may never exist within the life of the sex addict. The mask of the lower self is hidden from the world. Sex addicts have poor boundaries. With a damaged inner child emotionally in control for much of their adult life usually results in a poor and confused sense of self that leaves the person alone, misunderstood, feeling hopeless and ashamed to know where to turn for help.

Many times, I treat sex addicts whose addiction originated from a past life sexual trauma. The trauma can be triggered by an event or sexual event in this lifetime. The way to determine if a past life sexual trauma was inflicted upon the person will show itself in the language the person utilises in ordinary conversation e.g. I could not get the thing out of my mouth, I cannot bear the taste etc.

It is heartbreaking to complete a few weeks of work with a client who finds their inner strength emerging who matter of factly says 'I was abused weekly by 'x' for the first few years of my life, do you think that has me feeling the way I do? Maybe I am just a bad person.'

The key is to re-associate the person into their light body is by utilising the cauldron energetic system of human development. This will lead to inner child work which may require a power or soul retrieval to return the lost soul essence. The emotional light body will then be healed to balance the male and female essences into the true self. This will probably take between one to three years of therapy.

John.

John was two years into his therapy. He was progressing very well and had developed his intuition to the degree that he could see through external events as energies expressed through the laws of the universe. John was becoming a master. John knew that he desired female love and had an ache in his heart because his mother could not give him the energetic quality of love that he desired. John knew that this imprint was being transmuted energetically and therefore he was predominantly a type 1 and 2 personality (oral and schizoid personality). John refused a number of relationships over a few months but when visiting a new therapy centre he got taken by surprise. He met a girl that was alluring, soft and feminine. They spent the day talking and went to lunch together. At the end of the day, John asked if the girl would like to exchange telephone numbers. The girl replied 'No, I had a great day but I feel a little trapped in your company? John realised that he was still energetically operating from the standpoint of his lonely little inner child protecting himself from female vibrations that cannot give him what he desires – unconditional love. It was this special woman that entered his life that managed to break through his defensive barriers to expose John to his core. John walked away and internalise his sadness, realising that it was not about the woman but about him uncovering his deep childhood sadness within the cellular memory of his body. Energetically this heralded the treatment stage of the mysteries of fire and water. The fire is the Kundalini energy transmuting the water which is the suppressed cellular tears of sadness.

Oh no, where am I.

One night after a night club, John who was really drunk, met Joan in the queue for a taxi when they were trying to make their way home. John was in his mid twenties and Joan was in her late forties. Joan looked more like a fifty year old woman who was big into women rights and self expression. John was a soft easy going guy who went with the flow of life. They both headed back to Joan's house after which they made drunken love. John woke up the next morning, looked out the side of the bed and thought 'Oh no, where am I.' John remembered nothing of last night. When John turned over in the bed he shuddered to think that he went home with a woman in her late forties. They both woke, had breakfast and John agreed to meet Joan later that week.

John was between two minds about keeping the date but decided to go anyhow. They met at a bar and after an hour the alcohol took control and they both were having a fun time. They decided to go back to Joan's house and John said that he had no contraceptives. Joan laced into him and told him how irresponsible he was for not thinking that far ahead and asked him 'how did he expect her to sleep with him considering he was so careless and irresponsible.' John let this situation go as he knew that no one ever won an argument with a woman when sex was on the agenda. The following morning John went with Joan to her Mother's house for Sunday lunch. This was the first time that John had met his prospective Mother in law. After an hour or so, John found himself with a knife cutting the weeds from the paths and driveway. Joan and her Mother sat inside the front window of the house drinking tea while looking out at John clearing the weeds from the pathway. Two weeks later Joan hit John across the face for the first time in public while at a funfair. Joan remember, worked in the area of protecting human rights. Joan cried as she ran away as John followed her and hugged her as he hated to see her so upset.

Joan's Dad left when she was small. She was holding deep resentment and anger which surfaces when she enters little child mode. This love hate relationship with men is masking her deep insecurity with regards her essence being rejected by men. Her emotional behaviour alternates between love to hate/ rejection as she access her own inner world. Joan has attracted a warm, caring, loving man who is triggering her inner rejection that Joan is then projecting back onto her boyfriend. John's Father worked away from home for many years and he witnessed his mother cry with fear and loneliness at having to bring up her children alone almost as a single parent. John is therefore projecting his own mother issues onto Joan which is why he cannot leave this abusive relationship. The spiritual laws are complete through the laws of attraction and resonance.

There is nothing that John can ever do to make Joan happy. This co-dependent relationship is untimely doomed. The female is the male and the male is the female in this relationship. Their shadow sides are being projected onto each other. This allows their dormant aspects be reflected back onto each other in that Joan requires sensitivity and the development of her female essence while John needs to develop his male essence and integrate his shadow female anima. John eventually realised that the relationship was doomed and that he could never do enough to make Joan happy. John left the relationship after six months. Joan sends him texts every few weeks from her deep sadness of her inner child trying to win back the affection of her lost father from all those years ago. Throw away remarks are the subconscious minds method of talking to us – 'Oh no, where am I.'

The above example is where John had to learn not to revert back to little five year old 'Johnny' and react to women as their carer and parent. You cannot be a parent/father and a husband at the same time. John has also to transmute his shadow fear of women as he relates to women as they are powerless beings needing to be cared by the male. While this to some degree is true as males being a protector and carer, it is his fear of viewing his Mother when he was a young boy that energy is being reflected and not from a position of strength as an adult male. John swings energetically from being a father figure to women, to being a little boy afraid to put his needs first in case he upsets women. Utilise the cauldron system of development, bring in Stag energy, secure the inner child, integrate the fragmented inner child fragment if needed and open the heart chakra which will then release fear. This is the path of therapy required by John.

<u>*Casey: They will never do that again.*</u>

Casey was emotionally abused by her parents when as a child. She had to cook and clean for her younger siblings as her parents drank every evening in the local bar. Casey had to prepare the food for her siblings and have them ready for school for nine am. At seventeen, Casey left home and went to work in the city and lived with a favourite aunt. Casey started to feel good about her self as she was promoted in work and was popular in her social circle. At age twenty, after dating her boyfriend Sam for two years, Casey married and moved into her new home with her Mother in law. Sam was spoilt being the youngest child and could do no wrong in the eyes of his mother. In times of conflict he ran back to his Mother as a referee to win support in his arguments against Casey. To make ends meat Casey eventually had to take a second job to finance the family home.

Through therapy, Casey realised that energetically she married one of her younger siblings from her childhood. She had to be wife, mother and father to her husband and mother in law. Casey had to energetically remove fear from her life in order to stand in her own power rather then put her husband's needs before her own as per her childhood. Spiritually Casey had to learn that giving your power away was a weakness that was building silent anger inside her. Once she found her foundation and voice she realised that it is acceptable to have these feelings but also to take action with these feelings in a positive constructive fashion. Casey realised what it meant to be a woman as Morgan worked with Casey removing fear and finding Casey's inner woman. At work Casey realised that she was entitled to be her own woman as a sexual chemistry developed between Casey and a new co-worker. Rather then have an affair, Casey turned her attention to Sam to focus on the type of man that was missing from her life. Sam eventually had to take a job because Casey stopped supporting him financially. Her Mother in law got a new apartment built as an extension on to the back of their house. Casey realised that being soft and gentle did not mean that one had to be weak. While Sam never entered therapy he learned enough from Casey that he found himself to be his own person.

Cathy.

Cathy came for therapy because her new career was not successful. She trained as a therapist in a particular field, proved to herself to have a gift with her therapy and commenced trading from a beautiful building in a large town. After three months Cathy was nearly broke. Her earnings barely covered her rent and travel expenses. She produced brilliant work buy yet the flow of abundance and success eluded her. Interestingly, her three year old son found it difficult to talk and was a very restless sleeper. Through the law of attraction her son mirrored Cathy's energy which correctly projected the difficulties in her throat chakra. The throat chakra governs the professionalism of our voice, the expressiveness of our nature and holding onto money.

Cathy described the negotiations with her landlord as 'I couldn't get the thing out of my mouth, I mean words out of mouth,' and 'all he wanted to do was literally rape me.' Her previous career was littered with authority figures that were extremely masculine who dominated her gentle soft essence. She had a fear of snakes and heights arguably past life issues indicating fear of success and intimacy. Eventually she explained about her obsessive cleaning and washing of her hands which she described as 'have to get the filthy dirt washed off my hands in order to try and clean them.' Notice how she projected the failure of the task in cleaning her hands by utilising the word 'try.' No abuse was present in her history in this lifetime but Cathy had Fairy energy in her essence. A week ago she locked herself out of her car and light bulbs constantly broke in her house. Cathy was a schizoid personality with subtypes of the oral personality. Her biggest emotion to transmute was fear and inner rage.

Cathy's neurosis was disproportionate to her presenting case history. I suspected a past life issue as a healer or therapist who experienced sexual abuse. Her past life trauma of standing in her own power as a healer was projected onto her career in this lifetime. I commenced utilising the cauldron system of human development to anchor her essence within her body. I addressed her self defeating cognitions with regards her low self esteem being projected onto the universe through the law of attraction.

Cathy's business improved with her practise attracting clients who experienced childhood sexual abuse over the next three weeks. I decided not to explain my theories to Cathy until at least a specific trauma presented itself for transmutation. Cathy attended monthly until she asked 'was I abused Gerry….I mean….I have the same fears and behaviour as one of my sexual abuse clients? It was time to be honest with Cathy.

I explained the nature of reincarnation and how people bring past life issues that require healing into the present lifetime and that releasing the past will free the person in all areas of this lifetime. Cathy started believing in herself which was reflected in her blossoming career. Cathy discussed sexuality in which she enquired as to why she never experienced an orgasm in her life.

Cathy: Why is it that I love my husband but yet never experience an orgasm with lovemaking with him or for that matter with any previous boyfriend?

Gerry: That is very common Cathy. Orgasm is the explosion of the energy of the sacral chakra up to the heart chakra. Your sacral chakra is bound with the energy of your past life which means you are not free with the expression of your emotions. Your femminity is damaged which shows itself in you trying to think your way through life rather then feel the essence of your life. Your obsession with cleaning is simply a control mechanism fuelled by fear. It's easier to busy yourself with cleaning rather then put on a beautiful lingerie outfit with a pair of red high heel shoes and walk into your bedroom like a peacock to your husband.

Cathy: Yes, that's just it. Its not just about the sex, it's about me, the atmosphere, my feelings. How I actually feel about the woman I am.

Gerry: Well said. You got it.

The next session Cathy explained how she found mixed results in relation to the expression of her sexuality. Her husband didn't know how to react at first to the new Cathy in the bedroom. I explained that some men may become intimidated or may be unsure how to emerge from their own comfort zone. Cathy agreed and enquired as to how at times she found sex enjoyable and at other times she still struggled to orgasm. I explained that a flower opens in stages and does not blossom overnight. I focused on her emotions in which Cathy explained how she argued with a friend who was too controlling in her attitude towards Cathy. I asked Cathy to contemplate on the word 'controlling' and to see why such conflict was presented to her externally. She stopped and nodded that she was also controlling. We talked about her cleaning which subsided to some degree. This led us to a visualisation of her inner child when her home life was out of control hence her compensation to control her adult life on a micro level. I talked about a fictitious client who I described as covering her head with a pillow every time she made love to her partner. She was too embarrassed to show the expression of ecstasy on her face.

The next session saw Cathy attend in a strikingly red dress. I passed no comment but casually remarked during the session 'did you find yourself behaving differently during the month? She replied no but later said how she had this 'thing' in the wardrobe for months and just threw it on today. Morgan was conducting energetic treatment on her light body during her dreamtime state. She had moved on from her fearful dreams of battle scenes and was enjoying dreams of a highly sexual nature. She laughed at how I was correct in predicting such dreams. Her business was constant but she desired it to be busier. She remarked at how her client base was changing and how she was conducting more talking therapies in her work. She had three sexual abuse clients in a week in which she found herself counselling the women. Cathy cried thinking about their stories. The energetic vibration of her clients, through the law of attraction was opening Cathy's own emotions.

I found the way Cathy walked in to the room very elegant, confident and open. She had an air of sexiness about her that was intoxicating. I enquired to cross reference the energy by asking her did she notice anything different about male attention during the weeks. She laughed at how she attracted an 'old guy' in the supermarket during the week. On a girls night out when in a restaurant, a man the other side of the room changed his seating position in order that he sit facing her. Her friends pointed this out to her.

Cathy: He had a beautiful girlfriend you know, blonde, tanned, long legs, mini, red lipstick, I could go on.

Gerry: I am sure you could but….?

Cathy: But what?

Gerry: I can wait her all day if you wish but you know you have to finish this sentence.

Cathy: She was not me?

Gerry: *(Pause) Yes…She was not you. Feel that vibe you are sending out. Feel that tightness below your belly button?*

Cathy: Yes, I had that the last few days, what is that?

Gerry: *Its Kundalini energy. As you place your feet flatly on the ground you can feel as if a fire is placed underneath your feet. It's proceeding upwards but also notice how the tight energy under your belly button is unravelling upwards. This is the path of the serpent which is igniting sexually all your body and chakras to receive a greater degree of intimacy within yourself. This is what happens when we make love; the pulsations of the sacral chakra vibrate the energy upwards to the heart chakra. Feel it flow around you, up the back of your body and around the front of your body until a complete circuit is formed. You are now infusing yourself with a deeper degree of your sexuality which is what the men in the restaurant and the supermarket were illuminating to you. Hold the feeling for a few minutes but also reverse back the energy, back around your body to its home in the sacral chakra. This was also replicated in the wearing of that red dress today. It's the emergence of the real you.*

Cathy smiled and felt a little embarrassed. In the final therapy session Cathy said how her husband decided to attend a self development evening class while Cathy said she wanted to study psychotherapy to heal her new client base that was emerging within her practise.

Serpent Energy

Integrating from the Left.

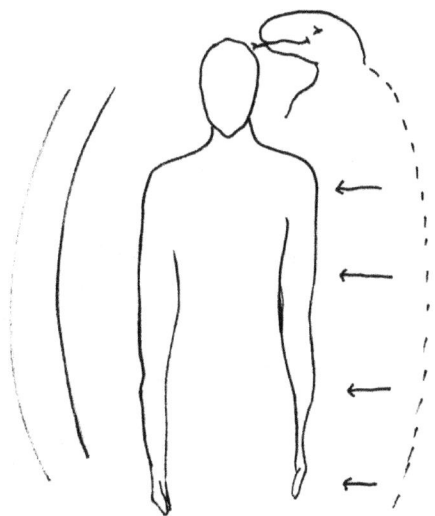

Serpent energy is the full force of the universe integrating the hidden essence into your psyche. It usually enters from the left to merge with the light body.

"Whatever is going on in your mind is what you are attracting."

'The Secret' Rhonda Byrne.

9. Spiritual Laws That Govern The Actions of Mankind.

The Spiritual Laws governing mankind are universal laws in that everyone is bound to these laws no matter what religious denomination you practise. Understanding these laws will allow you penetrate human behaviour to the deepest level of our being. Earth is a free will zone. It has a particular function in the grand scheme of the universe in that all the beings of the universe have access to the Earth plane as an experiment in free will. We are left to our own devices as to what we decide for ourselves as energetic beings on this planet. The trouble with this system is that different beings from all over the galaxy wish to control the energy of the planet simply because they can. Control is exercised by energetic vibrations. If we live in a particular mindset then we give off an energetic vibration of that mindset. The beings that control us can manipulate the human race through such emotions as guilt, fear and anger. This has the advantage that as we receive information as energetic vibrations, we become trapped in those vibrations and so become controlled by those beings sending those particular vibrations. Beings that want to control us i.e. particular people and organisations utilise the media to bombard us with events that keep us paralysed by fear and therefore easily manipulate us. The object of this book, Soul with a Mind, is to increase your own natural vibration and so take back ownership of your life. This in turn will change your psychology and behaviour so that you can see through the concept of what you perceive as reality.

The spiritual laws governing mankind are the yardstick by which you can access true reality. Once you get accustomed to applying these laws to your life you will then be able to take back control of your life and feel the freedom that is your natural birthright.

It is by increasing your vibration through earth connection that you rise above such lower vibrational energies as fear, guilt and anger that you can see control and manipulation tactics being bombarded at you. It is akin to climbing a mountain in that the more you climb the mountain, the better the view. Your elevation is your increasing vibration as your view is your discernment with regards analysing all incoming energies. The low lands are the lower vibrations of such people that live in the marsh wetlands that want to keep your view and vibration at such a low level.

The following are the laws that govern the actions of mankind.

The Law of One.

This law states that we all originate from source as a manifestation of Spirit. We may have varying degrees of light from spirit operating within each of us but we are all one. This concept is further expanded in the laws of resonance and attraction. Even though people may try and control us, it is coming from a position of darkness and not light. Absence of light is ignorance.

Case Example: Who would have believed it?

While giving a five day workshop I began to notice two students within our group circle that sat directly across from each other. They sat expressionless staring at each other, not even blinking as the atmosphere between them became heavy and thick. At the morning break, both students expressed discomfort at the presence of the other student. I passed it off telling them to see what their energies had in store for them over the course of the five days. That afternoon, I drew numbers from a hat to pair off the students to practise the teachings of the morning session. The two opposing students were matched with each other and amid great reservations they paired off and conducted the session of therapy on each other.

The following day, as a continuance of the teaching, the two students again had to pair off during the practical session. They only managed to conduct therapy on one person such was the depth of disclosure in the session. On day three, therapy again continued on the previous day's student but during administrating the healing energy to her 'client,' it was the therapist that started to cry uncontrollable.

On day four, the energetic practical sessions were received by the student who was the therapist during the previous days training. Both students hugged and cried at the end of that day. On day five while giving feedback about the course, both students surmised at how similar each others life had been with regards the experience of heart ache. Each student had very similar experiences but formulated a different personality as a coping mechanism to the same experience. In essence they were one and the same person who also mirrored each others energy. This is also the law of reflection in that we don't always like our own mirror image.

The Law of Cause and Effect.

This law is more commonly termed 'what you sow so shall you reap.' We are responsible for our actions. We drive a car at one hundred kilometres per hour, we loose control and we crash. We sustain serious injuries because of the excessive speed we were travelling. If we crash at twenty kilometres per hour then naturally we receive minor injuries. The damage to our body is in direct proportion to the speed we are driving therefore the law of cause and effect is evident for all to see. If we look at our actions during the Celtic Tiger years it is evident that its foundation was masculine based, quick profit, fancy holidays and flash cars. The economy was fuelled with borrowed money. Someday that money had to be paid back. The female aspect of contraction and correction emerged via the recession to correct the excessiveness of the false masculine side. The law of cause and effect in operation within their lives. The degree to which people found themselves identifying their masculinity through the falseness of the previous 'tiger' years is the degree to which their femininity is punishing them today.

<u>Katie and PJ.</u>

PJ was a builder who was very successful during the booming Celtic Tiger years. He had purchased building land to build houses over the next few years and thought he was set up to reap the fruits of the Celtic Tiger for years to come. They lived in the suburbs while their two grown up children was away in college. His wife Katie was a civil servant who enjoyed a cushy job with long holidays. The couple decided to sell their family four bed detached home in the suburbs and build a five thousand square foot six bedroom home in the country. The couple received a good price for their home and started the process of the planning permission for their house. The building of their new home dragged on due to delays as the couple rented accommodation until their new house was finished. The credit crunch emerged which saw PJ slash his house prices by one third. The building land bank became worthless. Their new home was now finished but came in fifty percent over budget. The holidays stopped, the jeeps were sold and Katie received three pay cuts in little over a year. As their home was in the country, their children in college rarely came to visit as they rented accommodation near college in the city.

The couple were lonely in their expensive big house and missed their 'home' with the family and old neighbours that they had known for years. Decisions had to be made. Will the head or the heart win?

The Law of Resonance.

I sometimes substitute the naming of this law with the Law of Attraction. Like attracts like? The vibration of the frequency we emit will be answered by other like minded individuals or energies. Who and what we resonate with will be in direct proportion to the energy we are holding within our light bodies. Simply look at your friends. Examine their personality, their lives, their happiness, their challenges that life presents to them. They are probably very similar people or essence to you and your life. Think of two thieves robbing a house. One will be dressed in working clothes etc while the other will not be dressed in a three piece suit. One thing they both have in common is the belief that the world owes them a living for free. It has never dawned on then that they possess the talents, intelligence and energy to become rich in all aspects of their lives without having to rob others of their energy.

The same is true for relationships. As we go about our business we attract in the energy we are holding whether it is our fathers, mother's or simply our attitude to life that we have developed over the years. We may not be in our own energy but may live our life as through the energy of another. Unfortunately we will attract a relationship to show us what energy we are holding that is clouding our essence. This dysfunction is fine as long as both parties enjoy living in such dysfunction but, if one party decides to look inwards through therapy, then that old relationship will have to be renegotiated. No one did anything wrong simply one person decided to change their vibration through self growth. At this stage of the development of the world old relationships based on insecurity are being challenged by the vibrations being sent into Earth. This unfortunately is causing great pain to many as dysfunctional relationships cannot survive but is necessary for self and the planets evolution at this time.

If a person treats you unjustly, condescendingly or in a harsh manner, do not seek retribution. Let your hurt dissolve and see through the persons actions. Part of their psyche was triggered and they projected out their internalised hurt onto you. This is because you both have similar life/energetic experiences or you both are carrying the energy of the person who caused similar emotional hurt to both of you. You are simply opening up the energy of your friend and it is being reflected back onto you.

Once you increase your vibration through energetic meditation a strange phenomenon eventually occurs. When challenged by an external energy you can feel as if time stands still. There is a pause in which you can stop and see the event unfold right in front of your eyes. Usually, it is a tool to help you reposition how you engage with the world as you integrate your male and female essence. Sometimes we are required to do nothing at all but let events dissolve naturally. This is the universe demonstrating to us the belief in the strength of our centeredness that allows the world revolve around our energy. I advise clients that these lessons come to us when we least expect them such as at the checkout at our local supermarket.

We are bound to the experiences of our life based upon the law of attraction or the law or resonance. This is what Jesus talked about when he said 'I give you power over Heaven and Earth. Whatever you decide on Earth you decide on Heaven.' What Jesus was talking about was the fact that we decide our own life's experiences based upon the emotionality we are holding based upon our past experiences. We therefore are Gods in our own right. The buck stops with you. How do you protect yourself from negativity? By keeping your thoughts and light body clean and pure. Therefore through the law of attraction only a pure loving vibration can withstand the lofty pure vibration of your light body. If you hold a grudge against someone and you decide to poison them by thought or deed then that is fine. But it is you who have poisoned yourself by your thoughts as you will resonate with other such undesirable people or situations.

As your vibration increases it can be akin to climbing a mountain. As you climb higher and higher your view increases over the low lands down below you. You now have a better view of the people, the games they get up to and how they operate. As you are experiencing the truth of your life you will no longer be party to other people's games or lies. As you progress on your journey you will become more centred and silent. You will naturally leave some of your old friends behind you as the law of attraction will repel their vibration away from you.

<u>Tonight 'God is a Lap dancer.'</u>

Marie Ann was a tall, striking beautiful woman. She had long blonde hair, perfect make up, tremendous style and a confident walk. I surmised to myself that Marie Ann must be inundated with suitors and that life must be easy for her due to her beauty easily opening doors for her. Marie Ann told me her story as the tears rolled down her face. She was alone and lonely. She had responsibilities above and beyond the call of duty. She didn't like herself. In fact she felt ugly. She couldn't see why any person would be interested in her as a person. She never dated due to the fact that 'what's the point.' Marie Ann worked as a lap dancer a few times a month the other side of the country. She told no one about this part time work as she used the money to keep herself in the style she was accustomed and to financially help her family.

I came down to earth with a bang as I contemplated where to start our therapeutic work. I felt ashamed at how I judged Marie Ann from her outside beauty rather then her inner beauty. I was blinded to think my prejudices came to haunt my thoughts in the therapy room and I felt that I needed to share my opinion with her as if something is not being talked about then no therapy is taking place. I saw her beauty but not her inner pain that she hid so well in the projection of her sexuality. My own projections entered the therapy space but as always the trick is to be aware what you are feeling during the therapeutic process.

Marie Ann cried after she listened to me tell my observations and prejudices. She agreed with me that everyone thought the same way as I did but the truth was very different. She paused, indicating I was to proceed with the therapy.

Gerry: Do you watch MTV Marie Ann?

Marie Ann: Yes, all the time.

Gerry: Do you know the band Faithless?

Marie Ann: Yes, I do.

Gerry: Do you know their song 'Tonight...... God is a DJ'?

Marie Ann: Yes, I was just watching the video during the week?

Gerry: Well, Marie Ann: Tonight God is a Lap dancer!

Marie Ann: (Stares into oblivion). I see what you mean.

Gerry: God finds expression in all things as nothing is neither good nor bad. Tell me what it feels like to be that other 'woman' dancing for your clients?

Marie Ann: That other woman. She loves it. She feels free. Not a care in the world.

Gerry: What lies behind those words....'not a care in the world?

Marie Ann: Responsibility. I always have to get it right, sort things out; be the best...I guess I never have time to be a woman in my daily life.

The rest of the session was spent illuminating the divergence of how Marie Ann felt she had to be masculine at all times and not be a powerful feminine woman. Our shadow aspect will eventually crucify us in that it will run us ragged in blindly projecting our ego fear and hidden shadow onto our life's actions. The task of therapy was to ignite Marie Ann's feminine side and rebalance her essence. The conflict within her subconscious resonated with her feminine side to be a lap dancer. The energetic treatments involved inner child work, the cauldron system of development and utilisation of cow energy. The solar plexus was developed as fear left the kidneys during the first session.

Emotions reflected through projection

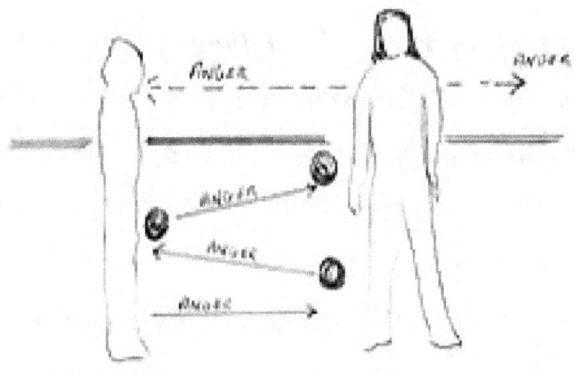

What you energetically emit will get returned back to you. The other person will take on that vibration and therefore will show you what you are holding vibrationally.

The Law of Affinity.

My advice to you is to not believe a word of what I say to you in this book. You must become masters of your own life and verify what I am explaining to you through the workings of your life. The law of affinity is the return of your vibration to you. This is the law I am addressing in the experience of the client's life in between sessions where I ask people what is happening in your life since we last met. As I develop the person's light body through energy healing in each session, the odd events in their lives are the attracting back through the law of affinity, into their lives the vibration they are holding.

If a person tells me they got angry with the postman, I realise that they are dealing with anger issues from their childhood and the event with the postman is simply an energetic agreement for each person to illuminate each others journey. The same is true of any experience in their life whether it is their heating system breaking down (warmth or intimacy problems), pipes being clogged (relationship problems) or sore teeth (issues with power).

After two or three sessions my clients usually become accustomed to these laws in operation in their lives. My style of practise is that I become an educator or mentor in showing people how to identify the energies operating in their energy field. The purpose of therapy is to bring the light to the dark and not to focus on the dark. We should endeavour to empower people in showing them how to change their own lives rather then rely on therapy to provide the answers to all their problems.

The operations of these laws are neutral in that they function to show both negative and positive energies in action.

Gerry – Entity Attacks.

In the early days of my hypnotherapy practise, I commenced learning about energy psychology once I knew that I was being called to work in that field. I was in training with my energy teacher but I found that I kept attracting entity attacks from my clients. I found this quiet frustrating as I was not trained to deal with such issues but yet, week after week, I kept attracting seemingly normal hypnotherapy clients who left their entities within my light body during the session. After I realised I was attacked, I had to close down my practise, attain an appointment with my energy healer and travel across the country for the treatment. This was a big loss of income and inconvenience to my life.

As I travelled home from my teacher who attended to my light body after one such attack, I was wondering why I was attracting such events into my life. I stopped to give a young man a lift in my car outside a town. All I could see was that he was wearing a base ball cap which was hiding his face. He entered the car and as he looked me in the eye, I could see that his eyes were rolling around his head. He had needle marks all up his arms, was tripped out on drugs after a hit and was walking alive with entities. I wasn't even home when I had attracted the same problem into my life. The session with my energy healer had not uncovered the reason behind the present situation with regards the entity attacks.

I thought about why this was happening and as to why I was sending out this signal. I reviewed my practice and life through the law of attraction. I then realised the problem. I wanted to be my energy teacher. As I was mirroring her energy I was attracting clients suited to the practise and energy of my teacher and not my own energy. I was loosing myself in my admiration of my teacher. This was my responsibility and the law of affinity and attraction was showing me the errors of my ways. I immediately connected to Mother Earth and asked my energy to connect to the energy of my practise. The entity attacks immediately ceased and I put an energetic block on entity work for my practise. This was a great lesson for me in the operation of the spiritual laws and an illumination as to the authenticity of the science behind the laws. The conventional viewpoint of reality is but a fallacy whereas the emotion of our feelings is the fuel of the spiritual laws in action in our life which is truth.

New Guides.

As your vibration increases so does your perception and understanding of energy psychology. Your healing capabilities will increase in that you can facilitate more complex treatments and realise greater perception in analysing case histories. This requires that you change Guides that have greater experience in the work that you will be conducting. Our Guides have their own hierarchy, if that is the correct word to use. The more experienced the Guide the greater the responsibility that they will be entrusted to complete through us here on the physical plane. Thus the law of affinity is completed in that your new Guide will resonate with your new higher vibration as you release negativity and embrace your enhanced spiritual gifts.

You can never Complete your Developing Work Alone.

Finding your true essence is not easy. It takes time, effort, commitment and money. The funny thing is there is no other show in town. You might think life is all about money, success or family but the facts are that we have come here to grow spiritually. Once your soul has called you to evolve you have little choice in the matter but to conduct the healing of your essence. Money and time usually corresponds to one appointment a month for a time span of between one and three years. The effort involves the restructuring of your life that would have taken place one way or another. It's just the matter of whether you want to willingly co-operate with your development or want to be dragged kicking and screaming through life. I know which one I prefer having visited both sides of that coin.

With the dawn of 2012, the Earth is being bombarded with different energies to free the emotions of the people on Earth. This is an evolutionary process that is already well under way. While your light body will be affected on a macro level, your emotions and energy will therefore be developing on a micro level. The work of understanding your energy requires that you seek the help of a person who has a higher vibration then your energy field. Again increasing your vibration is like ascending a mountain. As you climb you get a better view and perception of the people on the low lands. But how do you know where you are heading? What is the goal or end task as your changing energy will constantly attract into your life the conflicts within your energy system. Life can become very confusing at times as your inner compass changes as you energetically embrace spiritual freedom.

To complete this work you need someone to guide you on the correct path that is already at the top of that mountain. They can tell you what is happening in your energy field and relate those changes to the development of your psychological/ emotional life. They can advise you as to what emotions are going to emerge over the next thirty days until the next appointment. Therefore you won't start world war three in your private life. It is virtually impossible to complete this work on your own.

How do you realise a teacher that desires to build your knowledge as opposed to an ego based teacher who desires to rob your energy and keep you from developing. The answer is that upon leaving a good authentic teacher you will feel uplifted, strong and realise that you have a purpose in your life. They will not be threatened by you and will want to see you succeed.

Perception is projection.

We interpret the world through our senses or chakra system. We are designed that we interpret the world in such a fashion as energy flows inwards and outwards through our chakra system. Therefore, it is in conjunction with the energy imprints within our chakra system that we interpret the meaning of the external world vibrating towards us. How we perceive the world is therefore dependant upon the emotions we are carrying. Very few of us are a free open channel interpreting the world as it actually is rather then how we think it is. The world can be seductive in that we can choose to see only what we want to see or it can be dark, negative or hostile depending upon the darkness that covers our individual light.

This is the principle behind Jungian sand play therapy. Our energy is projected onto the symbol and so becomes alive to us. It is not strictly true that the symbol or play item chooses us but rather the symbol resonates with the projection of our energy. A complex that we are psychologically identifying through our energetic vibration is being projected onto the symbol. Every hook needs a hanger.

A particular energy cannot destroy a similar energy.

As all energy vibrates at its own frequency, each emotional frequency can be said to operate at its own frequency. There is no point fighting fire with fire with regards emotional energies as both energies will join together and create a bigger problem. The object of healing is to remove the negative energies therefore the same frequency of healing energy will not be able to displace an old negative energy. The solution is to utilise the highest frequency or energy possible to displace the low frequency negative energy. The greatest frequency of energy is love, acceptance and gratitude. There is no point conducting therapy through a 'tough love' approach as you would only be fighting fire with fire. Building your relationship with the Spirit world is an excellent method to develop your team of helpers that will greatly aid your practise.

Client Sarah has issues with her father. Sarah's essence is suppressed by her father's essence. The law of attraction is bringing people with her father's energy into her life to show Sarah the energy she is holding. Sarah is working with a female therapist who also had issues with her father. Sarah, through transference, is triggering issues within her therapist. Cracks are beginning to appear in the therapeutic relationship. Sarah's therapist is getting increasingly frustrated at Sarah's progress which culminated in Sarah being a half hour late for one appointment by 'accident.' Sarah's therapist becomes outraged and uses Morgan energy in frustration at Sarah's inability to perceive the progress of therapy. The Morgan energy was the same energy that Sarah's father used all the years during her childhood. Sarah walked away knowing that she would never be back for another appointment. The hurt that Sarah imprinted as a child was the same energy that Sarah's therapist utilised in the therapeutic setting. The same vibration cannot displace a similar vibration so progress ceased. Love and understanding, a higher vibration then anger, was required to move therapy forward.

The Law of Recording.

Once the death process commences your Guides present to you the events of your life. This is the where the saying 'my life flashed in front of my eyes originates. As you will not be judged by a God, you will simply be shown all that you have or have not completed here on Earth. The law of recording states that you will judge yourself through the presentation of your own life through the help of your Spirit Guides when integrated into the Spirit world.

The Blame/Victim mentality must end.

As spirits in our own right manifesting as the creation of God, the role of victim or blame game does not serve mankind. If we blame others we see ourselves as a victim. We are not living as co-creators of the universe in our own power. Likewise, if we are victims we will cultivate an attitude of powerlessness which is not the reason as to why we came to earth in the first place. I cannot watch soap programmes on TV due the terrible anger, hurt, betrayal and powerlessness that they are influencing within society. This energy is very easy to grab on to us as per the pack mentality. No one wants to be alone or left out. But that is what is needed. I sometime ask people to think of the soap actors and how they will judge themselves when they die seeing the reality that they influenced the spiritual crime of powerlessness to the mass's.

What you resist persists.

As we are a conductor of energy, the natural evolution of our energy is that we become God like in all our expression. As universal energy is abundant and is our birthright, this energy flows through us and sends the emotionality of our light bodies' experiences out to the world for the return of that energy to us through the law of attraction. Therefore the law 'what your resist persists' is true. If you decide to not deal with something in your life then you will be constantly faced with obstacles to illuminate that inaction in your life. The sad fact to remember is that it is we that have formed those obstacles even though it may be fear that is stopping us deal with those obstacles in the first place. What you consciously submerge within your psyche you will subconsciously project onto the outside world through your shadow.

Bump in the night.

A client consulted with the problem that an energetic being was present in his house. He got his house blessed and protected by getting someone to conduct a geopathic healing on the house. Crystals was placed in every room as an extra protective measure. After two weeks he was woken during the night with the feeling of a person at his back in his bed.

As he described his story I asked him to recall the last few years of mishaps in his life. He described how his new ride on lawn mower would not work after its second time cutting his lawn. He described incidents of the TV turning itself on and off. He described how a bat (Bat as a power animal is concerned to sense without seeing, psychic abilities and healing) came into his house and resided in his house for days until they found him in his hiding place. He described how his new car would break down at critical moments in his life. He began to see the pattern.

He described his fear of being himself. He knew he was good with people but did not have the confidence to stand on his own two feet and start his journey of self development. I asked him to call in the shadowy figure annoying him at his back while in bed. The room turned cold. He got a pain in his right shoulder and arm. His kidneys started to pulsate with dense energy as I linked in somatically to his energy field (indicating fear). It was Morgan or Crow energy. At some level his soul wanted to commence his healing work but his fear overcame him. His Guides gave him messages for some time but he ignored the fact that his life had to change in order that his soul experience growth. He was quiet psychic and he admitted that fact to me at the end of the session. He knew that he was being backed into a corner to make a decision. I advised him that his gifts were not his gifts but he simply only had the use of these tools as per the permission of his Guides. He would only be allowed a certain time limit to make up his mind and if he refused, access to his gifts would be rescinded. I also advised him that his soul would regret not accepting his gifts by going on a therapeutic journey with an energy healer, which did not necessarily have to be me.

The more we give the more we get.

This is one of the principles of abundance. We are simply a channel for energy to pass through us and if we stop that flow then we are unable to give to the world. When we give we create a vacuum within our energy field. As there is no such thing as a vacuum in nature, more energy has to rush in to fill the void. Therefore we will never be short changed in that what we give we get in return. If we give with an open heart as a gift for the good of all mankind then we will be given more responsibility in receiving knowledge and abundance from our Guides to share with the world. A sign that a person has a closed heart is that when you address them, the first word out of their mouth will be 'No.' They have blocked off the energy of the energetic vibration that you have sent them. They will then go up into their head and possibly repeat your words and try and think through the process of what you are communicating. This process is particularly evident with people engaging in counselling. One person put it to me that her counsellor would ask after a revelation 'what do you think about that? While this allows objectivity it also disconnects from the emotionality of the issue which is the driving force behind the spiritual laws operating in our life. Counselling is good but a deeper level of therapy is required as evident by the science of energy psychology.

As like attracts like, scarcity or poverty consciousness will only attract poverty. Our inner feelings must be aligned with our highest good. We need to have an open heart to share with others and to know the difference when we are caring for others rather then taking their power away from them. We will not be supported by the universe if we help others to be liked, to be needed or by disempowering others. That energy will be lost forever.

Bring Light to the dark and grow the spark of light.

With energy healing we focus on supporting and growing the light with the psyche of the individual. Think of the song by Leonard Cohen – 'There's a crack in everything, that's how the light gets in.' If a client consults with terrible problems, we destroy as per the evolution of their light body the darkness that is manifesting in their life. This energy is there for a reason and needs to be transmuted in order for the client to be free. This transmutation and release can only occur when the client is ready to change and the vacuum left by the darkness be replaced by the light. I see many therapists get frustrated with the results of their work with clients which in reality, is illuminating their own personal journey that is being replayed in the therapeutic setting. The speed and rate of change should be determined by the client. This is best achieved by the fact that since no vacuum can exist in nature; we focus on expanding the light through spiritual healing which will transmute the darkness within the psyche of the client.

Energy follows Intent.

We can say we wish to complete a task or plan our future but reality is fuelled by the energy of our intentions. The greater our belief is invested in our intent, the greater the chance that our plans will come to fruition. The emotion we attach to the intention can be directly attributed to the degree of success in out future. We may incur obstacles in our path to success but these should be regarded as merely learning experiences within our energy field. Success is guaranteed if the plan is agreeable with our higher self and we invest the necessary energy in the project.

"Watch your thoughts, for they become words.
Watch your words, for they become actions.
Watch your actions, for they become habits.
Watch your habits, for they become character.
Watch your character, for it becomes your destiny."

Unknown

10. Personality Development.

Our individuality concerns our soul's essence that is constant from lifetime to lifetime. It is hidden within the core of our being and is waiting to express itself once the influence of our personality is transmuted. It contains our true love, acceptance and caring for humanity in the realisation that we are all one. Our personality is the mask of our individual essence. This is formed through the realisation that we are energetic beings that form defence mechanisms according to the stage of development that trauma enters our light body. Trauma is simply an energetic vibration that interrupts the flow of energy within our light body. It can originate from another person, experience or can be formed due to a thought or belief that originates within our own mind. Depending upon the stage of development psychologically and energetically that we experience trauma, it will result in the development of our personality. Therefore, we encode trauma within our psyche according to two methodologies: energetically within the light body and psychologically according to our chronological development.

As we grow up our chakras energetically mature according to the stages of development of our light body. Naturally it is desirable that our chronological age and energetic age mature in tandem which for many people is not the case. This results in such psychological conditions as dissociation, depression/grandiose polarities and inner child conflict. According to when trauma enters our light body we interpret this trauma in the formation of one of five personality subtypes. By the very nature of us being human we will be a personality subtype or more accurately a mixture of up to three subtypes. We will have a dominant type of one particular personality. Each personality has its own individual merits and neither is better or worse then the next. We can experience the conflict between our shadow and ego within each personality to the degree of dissociation from our true essence which will be the cause of great pain in our life.

Unconditional acceptance of self through self love is at the root of each personality. We are required to learn to love ourselves unconditionally which if accomplished, will result in us finding our oneness with the God within us. We will then have accomplished our soul's personal task and probably have moved on to our world task which will be a gift from us to humanity. The degree to which we associate our identity with our defence mechanisms is the degree to which we invest in the upholding of our ego or lower self. Our ego is formed through separation and fear which will have to be integrated back into the self to rebalance our male and female essence. Therefore, the true individuality of the person can merge with the inner and outer being. Our ego, particularly its operating systems may have kept us alive for ten, twenty or possibly up to forty years. To denounce this position involves reliving the emotional pain from the sensitising events that occurred years ago along with the fear of developing a new way of living our life.

When we begin to integrate our higher self we commence opening our heart chakra at a very deep level. This usually involves fear and sadness being released after which a very deep dense ache will appear in the chest area. This is the various levels of energy transmuting within the heart chakra. When a person experiences this level of love entering their life their first reaction is to be scared. They energetically run away because they fear love, abundance and self acceptance. They never previously experienced love in their life so they retreat from the heart chakra and their life grinds to a halt. It can be akin to filling a hot bath of water. Often we may stick our toe in the water to test the temperature before jumping into the water. The key is to advise the person to place their attention in the heart area as opposed to the head/ conscious mind or sacral/ lower self. As they infuse the heart with energy and learn how to hold the space of the heart chakra they will then trust themselves living from the heart space. I have a friend who recently opened their heart chakra after a very long therapeutic journey. They were offered a very good price for a classic car that they were trying to sell for years. Once the offer was made, they sat in the car to think about the offer. They immediately had a panic attack. The shock of having their dream and financial abundance materialise was too good to be true.

Think of a friend you have known for five, ten, or maybe twenty years? How happy would you be if I asked you to renounce this friend after such a long friendship? That is why personality development should never be rushed in therapy as with energy healing the client always does the best they can.

It is through personality analysis that we can begin to energetically understand the challenge of life in the unfolding of the individuality of the true self. We will now examine the five personalities subtypes and the challenges that each present in the development of the individuality of that soul.

The Schizoid Personality.

Typical Schizoid personalities: Hamlet, Marylyn in Finding Nemo. Lightening McQueen in Disney's 'Cars'.

The schizoid personality is the personality that was formed the earliest of the five personalities i.e. during its gestation period in the womb or at birth. The child felt abandoned by its mother and hostility from at least one of its parents. The trauma experienced in the womb could be a result of a shock or injury to their mother or hostility towards the child from a parent. A difficult birthing process could be the umbilical chord wrapped around the baby's neck or the child's nasal passages left partially blocked after birth. This resulted in the child feeling abandoned and fearful to such an extent that the light body of the person only partially merged with the physical body. The remaining essence fled in fear back to the spirit world as a defensive escape mechanism. Thus the schizoid personality is absent to some degree from their body which makes them seem soft or brittle. They will be 'airy fairy' type of people, stuck in the clouds, scratching their head, not getting it together, looking around them unable to make up their mind type of people. They will not be grounded to such an extent that they will feel disconnected from the physical world. On a hot summer day you will see them walk up town wearing a big coat buttoned up to the neck. It's not that they were cold but, simply 'they never thought to think about the clothes to wear at the time of walking out the door. They will go shopping but forget the bread and milk. On returning a second time to the shop to fetch both those items they will have just purchased the bread – the headlines in the paper distracted them. This aspect of personality will drive an anal partner insane.

The schizoid person retreats from their physical body when under stress. They are so emotionally sensitive inside their body that they retreat up into the astral plane avoiding the physical harshness of being a spirit in a physical existence. The trouble being that to be successful in this world means to endure the discomfort and stress of ordinary life. We came down here to self develop in the first place but how can we grow if we don't wait around to experience that growth? They can have little mass on money and may simply give up on this aspect to life. They will tend to intellectualise a lot in that their interpretation of life will be dissociated in the contemplation of people and what they get up to. This avoids looking at what 'I do or can do' or in other words taking responsibility.

The schizoid personality holds fear but his fear is masking his inner rage. He will show his rage by grinding his teeth, clenching his arms and hands and not being able to look people straight in the eye. To touch his rage may trigger his fear of annihilation that nearly occurred at birth so he will be loath to get angry. He will also be angry at a parent who pushed him away at birth at his hour of most need. This anger will be held in the liver which needs to be released over a long period of time. If he gets stuck in therapy at this anger stage then all hell may break loose. He will require a flower essence or a liver detox to help move the liver/anger energy. A blocked liver meridian over time causes deterioration of the hip joint which usually requires a hip/knee replacement on the right hand side.

The conflict within the mind of the schizoid will manifest in their relationships. They are holding rejection from their parent(s) as per a closed heart chakra. They will not think well of themselves or others. They will not know how to share as the love they received as a child was conditional at best or at worst, non existent. Thus no flow can exist in their life emotionally, financially or energetically. In relationships they can be vacant and their partners will accuse them 'of not listening or not being present.' They may be able to repeat back their partners exact words to them but these are just words, nothing registered. The schizoid will have quiet a feminine aspect in that to live half your life in the energetic world will make you sensitive to people and energies. The schizoid will have to reclaim their masculinity. The danger for the schizoid in relationships is that they may attract a dominant masculine partner. Then the anima/ animus conflict will emerge through insecurity and jealously as a complete mismatch of essences will be present such relationships. In other words the male will be the female of the relationship while the female will have to be the male in the relationship. If one partner decides to self develop, a separation will be the likely outcome. Many couples decide to live in this dysfunction ignorant of the challenge that their soul requires which is to be an adult male or female in their own right.

The sensitivity of the schizoid's personality is that which allows them have exceptional natural psychic and mediumistic gifts. Mediumship involves a blending of the essences of the two worlds between man and Spirit. Schizoids with their finely tuned female aspect find it exceptionally easy to acquire the knowledge from Spirit provided that they anchor their male aspect within their light body. The female aspect is akin to the liquid within a challis while the challis is the male aspect that holds the emotionality of the female within its correct boundaries. Schizoids are very clever at times in protecting their emotional state in that they may reject a partner before the partner rejects them. This is the law of attraction in action in that to let someone into your heart runs the risk of feeling the rejection you experienced as a child at your hour of need. They usually have short intense relationships lasting only weeks due to the energetic methods they use to quantify the quality of relationships. This can seem to the outside world as if they are nit pickers and finicky. They are but not in a conceited way. They nit pick because they seek perfection in everything they do. When you live in the astral plane all knowledge is available to you in that you nearly know things before they happen. This is why they see no point in staying the distance with partners? This can lead to feelings of guilt which always masks the aspect of responsibility. They can feel responsible for the world in that their gifts of energy reading are a burden to carry. Once you start to reposition their boundaries in therapy, their world opens up for them.

Their fear will paralyse them into inaction with little or no forward movement. Because of their low self esteem, they usually don't attend therapy until many years of heartache has elapsed. They feel guilty at all aspects of their life and may apologise to everyone to such an extent it's just a way of life. They can be helpful to everyone which usually brings out the best in them. They find it difficult to organise themselves (being energetically out of their body) so a major task for the schizoid personality is to develop routine and discipline. They are natural healers, therapists, problem solvers and research assistants. They may hate paperwork and the mundane aspects of life. They find it easy to start projects but get bored easily and simply leave the task half completed. 'Stickability' is one quality that the schizoid needs to develop in that sometimes life is not pretty but is just about results. I tell clients that the team that wins the soccer premiership football league after a years work probably won the competition because the day they played bad away from home was the day they just battled hard and scrambled the ball over the goal line to score. Life can be like that.

Because the person is not within their body energetically, their hands and feet will be cold. This is because the spiritual body exists in the astral plane and their physicality exists as if it were a shell. As their energetic body spends half its life in the spiritual realm, they can read energy very well. They can be described as a conifer tree, green and healthy on the outside while broken and brittle on the inside. They can be experts in fields by having a superhuman knowledge of the field without having to hardly study the field. They can be sensitive souls who could masturbate quiet often in order to feel their own life force within their body. This can be at the expense of a real connection to another person as a client may often attend and say 'I have a gorgeous, sexy, beautiful, warm, loving wife. Why am I afraid to make love to her? Why do I masturbate? When we make love, the pulsation of the sexual energy rises upwards and heals the whole light body. Therefore with sex addiction, the person is trying to feel their own body. This is impossible for the schizoid to achieve as the trauma at birth has the physical and light body dissociated. Addicts become addicted in order to stop feeling the pain of their emotional history. Focus on feeling the emotions, remaining in your body and the addiction will cease.

The chakras that are most open in the schizoid personality will be the spiritual crown, third eye front/ will centre and the sacral chakra front. They will possess the ability to be spiritual, to see the future, to be emotional, sensual and sexual in feelings only. The front third eye will lead the person to intellectualise and be in their head which will further disconnect them from other people. This energy will show itself by the person growing distant in a relationship after a few weeks due to the fact that to feel closeness with a partner runs the risk of being rejected again. They will be attracted energetically to a partner that will reject them or where the woman can be the 'dominant male' in the relationship. The female will usually attract a harsh masculine partner. Both parties will have to enter therapy, find their true essence and learn to fall in love again. Relationships are perfect even in their dysfunction until a time comes when one party outgrows the others persons energetic vibration. It is somewhat a curse of therapy that inner work can destroy relationships but that is the price of not living a lie.

The complaint of the schizoid in therapy is that they suffer from fear and anxiety and so cannot be successful in life. The female partner of a schizoid needs to push financial responsibility back onto their male partner. This will illuminate the need for him to re-enter the physical world in order that he becomes present in the physical plane to enjoy success. The fear of failure has two sides to that coin which also encompasses the fear of success.

When the schizoid personality looks into their closed eyes they can see white energetic circles within the landscape of their vision. This is their essence floating around their aura as represented by the darkness of their closed eyes. Their essence floating around their energy field is not centred within their light body in the base cauldron as per the eye radar healing technique. The energy from the universe is abundant and unlimited and cannot be utilised by the light body if the essence is displaced.

The schizoid will suffer from depression, have a damaged inner child and may need soul retrieval. When you treat the schizoid person with energetic healing, the therapist needs to be careful with their boundaries with regards getting too close or emotional to the client. At the start of therapy their energy system will be huge and not centred. Since they are experts in energy they may read the rawness of the earth energies as a sexual energy. They are likely to be attracted to their therapist of the opposite sex. This will certainly occur if the opposite sex parent could not express love to their child.

The schizoid personality which operates their energy as if they have an elevator to allow them at will to float out of their body back to the spirit world is the predominant personality that commits death by suicide. It is much easier to remain disconnected then face life. The danger being that the schizoid may want to return home for good and not enjoy the riches of their education on earth.

Examples of Schizoid Personality.

Gerry: How did you get on with your parents?

Schizoid Client: Alright, I suppose. Look at the days that were in it back then, Sure it was the same for everyone of my generation.

Problem: Generalisation and intellectualisation. Client answered from the energetic plane. Did not get in touch with his feelings and avoided responsibility by intellectualising.

Gerry: Are you working at the moment John?

Schizoid Client: No. I had two jobs already this year. My new boss didn't like me. He was a brute anyhow. I was glad to leave. There's no work out there at the moment, look at the economy.

Problem: His vacant and female essence clashed with the dominant male boss essence. While he would be wise to leave such a job he answered by leaving his body and intellectualised from the astral plane thus leaving no room for success or examination of the real problem in the physical plane.

Gerry: Are you in a relationship at the moment?

Schizoid Client: Yes, if you could call it that. He spends every evening in the pub and comes home late and demands his dinner. He is gruff and a hard man. He walks on top of me. I wish I was stronger to deal with him.

Gerry: When did the problems start in the relationship?

Schizoid Client: After we got married?

Problem: The female is not in her body and has a soft but weak feminine essence. She has therefore attracted a masculine dominant husband. Once married, the true essence of both parties can emerge as the marriage contract energetically provides their true essence to emerge.

Gerry: Why is there conflict at the moment in your life?

Schizoid personality Spouse: He is no good. He sits around all day while I go out working to pay for everything. I buy him clothes, shoes and I purchased a new suit last Saturday for him. That evening, he criticised me publicly over setting the table when my friends were over for dinner. No word of my day spent buying him clothes only he humiliating me over a few knives and forks that evening.

Problem: Role reversal of the sexes as per the anima/ animus complex. The male waited to ambush his wife for her dominant masculinity in front of their friends in relation to a 'female' task as the cave woman of the home. The male's failure as the caveman was channelled to anger and he retaliated through humiliating his masculine partner in public. The wife by buying her husband clothes was taking away her male partners masculinity. (No love making tonight).

Gerry: Could you expand by what you mean by intimate problems?

Schizoid client: At first love making was great, exciting and new. But as time went on we grew apart...distant.....even uncommunicative. It has been the same for each girlfriend. It just fizzles away after a few weeks. I don't know what's wrong with me.

Problem: This client is in the grip of the anima complex and is dissociated from their light body. He interprets the energy of his girlfriends rather then let them be a real person in their own right. What this client is also not disclosing is that he continues to masturbate even while in relationships to feel his life force within his body. This client is highly likely to fall in love at first sight because he is energetically projecting his energy onto women. The phenomenon of 'love at first sight' will be the needle that may burst his bubble of the dysfunction he adheres to in the physical plane. He has, in other word narcissistic tendencies.

Gerry: Do you grind your teeth at night or get angry at times?

Schizoid Client: Yes, I do grind my teeth. I got a gum shield from my dentist years ago. It's funny. Sometimes a wave of anger flows up my arms down to the very tips of my fingers. It happens when someone does something demeaning or negative towards me. What is that?

Problem: This client is touching their inner rage. They will alternate from depression to anger and probably never think to question their mood swings. The teeth grinding is representative of anger held within their liver which also surfaces as clinching their teeth in times of stress. They will be afraid to express their anger which at times energetically engulfs their light body rather then journey inwards and access what is emotionally unfolding. It is through focusing inwards that awareness emerges which provides the opportunity to heal the emerging negativity. Secretly they know that their inner thoughts are full of bitterness and powerlessness. They also have narcissistic tendencies.

Therapeutic development of the Schizoid personality.

The schizoid person needs to ground themselves deeply into Mother Earth to anchor themselves back into their light body. They need to ignite the cauldron system of human development over a thirty day period with their bum sitting on Mother Earth. They need to utilise stag energy as their power animal to help call in their essence. They will then re-experience their fear which alienated them from their essence when in the womb or may go through a rebirthing process in order to complete their birth into the physical plane. After their fear starts to transmute, their power emerges which will then bring forth their anger. This can be projected onto others so advise the client to realise transference and projection issues are internal rather then external.

The greatest sadness that the schizoid client will release will be from a childhood spent being invisible to their parents. It may emerge from the fact that their parents had a different vibration from the schizoid and the child had no energetic space to 'breathe' as a child. No trauma need have occurred but the pain of emotional distance over so many years will be considerable. Through the law of attraction the schizoid would have been born into such parents in the first place as the schizoid is invisible even to themselves which has to be created externally in reality.

After their rage/anger surfaces then deep sadness emerges as they realise looking inwards holds the key to personal growth. Their sinuses may flare up or may get a chest infection coughing up flem and liquid which will mirror the withheld tears of their childhood. They will spend many months re entering their body with an emotional see saw of fear, anger, sadness, then heartache in the heart chakra and finally the emergence of self. Most of the first months of therapy will be spent dealing with the fear of re-entering their body. After the destroying phase of therapy which is releasing fear, they will enter the building phase of their life (through the laws of attraction) with their heart chakra opening via the connection to the emotionality of their lower chakras.

Remember trauma will result in the stopping of the flow of energy through the light body. If the child did not receive with an open heart then they had no choice but to close their heart chakra and not learn to give and receive. Through therapy there will be the continual opening of the heart chakra as the heart chakra is the link between the astral plane and emotional light body. This allows the person to accept and receive love in their life. The schizoid will be learning to accept and love themselves, to receive unconditionally and release guilt and feelings of failure. Their sadness will uncover the belief 'what was so repulsive and wrong about me that I was so unlovable.' They will have issues with their partner in that there is a good chance they married the rejection from their father or mother as per the law of attraction. In time they will be faced with a decision in their relationship – wait in loneliness or take a chance and reclaim love in their life. If they married a strong personality (the masochist, psychopathic or rigid personality) they will have to battle this person for ownership of their male or femaleness within the relationship. If their partner does not wish to pull back and develop their own essence then conflict will ensue. This will serve as a lesson to wait in their body and not retreat to the energetic world' as the waves of anger emerge from their partner. Their partner will be their greatest teacher.

The final stages of therapy will bring forth their inner bitterness and rejection from their spleen and gallbladder. Hiding behind the bitterness will be their fear, isolation and hurt of being ignored as a baby. This will be the time that they enter 'gallbladder mode' of eating sugar and sweets to satisfy the inner drives compelling them to powerlessness and isolation. They will re-enter their body probably with Morgan helping them with releasing fear from their kidneys and solar plexus. They will merge with the Wild Green Man/Woman energy and visualise what they want for their future. The symptoms they attended therapy in the first place usually involve fears, phobias, low self esteem, insomnia, insecurity, anger and rage issues will have been naturally dissolved through their inner energetic work. A quick fix of a mind trick as advocated by some therapies will only scratch the surface of the disorder. For instance, even if they cure their fear of flying they will not be tending to their soul's growth.

At the final stage of opening their heart chakra they will experience major fluctuations in their life with regards finances, relationships and work etc. This is because a chakra does not open fluidly but opens in spasms which will therefore be reflected in their life. Fear will also come to play as the schizoid will be afraid to experience their full force of their energy opening to the world. It is common to see a schizoid person enter the heart space, become fearful then retreat back to their old energy patterns before they re-emerge stronger into their heart space. It's like checking the temperature of a bath of water with your big toe before you completely dive in. A person who achieves an open heart space will have an 'energetic feeling of light' in their heart chakra. This is the mergence of their light body with their higher self or the end result of therapy.

Light Body of the Schizoid Personality.

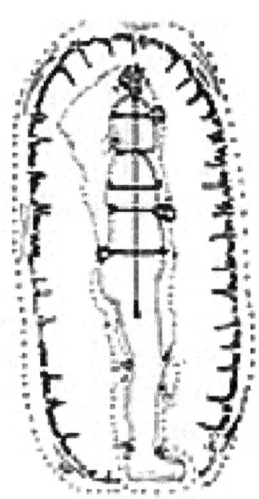

The Oral Personality.

Typical Oral Personalities: Dr. Wilson in House, Sally in Disney's 'Cars,' Watson in Sherlock Holmes.

The oral personality is very closely related to the schizoid personality. There will be somewhat of an overlap of these two personalities in that the cause of the oral personality's trauma was abandonment by their mother at the oral stage of development. This resulted in the creation of an inward energetic emptiness or neediness which they will try and satisfy through their external relationships. The lower self of the oral person will identify their existence through their relationships whereby someone is required to love them. One of the biggest problems with the oral personality is that they are afraid to ask for their needs to be met. Their needs were not met in their childhood which resulted in the closing of their heart chakra. A child is loved unconditionally when the parent's heart chakra channels energy unceasingly to the child simply because they are loved for who they are as a person. If that flow of love is conditional or non existent then the child will rebel with anger at first until eventually they will give up and close their heart chakra. As chakras are gateways for energy then no flow can exist in the adult life of this person. Always remember that parental styles will be heavily influenced by the experience of the persons own parents. If a parent only matured to the energetic age of twelve as a result of their childhood then that parent will not know how to parent their own children once they reach age twelve. There is no blame but simply karmic family patterns to be cleared. This causes the universe to stop flowing energy through their life which depletes their energy. The orals fear of further rejection results in a stalemate of resenting themselves for not asking for their needs to be met and so alienating their partner for not providing for their needs.

They usually enter a relationship with two suitcases of emotional baggage which translates into 'fill me with love.' They make love for closeness, to feel the warmth and love of the other person close to them and to be accepted. Unfortunately, as they have a huge empty gaping energetic neediness within them they find that another person is unable to adequately fulfil this need. They will have a damaged inner child, fears and phobias and a fear of losing control. They will usually answer a person with a question. Their language will be indirect and indecisive. This is a cover for not holding their own self worth in that to stand their ground means to value themselves.

As a result of their childhood rejection, the oral person feels that there is something 'deeply wrong' with them in order that they like the schizoid, are so unlovable. This may be projected onto their self esteem, their looks and the world that they inhabit. If they have not transmuted this deep inner sadness of self worth, the danger exists that they will attract into their life a partner that will reflect this deep sense of 'unlovability' of their essence. This also raises the problem that the oral personality may marry a father figure and have a parent child relationship with their partner as per the emotional/sexual maturing of the energetic light body.

If one partner enters therapy they will eventually stop looking outside themselves to emotionally fill their inner world. Their boundaries will become strengthened in that they will begin to view the world as it is rather then what they though it was as per their childhood. They will start making a life for themselves and will become annoyed at their neediness when a prospective suitor enters their environment. In a group setting where previously the dark hansom man would have been 'exciting and daring,' he now seems 'possessive, demanding and over consuming' to have to share myself with that person. Eventually the oral person will find solitude within their own personality and begin to like themselves. They will start to think of themselves first and realise that self love does not equate to selfishness. They will realise that the sex they had in the past was for closeness to fill their inner emptiness which now has developed into the expression of their joy of their inner being. They will open their heart chakra and realise that it's alright to receive from the world which will be a big realisation for them. Once their faith in their world increases they can begin to share their wonderful gifts with the world. Their relationship will be one of mutual giving so that they will realise that it's alright to accept nourishment from another person rather then a fulfilling of their inner neediness.

Towards the final stages of the healing of an inner child wound, the opportunity for a deeper connection with other people and, more specifically children, will emerge in the person's life. If a person was 'invisible' to their parents during their childhood which resulted in a damaged inner child then that child will be incapable of an adequate emotional connection to others when as an adult. That person, if they become a parent they will be robbed of the joy of an open heart chakra towards their own children. When the time will come that they can fully transmute their inner child wound, children present themselves in their life and will show them the beauty and love that they had hidden away in their closed heart. The children will smile, light up and hug the adult as if their life depended upon the sharing of the love. The adult will respond with a glow of the simplicity and purity of the connection which will indicate the person is now opening their heart at a very deep level. The actual act of sharing the heart emotion and the child returning this love through the law of attraction will open the heart chakra to even greater depths. This is a wonderful time during the therapeutic journey as sadness will be secondary to the actual act of living in the connection of their heart space.

The oral personality will carry the energetic baggage of the weight of the world on their shoulders. They will appear slightly hunched with an appearance of a hallow space within their chest area. They are usually quiet people with a tall slender build. There is some evidence to suggest through the book 'The Twinless Self' by Fr. Jim Cogley that the oral personality were originally conceived in the womb as a twin but only one child actually survived. The energetic loss of their twin will be mirrored in the creation of the oral personality later in life.

Their crown chakra, front of their third eye and front sacral chakra will be open hence their ability to feel love which will be reflected in their love making.

---

*Gerry: **What would you like to change in your life?***

Oral person: You mean what am I not happy with? Where do I start....have you got all day?

Psychological problem: The client has reverted to questioning as a defence mechanism in order not to stand in their own truth and conviction.

---

*Gerry: **What annoys you about your husband?***

Oral Personality: He never seems to know what to do or what to say? He can never press the right button. We have nice times of course but I feel hallow inside at times. He cannot seem to fill that deep emptiness inside.

Psychological problem: The client is touching their inner emptiness of the rejection they experienced as a child. At this stage the client does not know if the emptiness stems from their relationship or from their childhood. The client needs to be supported to wait in their relationship in order to

(1) Find their own internal essence and
(2) Then look at the essence of their relationship to determine if the relationship is compatible.

Oral Personality: I just left my boyfriend two weeks ago. But last week in a night club I met this gorgeous guy and we talked for ages. We are meeting again tonight. He is so warm and lovable. He makes me feel really good inside, totally different from that last guy who never saw me for the person I am.

Gerry: After just dealing with your last relationship which you were trying to leave for many months, how do you know that the emptiness that is being filled inside you is stemming from leaving the old relationship, which it could be, or from the desire of a new relationship that is masking your inner emptiness that you felt in your last relationship?

Psychological problem: The client is jumping headlong into relationship after relationship in order to fill her inner emotional void. The client has placed two suitcases of emotional baggage onto her prospective boyfriend that he simply cannot fulfil.

Therapeutic development of the Oral Personality.

The cauldron system of energy may need to be employed if the person is heavily influenced by the schizoid personality subtype. This will anchor the person within their body. The emotional blockage of their inner emptiness will be stored within the sacral chakra. It will contain layer after layer of hurt, anguish, disappointment and sorrow. It will be the seat of their damaged inner child as the oral personality may be living their life in an inner child mode. Their self worth will improve as energy enters their solar plexus which will then uncover their anger in their liver. After anger is accessed, their sadness will emerge through fear and emotions emerging from within the sacral chakra. After sadness comes the deep hurt of their soul not being nourished and loved. Once the heart chakra opens they will become aware of boundaries, become aware of the structure of reality for what it is and begin to not take life so serious. Their quirky, humorous side develops which illuminates their essence that warms to all people that they encounter. Once they find their true self they are surprised that they externally stop longing for love and acceptance and that the correct partner magically appears for them to fuel their passion for life.

I describe that the masculine energy is akin to a car while the female energy is the petrol that fuels the forward thrust of the masculine energy. Working solely on masculine energy or living in your head will eventually burn itself out. The mergence of true essence both internally and within your relationship provides bliss in your life. This will be evident within the development of the oral personality once they learn to take ownership of their life.

Light Body of the Oral Personality.

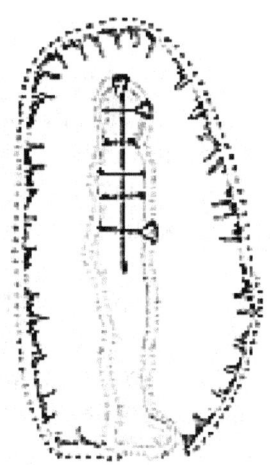

The Psychopathic Personality.

Personality people: Union negotiators, Company directors, Computer programmers, Police men, Accountants, Line managers, Soldiers.

The Psychopathic personality is a very anal controlling personality. As a baby, the child was engaged in a love triangle with their parents. The parent of the opposite sex was seductive towards the child in that the child was fulfilling some need for that parent. The child then sought support from the parent of the same sex which was not available. The child then reverted back to the parent of the opposite sex and found this support energetically unfulfilling as is all support from just one parent. As a result of that disappointment with that opposite sex parent they tried to manipulate or control that parent. The belief was then formed that to survive in the world was to control others therefore you will find the psychopath will use such controlling language as 'ought, should, and must' etc. In less extreme cases they will try and seduce you to enforce their will upon you. Their projected confidence and belief in themselves hides deep inferiority. They are scared of showing their feelings and may avoid sex. The anxiety the psychopathic personality feels in the expression of their life is great. They are extremely noble, kind and compassionate at times. They are expert negotiators and can see both sides of the same argument. They can thrive in employment situations due to their logical mind and tremendous will. Their homes can be effeminate with tremendous detail that shows the emergence of the conflict of the hidden anima/ animus complex.

On some level the psychopath personality is not in touch with reality. They can be like a volcano ready to erupt in contemptuous anger and in two minutes later be buying food for a homeless man on the sidewalk. This can be so frustrating to watch as they will dominate you one minute and give you the shirt of their back the next minute.

In playing with younger children the psychopath usually cannot loose. They always have to win. They do not understand the concept of development of the younger child through letting the child win. They will be meticulous with their belongings usually building up an expertise in a particular field. This is partly due to the fact that to make them irreplaceable to others is to strengthen their position in the other person's life. They will help people but it will be at a price. They do not trust themselves which is reflected in the front chakras being closed and only the will centre of the neck, head and throat being open. When they learn to trust themselves they will find peace in the world to share their natural and warm personality. You will be surprised to find that they admit to a large monthly donation to a charity or that since the last two years give four hours a week to helping needy people learn skills in their expertise.

On examining the parental relationship of the psychopath you will find that intimacy has broken down within that relationship. The opposite sex parent on some level required recognition for their essence or sexuality from their son/daughter. The pressure to be an energetic wife or husband is too much of a burden for a child to carry which will inevitably bring confusion to the development of the child. You cannot be both a parent and a partner to the same person.

Therapeutic examples of the Psychopathic personality.

Bear in mind that the psychopathic personality is usually closely related to the next personality subtype – the masochist. Often I see the psychopath enter therapy with feelings of defeat or just wanting to give up. The masochist (type 4 personality) consults with feelings of tension so the psychopath person will have tension to some degree in their interactions with people. They will be exhausted from the effort that they have to expend to hold their life together. Controlling life is a thankless task that will ultimately fail because life is a river that flows through us rather then we trying to divert the flow of the river through the coercive force of our will. Behind the manipulation of the psychopath are feelings of betrayal, insecurity and fear. They will wrestle for control of the therapeutic relationship in therapy which will be the start of the psychopathic saying to themselves 'why do I do that, is there another way of me to exist without this battle of wills.' The deep rooted anger will surface which, if the therapist does not take on the projection of the psychopath's anger, will lead to sadness and eventually heartache through the hierarchy of emotions.

Energetically the psychopathic' three bottom chakras need to be connected to the top half of their body. They will begin to feel emotions and connected to people in a real manner as the sacral chakra connects to the heart chakra. They will let themselves off the hook by allowing themselves to feel emotion rather then letting their inner tension build and explode from the pressure of their attitude towards life. The psychopathic will find much fault with their parents in therapy. They will consult with rage vented towards one parent but once the mask of the lower self falls they usually turn their attention to the opposite parent. This is usually an eye opener to the person as it never dawned on them to look at the essence of the second parent.

The aura around the psychopathic person will change to a more open and flowing energy system. They will communicate their needs and trust in themselves that they don't need to control another person to get what they want. They usually find their spirituality which makes great sense to them once they see the logic in the spiritual laws governing mankind.

Gerry: How were the last few weeks for you John?

John: Not bad. I was home the last weekend. It was only me, Mum and Dad at home. That was fine. I didn't go out on Saturday night. Dad drove me mad. He kept going on about his golf. I hate golf. Did he get it? No he didn't. I just made faces at Mum to tell her to change the subject. I don't know why I bother.

Psychological problem: The son is reaching his inner contempt for his Dad as he has energetically sided with his Mother. He is in effect, married to his Mother and in competition with hid Dad for the attention of his own energetic wife? Notice how he is trying to control his environment by asking his parents bend to his will. There is no space for a woman to enter John's life as this is evident by how he does not socialise on a Saturday night to hide his contempt for his own essence. He is still living his life in hurt inner child mode.

Gerry: How was your holidays Sandra?

Sandra: My back went 'again' on the day before my holidays. I was not able to go away on holidays and spent the two weeks at home being waited on hand and foot by Dad. The pain was so bad one night that he had to knock up the local pharmacist. At least I got to see my friends even though they had to visit me in my old bedroom unable to move a muscle with the fear of putting my back out again.

Psychological problem: More then likely a psychological response of her inner child expressing fear. Look at the inventive opportunity they conjured up of controlling their parents. Notice how the Dad waited hand and foot on their child and the public spectacle of everyone being controlled in sympathy for their back pain.

Gerry: How was the last few weeks John?

John: Good. I had a major row with my sister. We haven't talked in days. She wanted me to fix her computer. I agreed to fix it a few weeks ago which was fine. She got me a case of beer for fixing her computer but I never got a chance to fix it. I arrived home one evening and she had taken my laptop. She brought it to her house printing off some material she needed for work. I just walked in, exploded in anger, took my laptop and left. How dare she?

Psychological problem: The client is trying to be needed in his sister's life. He adores being needed but to fix the computer would spoil the control he exerts over his sister. The idea of being paid in advance for the work is secondary to his inner need to control others. He is projecting his childhood anger towards his mother onto his sister.

Gerry; How was your weeks Sam?

Sam: Busy at work. I had a meeting last week with the powers that be. They wanted to cut the budget and cut back on services to the homeless while the budget on trips to foreign countries was increased. I fought tooth and nail for hours at that meeting until the budgets were changed.

Psychological problem: It is evident that the big warm heart of this person battled for the homeless people who have no voice. Practically no other personality type would be as forthright in the protection of other people's rights. They probably won the argument due to the fact that they would not let it go and ground everyone down with their sheer force of will.

Therapeutic development of the Psychopathic Personality.

Since trust is a major issue that is absent from the psychopathic personality profile, the development of the psyche must involve strengthening the inner world of the person. This involves deep earth connection releasing fear in the kidneys, energetic shame and guilt on the head and, opening the feeling chakras on the front of the body. Deep anger will emerge as the chords from the past will be cut between child and opposite sex parent. The type of partner that they previously attracted in their relationships may change. They will realise that they are not in competition with the same sex parent as they will increase their perception of their own essence. It is likely that arguments will erupt as the person energetically matures while the relationship with their same sex parent will blossom.

In therapy, at some stage with the psychopath personality, a battle of wills will take place that will challenge the therapist to hold their own line of authority. If the therapist is unable to energetically hold the client in that safe position then the client will not go within their inner world to that very dark lonely place of deep insecurity. It is as if the therapist must become a surrogate parent to the child to show them how to trust themselves. Examination of the hierarchy of emotions states that behind anger lays sadness and behind sadness is heartache and, behind heartache is the true self.

Light Body of the Psychopathic Personality.

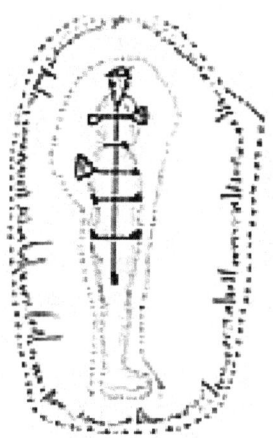

The Masochistic Personality.

The masochistic personality had a domineering and controlling mother in that their mother controlled all aspects of the child's life. The child was controlled to such a degree that self expression was non existent. Even if such expression was attempted, the child was made to feel guilty for such indiscretions and so the child learned to withhold emotions and their essence. This suppression from their childhood may not be evident to the client upon entering therapy as the way we shift ego states is camouflaged as a defence mechanism. This suffocation of their soul essence leads to internal boiling anger which is communicated through polite expressions usually administrated with whimsical disgust. The fear for the masochist is 'how can I be angry to someone whom I rely on for my survival? This anger is channelled into indirect communication which provokes teasing from others which in turn provides ammunition for the right of the masochist to be angry. Thus the person is caught in a cycle of anger, lack of expression, teasing, non surrender, whimsical disgust and then provocation by others.

In a room full of people engaging in conversation, you can sense a time when every person in the group energetically communicates with each other to almost alienate the masochistic character. It will appear as a communication within the group as a laugh, look, gaze, then a smile etc in which the group will be non verbally saying 'look at the vibe from that person.' To hide his inner feelings the masochist may have previously been sighing, yawning, stretching or directly confronting another person with their hidden boiling, seething anger. Eventually the masochist realises they are a fringe person to the group because they are lying to the group. They are not honest and open with their communication of their individual essence and a lie will always be found out in the energetic world. This alienation is usually the teasing of the group towards the masochist character. The masochist responds with whimsical contempt usually delivered in a contemptuous tone which alienates the person further from the group. This provides the opportunity for anger to be unleashed and so the internal emotional cycle is complete.

The masochist has a big heart full of warmth and caring. They have wonderful gifts and are naturally good with people. They can possess wonderful style and creativity. They usually are good with money and I often see luck follow them in their lives. They will have trouble in expressing their sexuality with the male vying towards pornography and the female feels she has little to offer sexually.

Gerry: What do you feel about the atmosphere between us Mary? How are 'we' getting on?

Mary: What do you mean by the atmosphere between us?

Gerry: Notice the air, the general feeling in the space between us and what is around both of us? More specifically what atmosphere are we creating as communicators in our aura that is being sent out to the world?

Mary: I think I know what you mean. The sense of the communication between us....I feel this is normal?

Gerry: I am so glad you used the word feel, that's exactly the word I wanted you to use. Now let's go a little bit further. I am feeling tense. It's not the fact that our sessions are a battle or confrontational but more so the fact that our sessions are quiet compact, intellectual! Dare I say it, enjoyable to the inner workings of the mind? Do any of your friends ever comment to you on your conversation or energy around you?

Mary: Yes, last week at work they were half laughing at me that I couldn't get this programme to work. It was very frustrating. I was mystified while everyone simply said' Ah Mary, just let it go'.

Psychological problem: Mary has been given feedback as to how her atmosphere, inner brooding and tension is communicated energetically to her world. Mary is not told as to how this is happening but is asked to reflect upon her internal emotions when she communicates with people. The more honest Mary is with herself and her own inner feelings the more people will trust her authenticity in her communication.

Therapeutic development of the Masochistic personality.

The energy system of the masochistic usually entails an open third eye and solar plexus in the feeling centre of the chakras. Their sacral chakra will usually be closed as will the heart chakra. The masochistic will need to connect to mother earth, support the lower three chakras along with inner child work, give themselves permission to feel and express themselves thereby releasing the constriction and anger of their youth. In learning to trust themselves they learn not to push people away.

Light Body of the Masochist Personality.

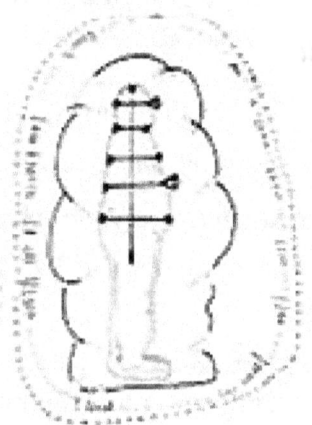

The Rigid Personality.

The rigid personality was formed due to the withdrawing of love to the child by the opposite sex parent. To a child, love, intimacy and sex are one and the same so this rejection caused the child to withdraw into themselves in order to withhold their essence. This is basically a protection mechanism as the child realised that it was safer to deal with life through their ego/will centre rather then their heart chakra. The child's feelings could not be trusted and so was deliberately shut off from the psyche of the child. Therefore they control the world using force through their powerful will and mind. Feelings are not to be trusted as to experience emotions is to revisit the pain of their rejection they experienced in their childhood. The answer lies in not surrendering to their inner pain which hides their biggest disappointment – their pride in their essence was rejected. This will result in the position that the rigid personality will make love out of contempt and not intimacy (into-me-see). You can see this person causing an argument and initiating love making after the conflict because energetically this is the making up of the rejection they experienced with the parent of the opposite sex. They will say 'the best sex is always after a row.' With such emotional suppression they will use qualifiers to achieve their own way in relationships. This is only competition in action which further alienates them from others. This will manifest as such language as 'yes but' as a defence mechanism to push people away thereby hiding their true feelings in order to control others.

The rigid personality, as per the law of attraction usually attracts a soft effeminate partner. Conflict will ensue as both shadows will become suspicious of their more developed partners shadow. In other words the female's shadow male side will be angry at her feminine partner's weak masculine side. Her inferior feminine side will feel insecure against her male partners highly developed female aspect. Therefore, there will be no balance in this relationship. They will constantly cut at each other indirectly through snide remarks which in reality is their shadow aspects rebelling against their partner's essence.

The rigid personality will not know how to say the word 'sorry.' Life is experienced through their terms in that their force must command and control their world. It is as if friend and foe is treated in the same manner. They can literally suck the life out of their partners as no emotional nourishment will be provided to their partner. If one partner changes and the other decide not to develop their essence, then the relationship will consist of two male essences or two female essences. This relationship is unlikely to last as both parties have reached an impasse and no further development is possible within that relationship.

The rigid personality with their force and temper are brilliant business people. They are the people that strip companies apart, don't see the people, take the cash and run. As they equate financial success with overall success in life they are too busy making money to attend therapy. Their poor self esteem will attract a similar character but many end up in their elder years alone, lonely, full of regret, physically exhausted from the sheer effort of life and their financial worth dwindling due to inflation and the passing of time.

As the mother principle is concerned with the softer feminine essence it is possible that their dad could energetically be the mum while the mum could be the child's dad due to mum possessing the stronger 'rigid' male essence. Attachment theory is concerned to the degree of sensitivity that is available to a child in order that the child develops secure attachments to her outside world. If mum was hard and domineering in the father role and possessed a weak, insecure female aspect then a female child could be rejected energetically by the parent of the opposite sex, namely her mother's harsh male aspect. This female child will mirror her mother's harsh male energy but feel the rejection from her mother's female side. The child will then attract a female dominated male husband and role reversal will consume the relationship through the anima/animus complex. Through the law of attraction, the adult female will likely create the repulsion of her own energy by energetically pushing her husband away due to her low self esteem.

Gerry: What would you like to change about your life Joe?

Joe: I have this terrible temper, I get angry a lot. It ends in a row and my girlfriend not talking to me.

Gerry: What do you row about Joe?

Joe: Money. That's what we row about. She spends all my money as if it grows on trees. She went to the shop last week and I told her not to spend more then €10. She spent €20. I blew a fuse. She says I have a problem.

Gerry: How does your girlfriend react to your argument?

Joe: She goes to the bedroom and cry. She remains silent for days. She doesn't even look at me.

Gerry: Did you say sorry for your part of the argument?

Joe: Were you listening to me....I have nothing to be sorry about? It's her that did the spending.

Psychological problem: Joe is completely closed on the feeling (front chakras) in his light body. His force is pushing his girlfriend away. He requires energy healing and will need to be told how his lack of feeling will affect him in his life. He is incapable of feeling for his girlfriend at this junction.

Gerry: Welcome Ann, how can I help you?

Ann: I have come to see you about (Phone rings) Sorry I will have to answer the phone?

Gerry: Where were we? Yes! What brings you here today?

Ann: Stress. This pain I have in the back of my neck. It's like a weight on my shoulders. Can you help me deal with stress?

Gerry: Yes I …..(Phone rings).

Ann: I will take that…I am waiting on a call?

Ann is so busy leading her life that she is unable to commit a short time to her emotional welfare. Her phone is more important then our conversation and is unlikely to be back for therapy. I advise Ann to go for a deep tissue massage. Feeling herself within her body is the best she can hope for at this time.

<u>*Therapeutic development of the Rigid personality.*</u>

The rigid personality almost never attends therapy. And why should they! With practically all the will centre chakras (force aspect of life) open at the back of their body which allows them to function without any feeling via their closed front chakras. They are thus suited to a career in business where they can thrive in the competitive world of making money. Many times they can have a ferocious temper that can accelerate from zero to ballistic in seconds. Their female aspect will be suppressed and will dress, think and probably feel like a man. Opening the feeling chakras at the front of their body will allow their emotions to flow. Introducing cow energy will ignite their female creative side. Once they start to release their hurt and inner fear they will find a wonderful world of passion and fun. The world can then be their oyster to experience their femminity and be successful and creative at the same time.

Again let me state that we are a mixture of personalities rather then simply a particular personality. Each personality will attract through the spiritual laws of mankind the perfect partner that will be our alter ego in transforming our emotional well being. Always look within to determine what lessons the other person is teaching you which will allow you freedom and grace in your life. In spiritual terms this will be the ending of setting down karma in your life. Other people will be free to be themselves with no threat from you or experienced by you. This is the object of relationships so that we learn from each other and become all that we can be in this particular lifetime. Relationships are always perfect even in their level of dysfunction.

It is very easy to be judgemental towards others. If you reflect upon the words of Silver Birch, the Spirit Guide – If you could see another person's past incarnational lives then you would never judge them.

Light Body of the Rigid Personality.

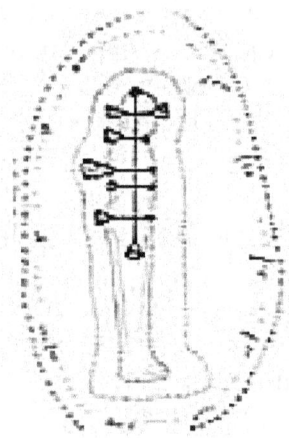

11. The Hierarchy of the Processing of Human Emotions.

There is a pattern to the execution of the processing of our emotional intelligence. Our emotional intelligence can be mature, responsible and in sync with our chronological age or can be stunted or misaligned with regards our age. We can find ourselves reacting as per our inner child aged five if an external energy triggers an old emotional experience that is lodged within our energy field. The spiritual laws will ensure that such particular triggers keep coming towards us in order to illuminate what we are withholding. This is quiet painful to watch but usually the person is caught up in the drama of life rather then to turn his attention inwards to his inner world to determine why this is occurring in his external world

Look at very successful businessmen. Many are really confident and masculine when in work. Once they get home to their wife (maybe I mean…. Mother Energy), see how they energetically react. Their wife goes into 'Mother Energy' and their husband becomes the 'son.' The processing of emotions in this instance will involve the husband energetically going back in time and processing the emotionality of their relationship with their mother in order that he can energetically grow into maturity.

We can realise the maturing and processing of the energy in our light body by the somatic energetic feelings within our body whereby we can check the movement of energy within our light body.

Question: You realise that you have regressed back to an earlier traumatic energetic state of mind. Analysing your emotions, how do you know if you are actually transmuting that energetic emotional state from your psyche?

Answer: You feel the processing of the negative energy imprints by bringing the emerging imprints up to the heart chakra. The heart chakra transmutes energetic imprints from all levels of our being. Then examine the developing emotional states that emerge with the transmutation of those energetic imprints.

In other words there is a process or hierarchy to the pattern by which we release negative imprints and their corresponding emotions from our psyche. The hierarchy of emotions is as follows:

Shame

Guilt

Depression/ loneliness

Fear

Rage

Anger

Resentment/Sadness/Bitterness

Powerlessness/ Stress

Positivity

Hope/ Enthusiasm

Excitement

Freedom/ Expression

Love

Gratitude

As we receive the healing energy from Mother Earth, it enters via our Earth chakra in our feet and proceeds to dissolve the negative emotional imprints stored within the light body. The storage of these imprints releases their corresponding emotional charge. Behind each emotional experience can be a myriad of emotions. Think of rejection as a little child. The child will hold the negative emotional charge of being rejected, unloved and being unwanted. As a child will internalise their external world, feelings of shame and guilt will emerge as thoughts 'there must be something wrong with me to be rejected.' The child will feel alone and therefore powerless. This powerlessness will lead to depression or a withholding of the persons essence. This internalisation will swing outwards from time to time as the inner conflict will be too much to bear and will show itself in anger if the person is masculine dominated in energy terms or bitchiness/contempt if female dominated. It will be much easier to remain in anger then to go into the sadness in the spleen and from there to heartache in the heart chakra. The releasing of heart ache will give rise to freedom, self- expression and self love. Ultimately this will transform into the passion for life in the realisation that the person will be grateful for the person that they are.

In psychological terms the person may be in inner child mode. They may attract relationships in which they will be the child and their partner will be a father figure. The possibilities are endless.

Forgiveness vs. Acceptance.

If we forgive someone it automatically conveys a position of dominance and strength over the offending person. It is as if we look down on them and judge them. It is us that agree to the releasing of the other person from the 'bad books' of our judgement. Energetically this is incorrect as we are all one. Acceptance on the other hand has nothing to do with our offender. It is concerned with the inner acceptance that we experienced a particular vibration but no longer hold any negative emotional charge towards the other person for their responsibility in this matter. Acceptance is concerned with us freeing ourselves from the inner slavery of bitterness, hate and anger. It is beyond self righteousness and is concerned with realising that we have scars from the past but the wounds are now healed.

The serpent path is concerned with the manner in which serpent energy travels its path up the light body to its home in the heart chakra. Serpent energy is the full force of the universe working with you. Surprisingly, this is the hierarchy in which we hold our emotional imprints and therefore release our emotional imprints from the past in the reverse order.

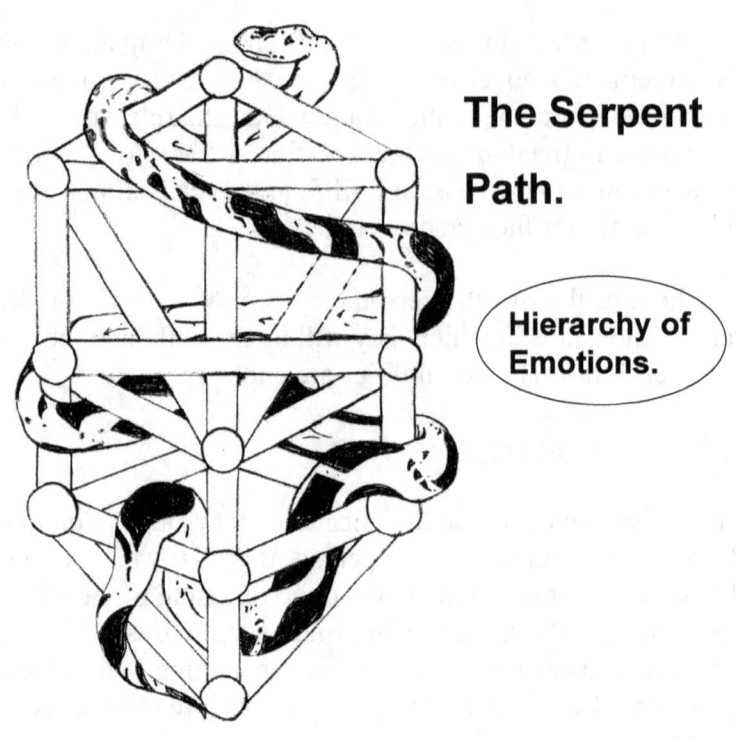

The Serpent Path.

Hierarchy of Emotions.

Base chakra releases shame which concerns our identity and meaningfulness from life. Shame is concerned with our identity whereas guilt originates from a specific action or inaction.

Sacral chakra releases depression, loneliness and isolation. It will highlight our relationship with the opposite sex.
Fear is released from the kidneys which gives way to powerlessness in the solar plexus.
Stress is released from the adrenals which influence the solar plexus.
All the above configuration of energy is concerned with power around the solar plexus.

Resentment (anger turned inwards from our female aspect) is released from the spleen which can alternate between anger in the liver. A blocked male side producing force reverts back to sadness/ resentment in the spleen.

This leads to heart ache in the heart chakra. This introverted ache ultimately provides freedom in the throat chakra releasing deeper suppressed anger and sadness.
Hidden behind the energetic swing of anger and sadness is rage. Rage is energetically held within the gall bladder.

The danger exists that we may get stuck at a particular energetic stage on the hierarchy. We can go around being angry or bitchy which for some time which is quiet common, due to the fact that we may be afraid to touch the sadness in the heart chakra in order to find freedom. Thus at each stage of forward movement along the hierarchy we usually encounter fear that has to be processed in order to move to the next level of emotional maturity.

Case Example: Jonny.

Jonny was eight when he witnessed his Mum and Dad have a major fight at home. Energetically Jonny dissociated from his body from the confusion of having to watch the two people he loved the most in the world destroy each other. Jonny went into school the following day but was still was not reconnected back in his body as his roots were left behind at the scene of the argument.

In class, his teacher asked Jonny to stand up and recite a poem. Jonny froze speechless with every student in the class staring at him. The teacher, being an insensitive soul, flew into a rage and ridiculed Jonny in front of the whole class. He hit Jonny so hard that he temporarily lost his hearing in his right ear. For punishment Jonny had to stand facing the corner until break time.

Years later, suffering from a damaged inner child, depression and relationship problems Jonny attends therapy. The incident from his school day is unearthed. Fear is uncovered which flares up his base chakra which helps strengthen his base chakra and foundations of power and security. The imprints flare up his kidneys which begins the processing of releasing fear of Jonny standing in his own power. Powerlessness is uncovered from his adrenals and solar plexus which after thirty minutes of energetic transmutation only then allows the sacral chakra emerge. This means that Jonny was living his life without any emotionality and was probably stuck in his head cognitively trying to process his way through life. His sacral connected upwards to his solar plexus which brought emotions into his thinking process.

His adrenals further released energy which released stress. Anger flared up in his liver which swung over to the development of his female side releasing bitterness and resentment. His kidneys flared up which released fear of opening his heart chakra. Jonny cried as he released the deep sadness within his heart. This brought peace, love and acceptance into his mind. Through one seemingly small childhood event is stored a myriad of emotions that are but triggers ready to be activated in the victims life.

I don't believe in the afterlife, but I am bringing a change of underwear just in case.

Woody Allen

12. Sending Discarnate Spirits to the Light.

If someone had told me when in my career as a supermarket manager that deceased people do not necessarily go to the heaven I would not have believed them. Equally if someone told me that I would one day send and train other people how to send discarnate spirits to the light, I would have said they were totally crazy.

I dislike funerals and dead people because when I was fourteen I attended a funeral where the deceased person attached itself to my energy field as a 'walk in.' The spirit, a lady who was very domineering, did not go to the light after death and as with all discarnate spirits required a new external energy source. My energy was similar to that of her deceased brother and was therefore a vibrational match to the time that she was alive in the physical plane. This was the law of attraction in operation as to why our energies became the perfect match. I always realised that I had a voice in my head which told me 'I was never good enough, had to do more and to think everything through at the expense of your feelings.' I attended a Healers Healer, Kieran Henson of Henson Holistic in Moat who made me aware of the external energy controlling my energy field. He sent the discarnate spirit to the light. Guess what type of partner/ relationships /employers I attracted over the years? Apply the law of attraction to the energy and you will see the answer. It's interesting to note that a symbiotic relationship existed between the two of us. I needed her strength and determination in my life therefore I was not able to release her energy back to the light until I started to believe in my own strength. Always remember there is no such thing as blame.

I am very comfortable with discarnate spirits that need to go back home to the light. Since I wrote the first draft of this book I have been told by a medium that when I was a little boy I got scared when I started to see dead spirits. I pushed my mediumship skills away but as I deal with my internalised fear of the deceased, my gifts will return. I mean no disrespect to the discarnate spirits as in energetic terms they are more 'alive' then us on earth. I must go to a good hypnotherapist to deal with that fear someday?

We have two energetic spiritual light sources, spiritual energy from the heavens and earth energy from Mother Earth. We are simply a conduit by which these energies are utilised by our chakras to formulate the corresponding psychological functioning in our life. Once we die, our chords connecting our light body from these energy sources are severed. The ideal situation when we die is that we merge with Spiritual light or proceed with our Guides or previously deceased loved ones back home to whatever you call heaven. The greatest risk we face coming back down here to earth via the process of reincarnation is the fact that we forget who we really are and do not return home to the spiritual realm upon our physical death. We deliberately forget our previous incarnations in that remembering usually serves little or no purpose in facing the challenges we choose in this lifetime. The forgetting I am talking about is the fact that we are firstly spiritual beings and secondly physical beings. Our Guides would describe our physical birth as a death in spiritual terms in that we forget who we really are and leave our real home in the spiritual realm. Incidentally many times I hear channelled Guides describe our physical death as our 'second death.' The real trick is to complete our personal and world task and return home with as little Karma as possible. Should be simple I hear you say!

What about Grandma's ring? What about my two door burgundy red five litre Mercedes that my awful son in law has his eye on? What about my wife who was just dieing to get red of me so that she could move her lover into my bed after I am dead and gone? She thinks I don't know about him but I do!

Now you are beginning to realise the problems and danger in becoming human and run the risk of attachment to your physical earth incarnation. The problem lies in that the only difference when we are alive as opposed to when we are dead is the fact that we will have no physical body. Our internal emotions are still the same. Our logical reasoning is still the same. If we were a fool when alive then we probably will be a fool when dead.

This is what the Buddhists talk about when they refer to the term 'attachment.' Attachment is where we identify with our life on earth and we become attached to some material possession, being or emotion that keeps us trapped to the physical plane. We become blind to our Guides, loved ones and the windows of opportunity to return home to paradise. The Buddhists who renounce everything in this life do so with the intent to end the cycle of reincarnation which is fuelled by the principle of attachment to life on the earth plane. Those who become free of attachments in that they have released all Karma and earthly connections are obliged only to return because of service to mankind.

Once we die, we energetically hop out of our body and view our physical body lying lifeless. We are able to see and view everyone and everything but also on an emotional level. We can read energy and peoples thoughts which are simply the vibrations of energy patterns emanating from their light body. When we die we usually commence the spiritual light body death process up to five days before our actual physical death. A chakra closes down each day before death starting with the base charka. While our physical body is being discarded, our life is shown to us in full technicolor. This is the origination of the expression 'my life passed in front of my eyes.' This is why many people close to death will become really exhausted five days before death as the light body commences its journey homeward. You will see all your life's deeds, actions and inactions presented to you. This may or may not be a pretty sight depending upon what choices you made in your life.

As we require an energy source to comfortably survive, the deceased person will seek a new energy source if they do not proceed to heaven. Guess how the deceased person will decide upon which living person to rob their light body's energy and so use as a host?

They decide via the law of resonance from the spiritual laws governing mankind. Like goes with like. If you were angry in life you will be angry in death. The greatest compatibility of an energetic vibrational match will be to find a living host who is also angry. You will, as a deceased person, feel right at home in your host's energy field. And so it is will alcoholics. A deceased alcoholic who has not gone to the light will probably take refuge in his local bar. He will wait until the bar patrons become drunk and then jump on their energy field to re-experience the feeling of what it feels like to be drunk. Like goes with like.

Being used as an energy source means that the discarnate spirit attaches itself to the energy field of the living person. As I developed my sensitivity to energy fields I started to see a blue mist or face on the shoulder of the living person. A female deceased spirit will attach itself on the persons left shoulder and a male will attach itself on the right shoulder of the person. They will also have attachments in the throat chakra and an energetic chord into the solar plexus of their host. While Guides and Angels are warm in temperature, deceased people are cold in temperature. Such symptoms of spirit possession are as follows:

> Neck or shoulder pain.
>
> Fuzziness in the hosts head or thinking process.
>
> Nightmares, funny dreams, insomnia.
>
> A loss of energy or upset tummy because the deceased has a chord into the hosts tummy (Solar plexus).
>
> Unusual behaviour of the host e.g. eating during the night, developing a new taste for unusual foods e.g. pickled gherkin sandwiches at two am in the morning etc.
>
> Becoming emotionally agitated.
>
> Using words such as 'possessed, robbed or dead' out of context.

A common occurrence is where the host works in a hospital, morgue, hospice, police man or comes across a dying person as a result of an accident. This is the situation where the dying literally jumps into their host's body for nurturance.

In my early days working with people, I was not aware that my higher vibration was attracting discarnate spirits to my aura. My energy teacher would tell me that I had a spirit attached to my aura and would take them away to the light. The method by which I came to understand how you send spirits to the light was in accordance with the development of my vibration. A person's gifts are encoded in their energy system and manifest with the maturing of their energetic vibration. When their vibration increases sufficiently to handle the required vibration of a particular gift it is only then that the gift can manifest in consciousness. Weekend courses teaching mediumship etc generally provide mediocre results because you cannot encode such gifts into your vibration in such a short space of time. A teacher, who illuminates blockages to such gifts, provides the science behind the gift and how to develop its functioning is, in my opinion, providing the greatest knowledge of understanding in their teachings.

Once I see a blue mist on the clients shoulder and a person begins to talk about a deceased person or talk about being in an accident, I then know that it is a deceased person attached to their shoulder or neck area. As I somatically link in to my client I can feel the cold temperature of the discarnate spirit. A discarnate spirit will be colder in intensity then a power animal. You will know it when you feel both temperatures with practise. The universe works in strange ways as I referred out those clients with spirit attachments until I was faced with a deceased spirit in my own home.

A friend of mine with an amazing gift of spiritual vision came to visit me one day. Upon entering my house he asked for my digital camera. He proceeded to take pictures of my house until he stopped to look at the picture of the stairs. I was surprised to see a large luminous ball of energy with a face in the centre of that energy sitting on the second step of the stairs. My friend told me he could see the spirit before he entered my house and then went on to point out the hand marks on the wall beside the spirit. I could not see any of this before my friend came as I was not of a vibrational frequency to see these problems. I called all my energy friends and strangely received no reply. I left it a few days and still no one answered my calls. After a few days it dawned on me that I had to face this spirit and learn from our encounter about discarnate spirits.

I placed my protection in place and called in my Guides. I could feel my Guides around me letting me know I was not alone but still I didn't know what to do or what trouble I would bring on myself. I knew that this was a test and my spiritual friends would not telephone unless there was a good reason. This was why I knew that this was an educational lesson and not foolishness on my behalf to attempt to remove the discarnate spirit. The universe was testing me to jump up a gear in evolutionary terms. I tuned into the spirit. As I am quiet good at feeling energy somatically within my body I could feel the liver and heartache imprints flare within my body as I let the spirits emotions flow through my body into the earth. I knew the spirit was energetically holding anger, suppression and heartache. My kidneys then flared, releasing fear into Mother Earth. My hands moved kinaesthetically via my Guides directions as I took the discarnate spirits hand in my hand. After a few moments my hand raised the spirit to the light. I thanked my Guides, closed down my energy and went to my healing room to try and decipher what had just happened.

I realised that my protection and faith in my Guides held in place during the session which meant my attitude and faith in my team was correct. I realised that I removed the spirit by releasing his negative emotions which only left positive emotions or love. The law of attraction in the spiritual light of God merging with the discarnate spirit of the deceased brought the spirit to rest. The fear that was somatically released through my light body allowed the deceased merge with the light through the law of attraction. My own fear of conducting this work was my vibrational blockage which up to now prevented me completing this work. I realised that some fear that left via the kidney imprints was also my own fear of this work. I had learned a new skill.

I realise that in sending discarnate spirits to the light I work in conjunction with my strengths. It may not work for everyone but it does the trick for me. It can be tiring at times in that letting emotions pass through you drains you physically no matter how detached you remain. I am determined and completely trust that if I come across a discarnate spirit that there is only one outcome of the encounter – they are going to heaven. As energy follows intent, this is my intention. The difference being I believe this intention from all of my being rather then just saying it as a lie would get me into all sorts of vibrational trouble when encountering spirits. At times I think I have the task completed but to feel the spirit latch onto me a few hours later. This is because I can be too bullish about transmuting their emotions through my light body and do not give the spirits emotions the time and respect they deserve to sufficiently transmute. This is my responsibility as I know my system works. We are quiet attached to our life here on Earth and sometimes great pain is experienced by leaving children or a loved one behind. It's not all about who's taking my wedding ring. Think of families where children and parents die.

If you connect to a deceased adult spirit, I now usually build their light body in front of me. If they are reluctant to go to the light it usually means that their discarnate children are also present in the room. A parent will not go to the light before their children. Why should they trust me or anyone to send their children to the light as I can only feel energy and not see energy? When a spirit waits holding my hand or my hand refuses to lift them to the light, I then know that they require their deceased children to go to the light before them. The deceased child spirit will be found on the ground somewhere in the room around me.

As I somatically release their negative emotions through my own light body I usually bring down a beam of spiritual light to the crown of the deceased spirit. Often I walk with their energetic light body to my statue of Buddha and merge them with the spiritual light entering the crown of Buddha. In my early days of bringing down a beam of spiritual light to the deceased I accidentally and foolishly walked into the beam which burned the side of my light body. I needed to receive a healing from another therapist to repair the damage. Another lesson learned the hard way but one never forgotten. I can now walk into the beams of spiritual light as my vibration is of an adequate strength to withstand the force of the light. As always I tell people I provide them with this knowledge as a proven truth of mine as I have usually learned it by making many mistakes during the educational process.

If you fail to send a person to the light, then that spirit will reside within your energy field. This is because your vibration as a healer will probably be of a higher source of nurturance then their previous source of energy. As your client will always resonate with you energetically, the discarnate spirit will also be an energetic match. The client will already be weakened as a result of the deceased spirit robbing the life force of their previous host. Deceased spirits where attached to their hosts always damage the aura of the place of attachment. I usually bring a candle to the side of the client in order to bring the spiritual light to repair the damaged aura of the living host.

There can be no doubt in your mind as to completing this work. Remember your energetic intention of doubt will stop you completing this work. If you don't possess an adequate energetic light body which is your bank balance in the astral plane then problems will arise if you write a check in the physical plane from that account. The result can be a bounced check. A check being bounced as returned to sender will be a deceased spirit residing and living from your own energy field. You will have to pay the fee to another therapist of a higher vibration to cleanse your aura not to mention the discomfort in your life.

Because my house was being invaded with so many deceased spirits in my early days as an energy healer, I got my house protected against geopathic stress. These are basically lines of energy on the earth on which the deceased spirits can easily travel. They exist as energetic roads or highways. The protection kept breaking down and deceased spirits kept coming into my house. At last I realised that part of my life's work is to send deceased people to the light and that putting the protection in place was futile. I am constantly aware to look for deceased spirits to send to the light and accept this work by dealing with whatever comes in my door.

When people commit death by suicide they may go to the light. Unfortunately, those who don't go to the light wait on earth around their loved ones. As no one wants to be alone, their vibration communicating to their loved ones can have the influence of them also committing death by suicide. It is important to treat the victim of suicide by sending them to the light along with healing your bereaved client.

I get frustrated by The Catholic church who say at funerals 'it is dust you are and dust you will become.' Think of a religious person who died who is now listening to their parish priest for direction, burying them in the soil telling them to focus on the incorrect pathway to heaven. It is time this prayer was changed to reflect the truth, science and spirituality of our essence.

Procedure for sending Deceased people to the light.

1. Connect to your own energy and Guides.
2. Place your protection in place.
3. Ensure that your treat the work with care, attention and respect. Treat others as you would wish yourself or a loved one be treated.
4. Build the deceased light body in your room using the sign of infinity. As you give your hands to your guides notice where the shape of the head of the deceased is indicated. If the deceased is an adult notice if they go to the light or if their children or babies are present will be indicated by a pause in the procedure.

5. Let your body be their body by connecting to their emotions and letting the somatic negative emotions flow into Mother Earth. Removing negative emotions means leaving only our true essence which is love. The law of attraction will merge their light body with the spiritual light of God.
6. Your hand may move to kiss the deceased hands as their emotions flow away.
7. When indicated by your Guides by moving your hands and body to a window, alter or statue, go to the light energy source and raise the deceased to the light. This will be indicated by the movement of your hand via your Guide. I usually say the prayer; 'it is light you are and light you will become'.
8. You can usually feel their cold energy flow up your hand and away.
9. Take a candle and brush away any debris from the side of the client's aura where the attachment took place.
10. Ask the client what emotions need to be resolved whereby the law of attraction drew the deceased to them in the first place.

Sending Babies to the light.

Feeling the spirit of a baby will usually be the same as feeling the spirit of an adult discarnate spirit. The main difference with sending a baby to the light is that babies will need to be held in your arms and cradled before going to the light. The love a baby requires is nurturance through energetic food and touch. By cradling them in your arms they can receive both the human physical contact and nurturance they may never have had the chance to receive. This usually takes longer to administer then if working with adult spirits. I always ask a Saint or a deceased loved relative of mine to come and collect the spirit and look after them on the other side. On many occasions I have visited friends who had a short stay in hospital. Upon entering their house I usually check if they brought any discarnate spirits home with them. Often it is possible to send ten or twenty babies during that visit to the light.

It is interesting to note the emotions that people are holding that prevents them going to the light. Many famous people that I tune into to ensure that they go to the light are sometimes holding regret. It seems the greater the gifts we possess on earth the greater the sadness we feel that we could have achieved more with our time spent on earth.

There is nothing special about the work I have just described. I have trained many therapists to conduct this work. All that is required is that you trust your Guides, build your vibration, let go of the negative emotions of your own baggage and open your heart. I even find that I can now channel enough spiritual energy through my heart that can lift discarnate spirits to the light. The purpose of the method of me facing my fears and learning how to send people to the light was that I find confidence in my method of work. If you wish to complete any type of work then make sure you are confident in the work and know the limits to your competence. I learned the hard way in conjunction with my gifts. I advise you, dear reader to learn your method of work which may not be my methodology.

In the future I intend to set up an organisation of therapists whose purpose is to send people to the light.

Case Studies Sending Discarnate Spirits to the light.

One of my children was crying in their cot. They woke four times one night which I eventually realised that this was excessive even if they were getting their baby teeth. The fourth time I tuned into my energy, placed my protection in place, gave my hands to my guides and scanned the room. I eventually felt the coldness of a discarnate spirit in the corner of the room and tuned in to bring them to the light. They refused to go after which I proceeded to look for a baby spirit in the room. Eventually I found the baby spirit in my baby's cot. The reason my baby was crying was because he could feel and probably see the spirit beside him. I sent the baby to the light after which the adult followed their baby home.

Case Study: Sick child who refused to eat or Drink.

I received a call from a Mother inquiring about hypnotherapy to treat her sick child. The child would not eat or drink. They had to literally force liquids into his mouth to drink. He was losing weight and had a raft of hospital tests planned in the following weeks. Because of the symptomology of the case I referred the mother and child to a Homoeopathist thinking it was a medical problem. After a week the child's Mother contacted me again and I referred the child to another therapist. Another week went bye and I received a phone call from the Mother insisting that there was probably something I could do. It was then that it dawned on me that a Mothers instinct is very strong and I had often seen where my Mother and wife confounded doctors in insisting that something was still wrong with their children even tough preliminary examinations proved inconclusive. I arranged to go to their home.

Upon entering I just sat in the room where the children were watching TV. The child's milk was left untouched after which his Mother explained how he only drank a basic quantity of liquids the previous week. As I tuned into his light body I felt that the chords throughout his chakra system were non existent. I somatically brought earth energy up through my feet to rebuild his chakra system from the base chakra upwards. After a half hour I was treating his heart chakra upon which his throat chakra started to receive energy. The little boy went over to his milk and drank a full bottle. This was more then what he had been forced to drink in the previous two weeks. I arranged to call later in the week. Upon my second visit I asked about their lives and their child's life. They told me about a deceased relative who passed away months ago. The child was extremely close to this relative. As I then tuned into the child I realised that the relative had attached itself to the child's aura. I sent the relative to the light after which the boy sat down to his evening snack. There was a long road ahead of them in relation to reconstructing cognitions of eating patterns etc but at least the source of the problem seemed to have been solved. Never discount a Mothers instinct.

Case Study: Night Vigil.

As part of my training as an energy healer I was required to conduct a night vigil alone in the woods. I was allowed to take water but no flashlight etc. The energetic proceedings of the night commenced around 12 midnight where I saw the clouds in the sky part and a portal open to the night sky above the clouds. I then saw white lights float upwards to the portal and once they arrived at the night sky, disappear in a flash of light. I knew that they were spirits going to the light as the portals between the worlds were open. I tell very few friends about this experience as seeing is believing. It's very comforting and indeed humbling for my Guides to show me such special events in my evolution of the work I am asked to do.

Case Study: Client saw a Spirit in a church.

Sean came to see me even though he wasn't sure why he attended or indeed what I could help him with in his life. We chatted and eventually Sean told me about a car accident from years ago. He described himself as never being quiet right since the accident and I told him I would check his aura for trauma or a displaced aura when Sean went on the plinth. We continued to talk after which Sean remembered that he recently saw a ghost in a church who had a disfigured face. It was then that I knew that the discarnate spirit was attracted to Sean via the law of attraction. This told me that Sean's aura was displaced as was the face of the ghost in the church.

I decided to tune into the ghost with the damaged face to send them to the light. I rebuilt their light body in my room after tuning into my Guides. My guides used my hand to rebuild her face before releasing her negative emotions and sending her to the light. I thought it interesting that the trauma to the discarnate spirits face had to be healed and reconstructed before forward movement was emotionally possible for the spirit. Remember we hold on to our human emotions which have to be transmuted along with all other attachments. The law of attraction proved correct in that Sean's aura needed to be correctly put back in place.

Case Study: Death of pregnant woman in a car crash.

A client consults with the death of a friend who died in a car accident. Unfortunately her friend was pregnant with twins. As we talked about her friend, her light body came and stood on my left hand side. I tuned in and tried to send her to the light but she would not go as I expected. I was already tuned into my guides so I again let them take my hands as I took hold of one of the babies and eventually sent them to the light. I then took the second child in my arms and they went to the light. I then tuned into their mother and she immediately went to the light.

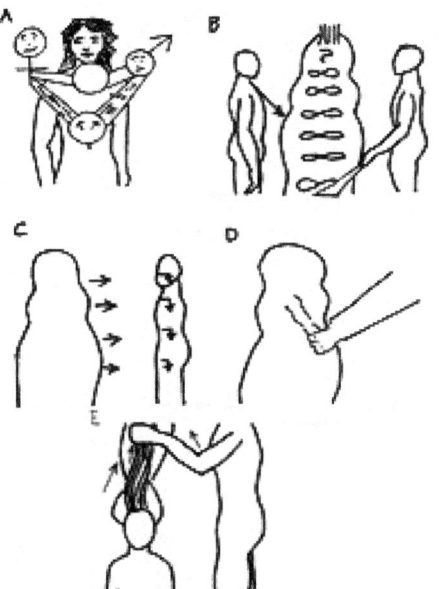

DISCARNATE SPIRITS TO THE LIGHT

A. Identify discarnate spirit hosting on a person.

A. Build Spirit's light body on Floor off client.

B. Remove Emotional Blockages.

C. Take Hand of Spirit.

D. Merge With Light of GOD.

Danger: Power of Light.

"We cannot change our past. We can not change the fact that people act in a certain way. We can not change the inevitable. The only thing we can do is play on the one string we have, and that is our attitude."

Charles R Swindoll

13. Past Life Chakra Energetic Bands.

Past life energetic chakra bands are bands of negative energy that represent similar past and present life issues that emerge from the astral plane that require transmutation. These bands which can feel like life belts wrapped around a persons body, correspond to the position of the five lower chakras in the light body. They signify that energetic progress is being made in the person's life but at that moment in time, a past life imprint has emerged for transmutation. Life unfolds in cycles. The most important of cycles probably occurs when we are cut off from the outside world and our life goes into shut down for a short period of time. This retrograde step or looking inwards involves changing our psychology at the deepest levels of our being. If we are too busy rushing around with the affairs of life then we cannot have time for reflection to determine what deep changes are being forcing upon us. Sometimes our journey requires us to do nothing but change our perceptions and not to fight the process. Remember the song 'you say it best when you say nothing at all.'

While sitting across from consulting clients I often feel past life energetic band wrapped around a particular chakra. I ask clients to hold out their hand six inches from their body and caress the energy upwards along the side of their body. They are usually astonished to find that they can feel these energy bands. We can identify the psychological and emotional issues that are resonating in the person's life at that time according to which band emerges for transmutation. The issues in relation to bands and chakras are as follows:

Base Chakra	Survival/ Identity
Sacral Chakra	Emotionality and Sexuality
Solar Plexus	Survival/ Powerlessness
Heart Chakra	Abundance/Flow of life
Throat Chakra	Self Expression
Left Leg (Knee to Foot)	Past life Issues

The bands exist like a life belt that permeates out through all levels of the aura i.e. not just around the physical body where you can easily feel the energy with your hands. The energy floats downwards from the outer layers of the aura to be processed by the chakra that is at the centre of the band. From there the energy moves up to the heart chakra for transmutation. The heart chakra transmutes all negative emotions as it exists to all levels of our being. Earth connection is vital to provide fresh energy to the light body at such an energetic stagnant time in order that the particular band dissolves upwards for transmutation to the heart chakra. An energy treatment from a therapist will also speed up the transmutation of the negative effects of the energy in your life.

The area from the knee to the base of the foot on the left leg will be the position of an energy mass that indicates that a past life issue is being transmuted. All time from the past and present exists within the here and now within the astral plane which will be reflected within the light body on earth. If you feel a mass of energy along this part of the body then that persons difficulties in their present life is mirroring a similar situation that requires resolution from a past life. There is an energetic chord linking all previous past life's to the present life which is being created by the similar unresolved emotionality of the challenges of that lifetimes. If you remove the emotionality of the chord then it will dissolve but you must also go back to the original sensitising lifetime or through the law of attraction the same situation will be created in your future. St. Germaine will help in this process.

At the early stages of a band the energy may feel cold dead and impenetrable. When a band feels burning hot then you know that the energy is ready to transmute but that band will be particularly felt in the person's life.

Even if a person receives an energy treatment, the band may still be in place but may feel weaker as sometimes time is required to transmute a band. Advise the client to take life easy if a band is in place and take a step back from life while the band is receding.
This is a time of growth, introspection and self awareness. There will be plenty of time for action when the new power of the light body is freer to move through the life of the person. Always ensure that no soul fragments emerge during the healing of past life bands which need to be integrated back into the light body.

Energetic bands should not be feared. In Native American Indian culture, the time of the women's monthly cycle was seen as a time of retreat into the darkness in order that new growth takes place after the cycle was complete. This is simply the ebb and flow of the world as such energetic bands, although difficult to transmute, is a time of progress and growth.

<u>Complete Case History: Obsessive Compulsive Disorder.</u>

Tom, a successful business man in his mid fifties originally accompanied his father to therapy. His father, suffering from anxiety, asked to attend as he had developed insomnia which was seriously reducing his quality of life. During the first session I energetically repaired his father's roots, solar plexus and closed his third eye. I showed them both how to press their hand and release trapped energy within their light body through the energy cone technique developed by Tom Wynn from Dublin. We chatted at the end of the session and as a matter of curtsey, conducted an energy treatment on Tom. Tom was also suffering from stress but left with his solar plexus strong and centred.

Tom's father attended in three weeks time with a flowing, strong light body. Great stress from years of a difficult marriage was entering his light body from the astral plane but no trauma or imprints was getting stuck within the chakra or light body channels. When I enquired as to how an elderly man was achieving such a great result under so much stress, he told me he played my energetic healing CD daily and practised the energy cone technique for a half hour after evening prayer. I smiled to myself as we sometimes underestimate the influence of our words.

I asked Tom how he felt. Tom was feeling much the same as before his first treatment but began to tell me about the terrible pain in his arm. He had x-rays, pain killers and a series of tests which showed no abnormalities but still the pain in his arm persisted. Again I conducted an astral healing session on Tom but during this session I lifted a splint of energy, about six inches in length from his shoulder. When Tom got up from the plinth he said he was able to move his arm above his shoulder for the first time in months. He felt the pain had subsided in his arm.

Three months later, Tom made an appointment but this time he came without his father. Tom described the fear that was taking over his life. At times he was afraid to leave his house as I somatically felt deep pulsating energetic fear in his kidneys. His solar plexus was shattered as he continually repeated that he was afraid of losing his mind. His roots were displaced and his third eye open indicating insomnia and excessive rumination. His heart was closed indicating he was being over whelmed by life. He had a big heavy band of energy around his solar plexus indicating powerlessness and the energetic stress around his neck, indicated a fear of speaking out and difficulty in receiving abundance. This was a man under a lot of pressure.

I asked Tom what was going on in his life. He worked in the food industry and was worried about hygiene, health regulations and health and safety. I asked Tom to link those thoughts back to a previous incident in his life as I somatically linked to the new developments within Tom's energy. His roots came back into his body as he let go of the fear of a past experience involving food hygiene when he worked overseas. His solar plexus relaxed, opening up to his heart chakra. Although receiving energy at the end of the session, Tom's heart chakra was still receiving huge amounts of fear from his kidneys. This fear was deep, pulsating and extremely heavy indicating this was a very old fear from childhood or a past life. Energy of this manner also indicates that rather then this fear stemming from a particular incident; it has been supported over the years from the way life was lived. That also means that the complete fabric of Tom's life is stained with this hidden fear. I advised Tom that life would not be easy over the next few weeks as he was still transmuting heavy energies. I advised Tom to walk the land to energise his body, complete an energy cone treatment daily on his hand and to try and relax according to his mood. I advised Tom to take a floral essence to help reduce fear in his kidneys.

Tom telephoned me three weeks later and said that he attracted a kidney infection. He said he was afraid of the depth of the therapy as at times he was engulfed in fear. I advised Tom to decide for himself if he wanted to attend but that releasing emotions from any methodology was the purpose of therapy. I advised Tom to continue working on himself and not to stop searching for other therapies that may be more agreeable to him.

Tom made an appointment six months later. This was Tom's fourth energy healing session in total. With a very worried look on his face, Tom described how his obsessive compulsive disorder had severely restricted his life. Tom was obsessed with hygiene and cleanliness. I let Tom speak as he described his life:

'I am afraid to use all but three knives and two saucepans in my kitchen. I am afraid of the germs on the sink so I only use a basin for washing and cleaning. I burned out three electric kettles in the last six months because I know or I feel that the hot water in the tap is not hot enough. Look at my hands, they are raw from cleaning. (Tom's hands were wrinkled and shrivelled). My dishwasher is eight months old but still in its packaging. I am afraid to use it in case the waste pipe backs up the drain and contaminates the utensils. I buy the smallest portions of food in case they go off or go out of date. That is so expensive. No one can clean or prepare food in the house but me. I might wash the floor a few times a day. In case the mop is holding germs I throw out the mop and bucket every few weeks. I spray my shoes upon entering my home after shopping. I feel sick to my tummy at times. I can only eat little bits of food. I am driving my family mad. I can't help it but it's just something I just have to do. Can you help me?

Tom's obsession has taken over his life. Tom is trying to control his life as his conscious mind has manifested this ego defence mechanism in order not to repeat a similar event in his past when everything was untrustworthy, uncontrollable and certainly fearful. Tom's solar plexus is spinning negatively, his roots are displaced, and his sacral chakra is as heavy and solid as a stone. His heart chakra is naturally blocked due to life closing in on himself through his thoughts and attitude. Energy is only circulating around his crown chakra leaving him living only in his head. Through listening to his subconscious as per his normal verbal choice of words, Tom just uttered a clue of his hidden emotionality of a previous experience that he has buried in the astral plane. Would this be the link to the energetic state of fear from his past that Tom was now stuck living his life.

Gerry: Tom, I am going to say something to you, (confusing his conscious mind), Blank your mind, close your eyes and float back to the past, to a time when 'it was something you just had to do?

Where are you, what's going on, what are you feeling?

Tom: I see myself back home when I was a young lad. We all had jobs around the house to complete. I had mine. There was no other way...you just had to do them.

Gerry: You just had to do them?

Tom: Yes, we had no choice. There would be trouble if we didn't complete our work.

Gerry: Go back in time and connect to your younger self. See yourself back there....feel what you feel...see what you saw....hear what you heard...be there now.

Tom: Yes, I can see myself there.

Gerry: How do you feel Tom?

Tom: Relaxed, just getting on with it. It's a normal day. (Pause). What is that....Oh, I forgot that. I see that dead animal at the side of the road. He is swelled up and his belly is burst open. It's disgusting. I ask my father what happened to him and he said he eat something. Maybe that's what made me nervous.

Gerry: Connect to your younger self now. Let all that fear, sorrow and revulsion go now. Feel it flow through your body downwards into the ground as you sit there in the chair Tom as the past and present are now. Decide now to let it go.

Tom: My tummy is starting to relax. I never thought of this memory, I am amazed that I forgot it.

We conducted an energy treatment on Tom using astral healing. A past life band around the solar plexus emerged which indicated that this irrational fear was driven from issues from a past life. I was guided to work on Tom's left leg.

My hands started to remove energy from the leg by lifting the energy to the light of the candle positioned on my altar. Eventually my hand brushed on some cold energy. I followed the line of the energy and realised that I was feeling an energetic arrow stuck in Toms past life leg. It was then I remembered the splint that I removed from Tom's shoulder months ago. I now knew that it too was an arrow. I called in Archangel Raphael, who has responsibility for all healing. I did not want to remove this arrow and find that energetic attachments were attached that could damage the fabric of his light body if I extracted the arrow incorrectly. I asked Archangel Raphael to oversee the treatment and to use my hands for him to complete this treatment if it was for Tom's highest good. My hands took hold of the arrow and I felt energy move into the wound and the arrow from my hands. After a few minutes my hands removed the arrow and proceeded to burn it in the light of a candle. To my surprise, my hands moved towards Tom's right leg and proceeded to remove two arrows from underneath his knee. As I looked at Tom he was changing past lives into an American Indian. We had uncovered a sensitising past life event.

Tom left feeling more relaxed then after any of the previous sessions. Tom telephoned me to say that his anxiety was reduced by half and was beginning to feel 'normal' in his kitchen.

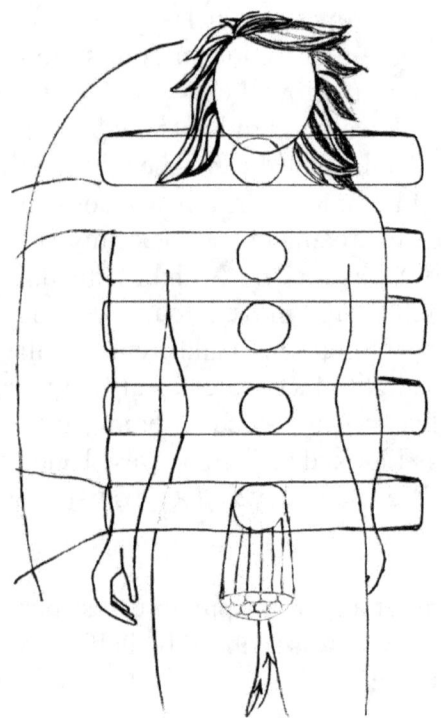

THE 5 PAST LIFE BANDS.

Transmuted through The Heart Chakra.

The unreflecting man can know no peace and lacking peace how can there be bliss.

Bhagavadgita.

14. Psychic Attack.

There is no such thing as an accident. Everything happens for a reason. Experiencing a psychic attack from an external source such as an entity or person is ultimately the victim's responsibility. A disciple or student is one who learns how to master the external world and therefore becomes a master in their own right. A student directs his attention outwards and points the finer of responsibility at others. He will try to control his surroundings but he is blind. Blindness comes from the fact that he chooses to ignore that subconscious emotions within his light body are at work through the spiritual laws of mankind which ultimately created the psychic attack. When one is a master, he looks inwards. By looking inwards they realise that on some deep level they have caused the attack and the other person are just simply the vehicle for that attack. So within, as without. Looking inwards involves examining their inner landscape to determine what was the attraction fuelling the attack. The attack will be energetically aimed at where there is a weakness within the functioning organ or aura of their light body. If you find that you or a client has been psychically attacked then proceed as follows:

1. Determine what emotions the originator of the attack is energetically holding.
2. Ask yourself what was the purpose behind the attack.
3. Ask yourself what responsibility for the attack had the victim of the psychic attack.
4. Once the resonance of the attraction of the attack is uncovered then it is safe to repair the damage of the attack.
5. Deal with the insecurity within the victims light body/emotions in order to remove the emotional imprints that can attract such a similar attack in the future.

As you look inwards you will find that the victim of an attack is not in his power or is refusing to listen to their inner voice which is asking them to address an issue in their life. This means that fear, insecurity, guilt, resentment or despair is such an emotion that attracted the attack. If the attack is aimed at a particular organ of the person then the emotional function of that organ is either the cause or the aim of that psychic attack. Many attacks are administered as:

A knife wound.

Psychic cover to stop the functioning of a chakra.

Take the representation of an animal within the light body of a person e.g. a snake.

Damage the reputation or thinking process of the person or people around the individual.

A knife left behind in the light body but secretly has a secondary devise attached to the tip of the knife.

Skewers or toothpicks lodged into a chakra. This attack is clever in that it is hidden from the victim. Usually the perpetrator of this type of attack is a female and the person is quiet bitchy or jealous towards the victim. A male will usually attack with brutal force and a woman will usually be cunning and sly.

<u>We can therefore view the aim of an attack as follows;</u>

Organ	Function	Desired Result
Left Kidney attack aspect.	Fear	Create Fear on Creativity
Right Kidney attack aspect.	Fear	Create Fear on Masculinity
Solar Plexus Rear	Power	Stop Forward movement
Heart Chakra	Love	Stop the person experiencing love

Base Chakra	Strength	Stop the person being grounded
Throat Chakra	Expression/ Receiving	Stop the voice or receiving in life
Sacral Chakra	Emotions	Sexual/Emotional expression

When you identify where you were attacked you now know as to the purpose of the attack. You also know that you have a blind spot in that particular functioning in your life that needs to be addressed after the attack has been healed. The consequences of not addressing the underlying insecurity in your life are that you will be continually vulnerable in that area of your life. As like attracts like you have the choice to address the issue or the issue will simply reoccur in the future through the law of attraction. There is no such thing as 'an opt out clause' because to do nothing is also a decision. There is no other show in town as the saying goes.

Often after removing the energetic vehicle of the attack such as a knife, chord or spear, the person's body will shake with the emotional pain of the removing of the trauma of the attack. Light and love flows in as you can somatically feel or see droplets of tears emerging from the victim's eyes. The clients light body is crying. If you focus on the side of the body that received the attack, left being female and right being male, you may find a huge amount of energy streaming into that side of the light body. You will somatically feel it. The pain of the attack served as a catalyst for jumpstarting the level of performance of the male or female aspect of the light body. The person will be regrouping to form a stronger, positive and secure aspect to their life. It's a tough way to learn a lesson.

To continually protect your light body involves looking at your own issues. This means facing your fears and looking at such internal emotions as guilt, fear, resentment, anger and despair. The removal of your negative imprints means that other people's negative imprints cannot attract themselves to you as per the law of resonance. A consequence of removing imprints is that your vibration will increase.

A method to protect yourself from attack is to cultivate pure thoughts in your life. Thinking negative thoughts only sets in motion the laws of attraction. Revenge is a negative emotion that will attract into your life people and events that you could be vengeful towards as a result of their actions. That is not life but only imprisonment. Your aura is like a crystal emitting a signal. The purer the signal you emit, the purer the expression of your life. Strength comes from connecting to your true self deep inside your inner being. If you live a lie or are covering up issues in your personality then take heed. The day will come when you will trick yourself into dealing with your own issues. The difference being, will it be on your own terms or the terms of another person via your energetic signal.

Professional energy healers/therapists can be very dangerous if working on behalf of the dark side. While attending a function, I realised that I was knifed in the heart by a jealous healer. I did not have my protection in place in that I felt lonely and vulnerable at that particular time of the day when I crossed their path. I attended a Healers Healer, Kieran Henson and he administered a treatment to me. My attacker plunged a knife energetically into my heart and Kieran told me that a chord and a hidden blade was attached to the tip of the knife. If an inexperienced healer energetically pulled the knife in order to release it from my heart then I would have been energetically tore all the way through my light body. Kieran asked his team to firstly remove the blade and its attachment and then proceed to remove the knife. Kieran also completed some work on special protection from the fall out of the attack. All healers need to have their own specialised healer to attend to their light body. Never remove a knife for the sake of removing a knife. Look to see the contract or reason as to the cause of the attack and to the inadequate protection of the healer before you remove the knife. Otherwise the attack will reoccur within minutes of the client leaving your premises.

My lesson from that attack was not to feel insecure or inadequate around other healers. I have my place and my childhood should be left in the past and not to retreat back into the past when doubting myself.

Psychic Protection.

I always talk through the life of the psychic attack victim in order to determine what caused the attack and how they are energetically open to such an attack. Once the person understands their responsibility towards themselves going forward, I invoke the protection of the Christ Energy to protect their aura. I bring it down on top of their aura and feel it lick into place like a shell over their aura. This is one of the strongest protections I know. I sometimes energetically position a cross at the front, rear, left hand side, right hand side, below their feet and above their head. A cross is simply a seal and not just a religious symbol.

Case studies involving psychic attack.

Case Study: Invading my body space.

A friend who was dealing with masculinity issues was projecting his issues on to me. He was looking for a strong, masculine, authoritative male to advise him what to do at a difficult junction in his life. I knew that he was projecting his hurt onto me from his inner child due to his absent father. I was not taking his power by telling him what to do but was rather forcing him to dig deep and find his own inner resources to deal with his present situation and thereby develop energetically as a man. Growth can be painful and my friend was only seeing male rejection reoccur a second time in his life. He glared at me as he put his eyes through me. He positioned his hands across his solar plexus protecting his power base. He sat forward in the chair with his head protruding towards me in an attacking manner. At times his anger flared at me with a barbed attack criticising my actions. I advised him to look inwards and feel what he would like to achieve from his present situation in his life. After he left, I could still feel his glare towards me as I knew he had left an imprint in my aura. I was not expecting his attack and had not protected myself energetically until it was too late in our meeting. The meeting showed me that I still had work to complete on myself energetically to develop my male aspect.

Purpose of Attack.

>By Attacker: To accentuate the masculinity of his personality and project his childhood anger.

> By Victim: For me to increase my masculinity and let go of issues in relation to being my own man.

Case Study: Knifed in the Kidneys.

A male friend who was an accountant was leaving his employment. This had the effect that his partner in his firm would be exposed and would be in danger of not being able to continue in business. While talking to him over the phone, I felt a sharp pain over my right kidney. I was linking in somatically and could feel a knife stuck in my friend's right kidney. As we talked I conducted a distant energy healing treatment on my friend with regards to who originated the attack. I energetically tuned into the knife wound. As we talked about his partners fear it was then that the knife was released. By deliberately tuning into the attack it allowed us specifically to determine the cause of the psychic attack. I repaired the kidney, light body, solar plexus and brought new energy from Mother Earth up into the heart chakra. I advised my friend about psychic protection and the cause of the attack.

Purpose of Attack.

> By Attacker: Insecurity and jealously with regards my friend advancing in his new employment. To paralyse my friends masculinity with fear by blocking his male right hand side.

> By Victim: Indecision and insecurity with regards moving forward. Feelings of guilt with regards to leaving his partner behind.

Case Study: Blocked rear solar plexus.

After deciding to leave a therapy centre, I was psychically attacked in bed one night. The attack, while not vindictive took the form of a person placing an energetic plate over the rear of my solar plexus. The solar plexus governs power and mental capacity while the rear of the body governs action. My business as a therapist literally died over the following days until I received a treatment to remove the crippling energy block from my light body.

Purpose of Attack:

> By Attacker: To stop me moving premises and moving my business away from the spin off to their business.
>
> By Victim: To be determined and confident about my business standing on its own feet.

Case Study: Snake wrapped around light body.

A client attended with a pain in their left arm. This client was an experienced healer with an established practise. As we tuned in, we felt a snake wrap around the persons light body. The snake was hissing and biting the side of my client's neck. I asked the client if they had any unusual thoughts or clients etc over the last few days. They eventually described a client who was dealing with inner child issues. This client was triggered back into their childhood during their last session and was choosing to wait in their hurt mode rather then take responsibility and deal with their past. We tuned in to Cone energy (Crow or Morgan) which took away the snake and cleared the aura only when we understood all issues in relation to this client.

Purpose of Attack:

> By Attacker: To revenge her childhood by projecting her anger onto her therapist. It is easier to remain in anger rather then go further into sadness and hurt.
>
> By Victim: To develop his masculine aspect of personality which means to have his protection and boundaries firmly in place when treating clients of a different essence.

Case Study: Skewed in the throat.

> A client attended with a large shawl wrapped around their body. It was a warm summer day and the clothing seemed excessive especially since the shawl was doubled twice around their neck. Upon tuning into the client, I could feel a pressure on their neck and a sharp pain in their right kidney. I removed three small

skewers from their throat chakra and a large knife from their right kidney. I advised the client that the attack was probably from a female that was 'bitchy and jealous' towards the client and that their friendship was decreasing over the previous few weeks. I advised the client that they needed to listen to their inner voice and start to trust their inner guidance.

Purpose of Attack.

By Attacker: Jealous of their friend getting stronger and moving forward in a new direction.

By Victim: The client said that I was correct in that a friend was jealous of their life moving in a new direction. The client needs to listen to their inner guidance, be mindful of them leaving an old way of life behind and develop their male/right side which commenced receiving huge amounts of energy after the healing.

Psyhic Attack

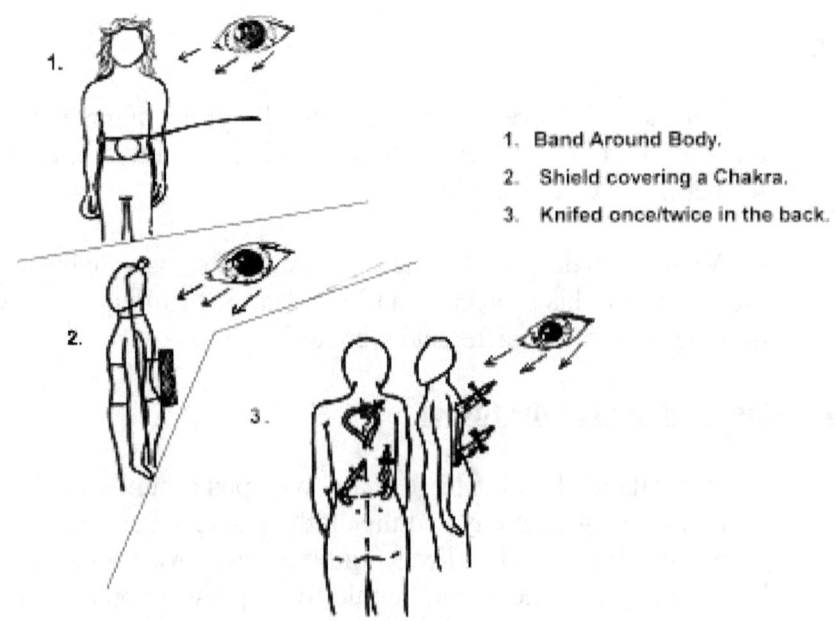

1. Band Around Body.
2. Shield covering a Chakra.
3. Knifed once/twice in the back.

Psychic Protection.

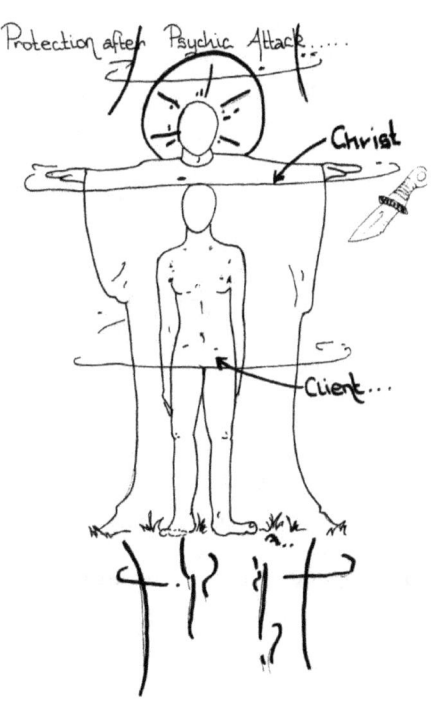

"A great silent space holds all of nature in its embrace. It also holds you."

Eckhart Tolle

15. How to Meditate Energetically.

A CD of this healing meditation is available to download at the back of the book.

We meditate to relax the mind and find our true consciousness within. Meditation connects us to our true essence. This is the returning home to the Self, our true nature. We do not meditate to calm down or take a rest. That is not meditation because we would then be approaching meditation as a means to reclaim ownership from emotional disarray rather then to enhance our true essence within our mind and body. We should commence meditation ideally from a neutral state of mind rather then from a negative state of mind. That is why it is a good idea not to meditate just after getting up from sleep as your mind may be continuing the drowsy/sleepy state rather then meditating. There is also no point in meditating when you are full of anger or bitterness. If you do so then you are simply letting go of these negative feeling rather then controlling the mindless state of your inner thoughts. Meditation is a self healing tool that reconnects the power within our light body.

Approach the practice of meditation in a calm and serious manner. Set aside the time when you are relaxed and calm. Try and allow no disturbances i.e. turn your phone off and tell the members of your family not to disturb your for the next half hour or so. Build up the time you spend meditating. Start with 10 to 15 minutes until the time increases to an hour. Quality is better then quality. My healing meditation cd is 25 minutes of duration as I realise people can find 25 minutes many times during the week but may not as easily be able to find 1 hour. The key is to enjoy the experience. I know of one very powerful spirit who described chanting as 'madness' but practises energetic healing on her light body all the time. What ever form you feel is correct for you then practise the exercise for the betterment of your life.

If you decide to incorporate a chant or mantra into your meditation then realise that you are engaging in an energetic exercise to open to greater depths of consciousness. The words of the mantra must be felt by you, mean something to you and not just words that that you rattle off without thought or contemplation. Breath in the words, let the energy of the words travel into your body and chakra system. Change the words until you realise that you have the mantra that is correct for you. A mantra such as

'I release the past and align my Life with Spirit' is a very powerful mantra. It directly gives control and direction of your life to your higher self. It also has the added benefit of allowing the laws of attraction operate at the optimum speed and evolution of your energy.

The advantages of the energetic meditation that I advise is that it provides the benefits of both meditation and energetic healing of negative emotional imprints within the light body. Therefore you can change your world with this exercise. You can let go of the past, return to your correct vibration and therefore attract corresponding positive vibrational frequencies into your life.

Remember our mind is a gift from Spirit. It is but a tool that is to be used by us in the achieving of our life's purpose. It should be empty and blank. Our thoughts that we think in our head is controlled energetically through our solar plexus. If you have an upset solar plexus then it follows naturally that you meditation will be undertaken from a disadvantaged position.

This meditation will help to give you back your control over your mind. Sometimes we require a specific energetic treatment from an energy healer. Remember the spiritual law – you cannot complete this task alone. At any rate, do not be discouraged from allowing meditation a way of life. Once you begin to bring more light into your aura, the light you emit expands. You become like a flashlight shining your love and light into the universe for all to see.

With meditation through the operation of the spiritual laws, more and more energetic beings full of love and light will be attracted to you. They will see your light and want to be near you. You can resonate with their vibration and take in their joy and warmth. You will find peace and love. You will radiate this feeling through your work, family and even leave your warmth behind you on the shopping trolley after you have finished your shopping. More and more Guides, Angels, Spiritual Masters and Elementals will come and bask in your aura which you can radiate their essence for the glory of mankind on Earth. You can be their ambassador here on Earth. This healing meditation will expand your aura to grow bigger and brighter. It will give you an inner strength that will be your rock upon which you will build your life.

You will realise, through all your difficulties and challenges of life, that you are a Spirit experiencing a human existence on this outcrop of rock called Earth, for a time frame that is merely a blink of an eye.

Preparation for energetic meditation is to ensure you wear warm comfortable clothes. Earth energies are cold so definitely wear socks. When you connect deeply to Mother Earth and bring the energy up into your heart chakra, you can actually hear a hum or beat pulsing through your body. This is the rhythm of the Earth merging within your body. You can sit with your back straight against a chair as long as your feet touch the ground. Lie on a bed if you must but imagine that your feet are going down deep into the ground. Do not place one foot on top of the other as it may cut off circulation and cause pins and needles on the pressurised leg. You can listen to the healing cd while you are getting used to the exercise but after a while your own meditation will be just as powerful and more likely more powerful. Simply use the healing cd when you would like someone else to conduct a healing on your light body with little or no effort on your behalf. There is nothing wrong with receiving. Standing, sitting or lying on Mother Earth is just as beneficial as the earth connection contains the healing energies.

<u>The meditation to reclaim all that you are is as follows.</u>

I call in the powers of Mother Earth and Father Sky.

I call in the powers of the North, South, East and West.

I call in the powers of Earth, Wind, Fire and Water.

I call in my Guides, Angels, Teachers and Masters.

I call in Archangel Michael, Gabriel, Uriel and Ariel.

I call in my power animals (personal power animal).

I protect myself with a bubble of light/Celtic cross etc. (Personal choice).

I send my toes, feet and legs down deep into the earth. I imagine a healing colour down in the Earth. I can feel its texture. I imagine the roots of the Earth come up and wrap around my legs all the way up to my knees like the roots of an old oak tree.

I feel the healing energy of the earth move into my feet, my ankles and shimmer all the way up to my knees. I feel the coldness of my body merging with the earth.

I imagine a beam of sunlight (Moonlight), come all the way down from the sky, enter my head, enter my throat charka, my heart charka and down into my tummy (solar plexus).

I breathe all the way down, down past my lungs, down past my tummy down to 3 inches below my belly button, down to my sacral charka. Feel my breathe wrap around the sacral charka as it gives permission for the healing energy to come up my body from Mother Earth. (Breathe with your open mouth if possible; a little practice is required to get accustomed to the habit).

Feel how the energy has a mind of its own as that coldness is now merging with your hips…forming a line across your body…gently rising upwards.

Feel the energy flow upwards now….forming lines or channels into your kidneys…pulsating and releasing the imprints of fear from your light body.
As that fear leaves, feel the channels open at your back, circling your sacral charka… and pushing energy into your solar plexus (Tummy).

Notice the spinning feeling in your tummy as your mind is now calm. The energy circles around your tummy….. Pushing energy sideways opening into sadness on the left and force or anger on the right.

Notice the feelings that envelop you as you release the past. Notice your breathe as it swirls the energy within your body upwards. Feel the circle of your solar plexus form as the energy from your adrenals subsides.

The energy slowly moves upwards, up into your breastbone or where your knowledge charka is located. Feel the energy seep through this charka that cuts your ties with the past and gives you the knowledge to free yourself.

The energy moves upwards along the sides of your body, into your liver on the right and spleen on your left. Release anger and resentment now. The energy flows upwards moving inwards all the time now as a pulse is forming in the centre of your heart charka between your lungs. It's like a candle being lit in the dark as if you are viewing your closed eyes, notice the different colours that are appearing to you as you open love into your life. Feel the energy flow from your left and right side now as you breathe deeply into your heart charka.

You may feel heaviness in your chest. Know that this is fine as you are now releasing old patters of heartache that have his behind fear, anger, resentment and powerlessness.

Decide to let it go now.

Feel the weight on your shoulders your spiritual team are around you directing the session.

Know that all is well.

Sit in this energy and feel your body quieten as the session comes to an end.

Thank spirit, Your Guides, Angelic beings, power animals for being with you today. Bring the energy back down to mother Earth.

This treatment may take up to 1 hour to complete or a number of sessions to bring the energy up to the heart.

During meditation your metabolism and your breath rate go down to a level of rest, twice that of deep sleep.

Mike Love

16. Meditation to Connect to the Wild Green Man (Woman).

The Wild Green Man/Woman energy represents our wild, free, true, unburdened essence of self that exists in the underworld. We change and develop through the mergence of the outer and inner worlds usually through the mistakes of being at the cutting edge of our energy. This involves making decisions from the most advanced mature standpoint that we have attained through the development of our light body. Our conscious mind interprets our energy which also avoids change at all costs. While we still feel that we are in control of our life, then we will make decisions based upon fear. When we reach the stage of not identifying with our ego then we will let our true essence or higher self allow the world come to us. This is where we will have a quiet mind, be calm and relaxed with our status in life, realise that financial worries need not erode our trust and believe in the journey that our soul came here to experience.

The peoples of the world develop through cycles of energetic development. The next ending of a particular cycle of development will be in December 2012. Thereafter a new cycle of development will commence for those that have not evolved within the time frame of this cycle.

In energy terms this maturing of our light body culminates through the realisation of the energy of the Wild Green Man/Woman. At this seeding stage of therapy, connecting our essence to this energy can help programme our future in that the vibration we encode into our essence will manifest in our life. The seeding stage of therapy is the start of the building stage of therapy when there are no issues left to be uncovered or destroyed. The therapy is concerned with strengthening and merging the male and female essence into one unified essence as deeper energetic levels of our past issues emerge for transmutation.

Even if you do not perceive energy when conducting this exercise, do not worry, as energy follows intent. Your intention is all that is required and so much the better if you can visualise the meditation in your third eye.

1. Ensure that you can sit in peace and not be disturbed for 30 minutes.
   Switch off all phones and settle yourself into a comfortable chair or plinth.
2. Connect to your energy. Feel the energy of your Guides around your head while your breathe brings up the energy from Mother Earth.
3. From that point behind your eyes where you think the thoughts you think, drop that attention point down to 3'' below your belly button.
4. Open your mouth and breathe from that new point in your abdomen creating a hallow energetic breath throughout your body.
5. Imagine yourself in a field of green grass. You feel safe, secure and at ease.
6. Look to your left and you will see a forest.
7. Approach the forest and as you do so you notice the trees, the ground, the shades of colour as a feeling of welcome comes over you.
8. Walk into the forest until you come to a clearing. Sit on the ground and connect deeply to Mother Earth.
9. Look to the other side of the clearing. Among the bushes notice a Green Wild person covered in Earth, mud and moss. Notice how carefree he is, how engulfed he seems within his own thoughts.
10. As you look him in the eyes, a colder deeper energy enters your body from Mother Earth. Breathe this energy deeply through your whole body until it reaches your Heart Chakra.

11. Let your thoughts flow to what it feels like to be free…wild…unburdened living in the woods. Being in charge of your own life as the energy enters deeper into your body.
12. As the energy enters your heart chakra, send out this free wild and unburdened vibration throughout the world to be reflected back to you in your life.
13. Know that this vibration is you and that this vibration is your destiny.
14. Bring the energy down through your body back to Mother Earth.
15. Say goodbye to your Wild Man as you feel yourself coming back into the here and now….. safe and sound in your body… knowing that all is well.
16. Feel your eyes relax and open, your feet securely on the ground and all parts of your psyche centred and safe for the rest of your journey.

"Forgive all who have offended you, not for them, but for yourself. "

Harret Nelson

17. Sexual Abuse Healing Methodologies.

Sexual abuse exists as an energetic imprint that we carry from past life to present life or imprints that are formed through the experiences of this particular lifetime. This can be as victim or perpetrator. The emotional abuse attached to sexual abuse is so severe that the person is damaged emotionally, physically, mentally and sexually. The cellular imprints of the abuse will be required to leave the body which is an extremely painful releasing of anguish that is encoded from the very depths of our being. Often abuse victims will describe how their body will tense if another person touches their hand or body. This is the cellular imprints of their anguish being reactivated in the present day. The emotionality of sexual abuse is recorded in the sacral chakra which governs our attitude towards the opposite sex, our emotions, sensuality and sexuality. Therefore, as sexual abuse will literally shatter the sacral chakra, the positive emotionality of our life can die within us from the day of the abuse. If someone experienced sexual abuse at age twenty five, the sacral chakra will be damaged but as our heart chakra develops at this age, will also experience the shock of the vibration of the abuse and will become stunted in its growth. Therefore sexual abuse will be recorded sexually in the sacral chakra but also chronologically as per our age of development of the chakra system.

If a child was sexually abused at six months of age then the base chakra will be damaged as well as the sacral chakra. In this case the sacral chakra will not develop but the person as they mature can energetically revert back to six months of age. The trauma may require soul retrieval through inner child healing at a later date. Many people who experience sexual abuse do not realise they were abused until they reach their puberty years. Then, as per their physical maturing with their hormones bringing their emotional baggage to the fore, may send their life into free fall. They may find themselves acting out sexual deeds or attracting 'peculiar' circumstances in which sexual acts seem to manifest in their lives. The person will find that the following attributes may be present in their life which is an indication of sexual abuse.

Indications of Sexual abuse:

Afraid to allow water run on your face i.e. in the shower.

Afraid to sleep in the dark.

Will suffer from nightmares.

Feels that something black is behind them.

Feels that they are being watched or peeped at even in their own home.

Will wear predominately dark clothes.

Will be a restless sleeper.

Will suffer from low self esteem.

Possibly suffer from panic attacks.

Will be prone to mood swings i.e. rage turning to depression.

Will naturally attract 'bad luck' into their lives.

Will usually attract a poor partner into their lives.

May be afraid to look at their reflection in mirrors.

May channel their trauma into addictions, compulsions etc.

May take up employment in the sex industry.

Will be reluctant to enter confined spaces i.e. basements.

Will have poor decision making skills.

Will have unusual fears of phobias i.e. custard or sticky things.

Will use language such as 'can't get that horrible thing out of my mouth' in an unusual context.

May stop and pause before entering a room i.e. rest on the door way.

Will possess much of the symptomology of a damaged inner child. This will require Inner child healing and possibly soul retrieval.

Will always feel out of place as akin to being an outsider.

It is important to remember that energetically the sexual abuse adult can be constantly living in the actual or subconscious fear of 'if I enter this room will the same abuse happen to me as before? They go into survival mode of which all decisions they make in their life is based around protection and not expansion. If a sexual abuse victim tells me that they have been abused at age twenty, I usually ask the client to regress back to their inner child. As per the spiritual laws governing mankind, it is highly likely that the person encountered sexual abuse at a much younger age then twenty. This person was sending out a sexual abuse signal in that we emit through the laws of attraction what we are energetically holding. This is no fault of the person but simply a matter of how we are built as 'Gods in our own right.' The regression to their inner child may bring up a youth of approximately fourteen, the age of puberty of when the body and mind comes together to commence the maturing of our sexuality. As with inner child work the person may have to regress to a younger age depending upon the time of the sensitising event of the trauma. With soul retrieval the inner child needs rescuing by removing the trauma. Once the trauma is removed, the lost soul essence will feel safe enough to come back home into its natural home within the sacral chakra. It is only then that the inner child can show himself and integrate towards maturity.

The timing of the rescue of the lost soul fragment may be different for each sexual abuse client. If the sacral chakra is healed solely by energy healing, the law of attraction will uncover their fear, emotions, hurt and sadness in their ordinary everyday life. The person crying about failing their driving test will in reality be their light body releasing judgement, fear and self esteem issues. I always start off therapy sessions by asking what is going on in you life? How was the last four weeks for you? In my therapeutic process, the victim of sexual abuse is not treated by me as a sexual abuse victim but a person who is developing their essence who occasionally will deal with sexual issues within our sessions. The enfoldment of their personality will encompass their sexuality as a matter of due course but is not the primary focus of any session. Many victims always comment as to how comforting it is to come and work through this particular process of energy healing. Going to counselling and regurgitating the same issues of 'what happened next to me' is barbaric. Even after such cognitive work the body needs to heal on a cellular basis and not just on a conscious level.

Even if visualisations and inner child work is completed over many sessions the lost soul fragment may only come back after a large amount of fear is released. The soul fragment will not return to the light body due to the overwhelming trauma of the sensitising abuse. The development of a person's energy has a plan of its own and should not be rushed under any circumstances. Remove the fear and the fragment will feel safe to return.

The victim of sexual abuse will suffer night mares. They usually consist of being chased often by a man or witch with a big knife. The person in the dream may have symbolic sharp teeth. They will have mood swings expressing itself from tempestuous anger to self loathing depression. A balanced emotional disposition will be impossible to achieve for any great length of time. They will be constantly looking over their shoulder which will manifest as 'yes, sometimes there is something black behind me.' They will be afraid to enter confined spaces such as toilets without a window or a basement with only one entrance/exit. They will be afraid to sleep in darkness. This may manifest as 'oh, I sleep with the light off alright but I must have the hall light on or see the street light with my curtains open.' They may find it difficult to remain in relationships and may attract a partner that was also a victim of sexual abuse. Usually they subconsciously make decisions from the position of their internalised guilt and shame i.e. their low self esteem which may feel as if bad luck follows their life. This may also manifest as addictions e.g. drugs, alcohol or gambling. Gambling is a disease to pray on the weak to prove the existence of their low self esteem. Gambling premises contains some of the lowest vibrations of energy on earth.

Many victims of sexual abuse, due to their heightened sensitivity in protecting themselves acquire their spiritual gifts after such abuse. They begin to exist on two realms and can utilise psychic or mediumistic abilities. They unfortunately have to get used to the difficulties of growing up with such gifts along with dealing with the pain of their heartache. The abuse would serve as an energetic awakening of one of their life's purpose.

Healing Methodology for victims of sexual abuse.

Victims of sexual abuse will either be energetically out of their body with the fright they received at the time of their abuse or can have an attitude such as 'I will get you before you get me.' It's as if their soul fragmented in order to not remain in their body in order to not experience the pain of the abuse. The person needs to be centred and grounded in order for a stable chakra system to be developed. Once this has been achieved through the cauldron system of energetic breath work, the anger and sadness can emerge. (See hierarchy of emotions). The person will find clarity developing in their life and will begin to know when they operating from an inner child state as opposed to a balanced adult frame of mind. This knowledge provides power. Soul retrieval may be necessary through inner child work to reclaim back their inner child which will reconstruct their sacral chakra back to normality. Then the healing energy and self development can naturally restart to take back the persons life from their abuse.

The sexual abuse person who adopts a curt, angry, venomous disposition will be projecting their inner venom onto the world and usually is a very dangerous person in their own right. They can be very self centred and cruel. They will have an air of haughtiness as if they look down on everyone else which is what they exactly do. They usually dress in a highly sexual fashion and may use lewd talk. In a night club where someone might casually remark 'there is a pole where someone could conduct a pole dance' will usually end up with this person dancing around the pole and conducting a very powerful raunchy strip. They will like nothing more then have the crowd adorn them with attention but God help the man who gets to spend the night with this person. Unless he is supremely confident in his inner strength as his own man then he will get chopped up and spit out in the morning. Think of a tarantula and how it mates with the male. This person may prey upon the unsuspecting immature vulnerable therapist in such areas as wearing a very small tight mini skirt and sliding down the seat in front of the therapist. It is best to refer out such clients to female therapists. As a therapist, never work with a client who devalues your therapy space in this fashion. This personality subtype described above is usually female and may be unaware that she was sexually abused.

It is my wish that such organisations as the 'Rape Crisis Centre' and women's counselling support groups further their education and learn about the true nature of trauma in the recovery of human sexuality.

I know what I am talking about with regards sexual abuse. I brought a past life imprint of sexual abuse into this lifetime. The healing of that imprint was the making of the foundation of my life in this lifetime. I may not necessarily sign up for that trip another time but it is possible to reclaim your life after such events in ones life.

I advise many clients but particularly abuse victims to conduct deep energetic earth breathing or rebirthing while lying on mother earth to reclaim back from the earth their lost soul essence. This can be very difficult and may take a number of months to succeed. Morgan and the persons Guides will be particularly felt in the person's life to heal, support and love on their journey back to self.

Case example of Sexual Abuse Client utilising Energy psychology.

Session 1.

Client attends for therapy describing insomnia, worry and anxiety. The client is being bullied by her boss at work which we identified as having the same energy as her 'Dads best friend when they were young.' We conducted a visualisation separating the two peoples energy by getting the client tell each person how different they were from each other. We surrounded a gold ball around the client and practised the client hold her energy when interacting with their boss. We completed an energy session on the plinth. The client clothes were all black and she slept in the 'dark' but with the light on in her hall at night. I gave the client an energetic healing cd and advised her to connect to Stag energy.

Session 2

Three weeks later the client attends complaining about her mother in law. She describes how small and belittled she feels around this person. I ask the client to connect to their past as to when they first realised they felt the same way about themselves. The client went back to age fourteen. We integrated that memory after which I asked the client to go back in time to age three, four, five or six. The client was unable to connect to herself at that age. No memories or emotions presented.

This showed me that the client was still too hurt and dissociated to connect to her younger self. The client may not have yet trusted me or have found the inner strength to reconnect to he own emotions. It is the clients issue and not to be taken personal.

Session 3.

The client attended three weeks later after making the appointment in a hurry requiring one day's prior notice. The client attended a wedding in which she was the object of attention for two married men at her table. One of the gentlemen's wife's noticed the attention and later accused her of 'being a slag.' The client couldn't get the words out of her head. When I asked her to link the words back to her past she described how she was sexually abused by her 'Dads best friend' when she was five years of age. She confronted him years later and he lashed out at her calling her 'a slapper and a slag.' She forgot these words until the link of the association was made. The law of attraction illuminated what emotionality she was energetically carrying.

The client was bewildered by the sexual attention she received from the men and also the guilt she experienced from the attack from the other women. Her anger now started to emerge with her thoughts from her abusive past.

The earth energy, specifically Morgan energy had entered her light body and had removed enough fear that the client began to reintegrate her sexuality. The spiritual laws illuminated her new found sexuality/self esteem via the men and women at her wedding table. Now that her sacral chakra was developing she was able to make sense of her emotionality of her world. The anger, guilt and shame she experienced was representative of her self esteem from the sexual abuse she suffered as a child.

Inner child work was completed after which the soul fragment of her sacral chakra was returned via an energetic treatment. I advised the client to place a photograph of them as a child in a beautiful picture frame on their bedside locker. They can lovingly connect to their younger self last thing at night and first thing in the morning. I also asked that she gives herself permission to beat a pillow, walk in the forest, curl up in a ball within Mother Earth or just sit in front of the TV with a big tub of ice cream. The client was advised to attend in a few weeks.

Session Four.

The client attended and the session was dominated by a row she had with her boss in which he ended up apologising for his behaviour. My client was vindicated in front of the whole department. Two other ladies came and congratulated her that she had represented all of them by 'sticking to her guns.' She feels exhilarated and uneasy at her new found power. Her history of sexual abuse was not mentioned during the session but Morgan conducted many treatments on the client during her dreamtime.

Session Five.

One month later, client attends complaining that she never cried as much in her life. She was unable to meet anyone or socialise the last two weeks and was wondering was the therapy causing such upheaval. Two weeks ago she took in a stray kitten who she found all bloodied and cut outside her house. The client casually remarked 'At times, I feel I am that kitten.' The client said 'I was doing so well. I have failed again. Look at the state of me! The client has just reached another level of energetic development that needs to be removed through astral trance healing. The cyclical nature of therapeutic development is progressing as normal.

Session Six.

The client attends commenting 'the world is a funny place.' I was at dinner the other night with six friends and after I came back from the restroom I realised it was just me alone with Jason. We went to a bar to meet his friend as he was driving me home and then it just all seemed to flow? Jason ended up spending the night with me. It was wonderful, great. He asked to see me again but this time only dinner. He says he wants to get to know me. I went shopping last week and bought some new clothes. I don't know why but my friends laughed so much when they saw my clothes, they said it wasn't me. He said he had his eye on me since I walked into the pub. He is really good looking you know! He told me that he made up the story about meeting his friend as he was 'crazy' about me.

The client's sexuality has entered her light body – specifically Kundalini energy. This is represented by men responding to her natural sexual signal that she is emitting and her new found confidence in her sexuality being expressed in her new choice of clothes.

It is wonderful to see the client describe the expression of her sexuality as 'wonderful and great.' Sexual frigidity can be caused by the sacral chakra not being connected to the heart chakra therefore the client describing her sexual performance with such words indicates that love and sex are flowing in harmony into her heart chakra.

Session Seven.

Client attends saying she no longer sees her boyfriend saying he was 'clingy and possessive.' He was great fun but was unreliable. I describe the development of peoples sexuality in which the Youth, Father and Tyrant as an energy enters a persons life. Client laughs as she says she had a lucky escape. Client describes Morgan providing intense sexual dreams during her dreamtime. The session is filled with laughter as I remind the client about the ebb and flow of energetic emotions as per the emotional upheaval of session five.

Clients realises she has matured and is rebirthing herself as her own woman in the world.

Session Eight.

Client has a major argument with her Mother. Client admits she was a surrogate mother to her mother which was preventing her attain the energetic freedom of existing in her own adult female energy. The atmosphere is frosty between the two of them but also realises that many of her friends are in similar child energy. Client is distancing herself from her two friends but another good friend is emerging who is more balanced and supportive. Client remarks that 'Mum was never interested in bad public relations – she turned a blind eye when I needed her most.'

The mother complex is being destroyed as I describe the natural energetic parting of the child away from the mother complex.

Session Nine.

Client has let go of two of her friendships but has commenced rebuilding a new relationship with her mother. Client projects her inner rage towards her Father who had her abuser around to visit one evening last week. She left disgusted stating he should have known something was wrong about this person and he never took responsibility for his role as a father in his life.

Client is reconciling her feminine aspect and has commenced integrating her masculine aspect through the emerging of her anger and rage on her right/male side. I advise the client to internalise and release her inner feelings as opposed to channelling her rage outwards towards other people. I explain the hierarchy of emotions and advise client not to get stuck in anger/rage mode but to progress to energetic freedom via stillness within the heart chakra.

Session Ten.

Client consults feeling balanced and together. She described her inner turmoil and sadness that had come through the opening of her heart chakra. She agreed that her past was nothing to do with anyone any longer but that she had the task to release herself from her own feelings. Client had learned the lesson of acceptance vs. forgiveness.

Client utilised very deep energetic breath work from Mother Earth to breathe in the healing inner to replace the emerging sadness as it emerged. The curling up in a ball in the forest is the rebirthing from the womb of Mother Earth into the next level of their true self. The client became a master in her own right and took responsibility for her own journey.

Consequences of sexual abuse on the light body

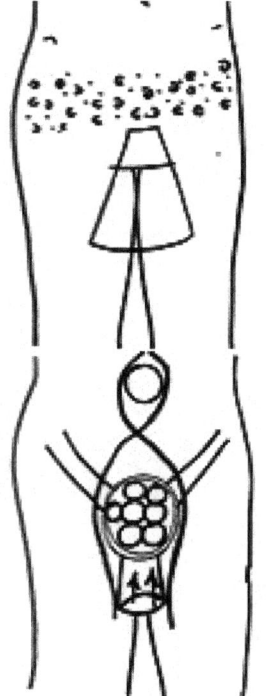

After Sexual Abuse

After Healing

Sexual abuse shatters the sacral chakra. Sexual experiences at an age before we can deal with such experiences can also incur the effects of sexual abuse for both men and women.

Removing Imprints

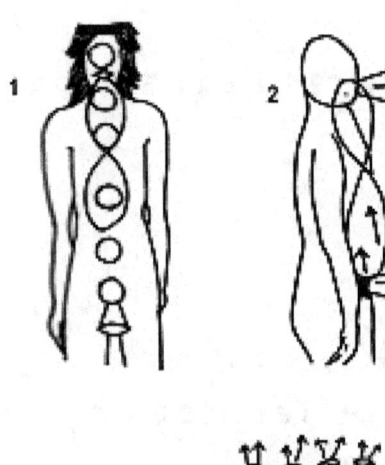
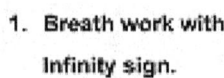
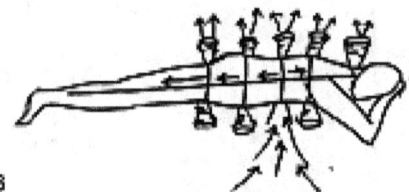

1. Breath work with Infinity sign.

2. Breathe/Cough away.

3. Earth Connection.

Depression is when you have lots of love, but no one's taking.

Doug Coupland

18. Understanding and Treating Depression.

One of the problems with depression is that it doesn't discriminate with regards age, sex, occupation, wealth or class. Symptomology vary from person to person and for many it's difficult to describe what is for them a way of life. With regards my own journey with depression, I remember thinking when I was in my mid-twenties 'Is this right? Should I be feeling like this? Is this how life is meant to be? The thought never crossed my mind back then if I should talk to someone about how I was feeling. I buried my head in the ego defence mechanism of the workaholic with a wounded inner child. It was only in my training as a therapist that I began to acknowledge feelings that I had become accustomed to denying. It was simply a way of life for me as I knew no better.

Many of your clients won't realise how life should feel. A problem shared is a problem halved. With a damaged inner child or with depression, your perception of the world becomes skewed. You don't know what you're looking for or indeed where to find it. The internal compass you use to navigate your way through life becomes dysfunctional. The Holy Grail of happiness eludes you. Happiness exists only through external manifestations. Journeying inwards involves pain and bravery, something you may be short of just keeping your head above water. For many clients who attend energy healers they find that the old structure of reality no longer makes any rational sense and the spiritual energetic view point is the only methodology by which their world can seemingly appear rational. Many people have an encodement in their energetic development that their life will implode between the age of thirty six and forty two. This is usually the time when the depression they endured for so long will not be tolerated by their higher self any longer. Change is inevitable.

This is why I have the greatest respect and honour for the people who come to see me. And I make no secret of the fact that I still consult an energy therapist/teacher myself. This helps me become all that I know I can be; it helps me cast aside the masks I've hidden behind for so long –

for centuries! I realise now that I don't need to be perfect but I do need to be gentle with myself as I travel the sacred path that is my life.

Depression is a lack of self expression of a person's life force. If a person's life force is introverted then no creativity can express itself for the person to enjoy within their life. Life will be stale and monotonous. The key to unlock depression is to analyse what caused the person to feel so fearful that self expression was so futile.

The symptoms of depression are vast and varied. They can appear in multiple forms within the psyche, affecting us mentally, emotionally, physically and spiritually. The following is a list of some of the symptomology. When talking to your client you may sense or know the answers to some of the questions but may decide to discuss the points with the client just to let him know you understand what they are experiencing.

Symptomology of Depression

Feelings of sadness and hopelessness.

Insomnia, early wakening, difficulty getting up.

Loss of pleasure/interest in activities once enjoyed.

Diminished ability to think or concentrate.

Fatigue, weakness, lack of energy, decreased levels of energy.

Chronic pain that fails to respond to treatment.

Eating disturbances/habits. Loss of weight or over-eating.

Restlessness or irritability (especially with young people).

Thoughts of suicide.

Low self-esteem or guilt.

Lower-back pain.

The Homeopathy personality type Arum Metallicum, is an intense person who suffers from depression and is capable of taking their own life. The homeopathic remedy arum should be given where possible to help alleviate the symptoms of this personality subtype. These are the symptoms of such clients:

The Arum Homeopathy Personality Type (personality type susceptible to depression and suicide).

A typical Arum personality would be Hamlet.

Scratches the side of their head when thinking/embarrassed.

When driving are constantly changing radio channels.

Full of self-reproach through negative inner critical voice.

Possess a gold, sunny disposition to the external world.

Bright, pleasant on the outside/crying on the inside.

Extremely helpful – would do anything for anybody.

Would never hurt anyone.

Have an extreme drive to prove themselves but is never good enough – the successful businessman who is never fulfilled.

May find it difficult to work with others; believe they are the only ones who can do the job correctly. Delegation is almost impossible so they have to do it all themselves.

Carry the weight of the world on their shoulders.

Ask a question but answer it before it is answered.

Have weak knees.

Fidget with their knees or feet, always moving, cannot sit still.

Mind may be miles away when talking to you or watching TV but will not know what the show is about.

Fidget with their hands.

Favourite colour is gold or shiny chrome.

Talk to themselves through their inner voice.

Will live in their head and find it difficult to fit in with the real world.

Will be governed by fear. Their fear will manifest as deep thinking or a benign control freak.

Are intense and find it difficult to have fun. This can make them difficult to live with. On another level their intensity can be viewed as the benign dictator. They can be bullies without raising their voice.

Dislike the mundane things in life – paper work for example.

Are great to begin a project but lack staying power to finish it.

Can have very entrenched beliefs due to their over analysis of events. It is usually the law of attraction over an extended period in operation in their life when they allow transformation in their cognitive processing.

Usually the energetic and oral schizoid personality.

Energetically they experienced a trauma in the womb or immediately after birth. This trauma caused great fear which they are holding on to energetically which resulted in their light body not fully integrating into their physical body. Thus when trouble emerges, their essence exits their body and so they become as a shell. Their essence spends much time back home in the astral plane and so is not fully integrated to make a success of life in the physical plane. This creates the desire to go back home by committing suicide. They also experienced rejection from at least one parent at the time of their birth. This rejection is internalised as a way of life as 'I don't deserve love….look what's wrong with me.'

When one is not integrated energetically in their physical body, their essence is floating around their light body. This projection will give rise to such thoughts as 'Am I real, how I know I am me and not someone else or am I my pet dog….what is the difference.' Notice the lack of boundaries as the aura is wide open. Connection to Mother Earth to breath in their essence from around their aura into the abdomen of the person will start to ground and integrate the person. This can be shown in their vision of the eye radar energetic healing system. Their roots will develop and so a foundation will form upon which to build the person. As the person integrates back into themselves, their hidden fears will also be pulled in from the astral plane. Behind their fear will lay powerlessness and therefore anger? At the early stages of therapy they may have a victim mentality rather then feel their power or masculine aspect. Their anger will express itself as blame such as why did that have to happen to me? Anger develops responsibility for their life and so the heartache of their life is felt. Releasing heartache means stop being a victim or blaming others. This will be how the person will start to take responsibility for their emotional well being and life. This is the start of the person looking externally to the world in the expression of their energy.

With self empowerment develops self expression or the ending of the old way of life that was called 'depression.' The manifestation of the energy of anger is to take action in their life in a powerful and loving manner so advise the person to not feel guilty about being powerful. Much of life is simply our attitude or sensitivity towards life which needs to be developed as per our maturing cognitions of the workings of our inner and outer worlds. It is better to be angry then depressed. It is an emotion that is nearer to love and gratitude then depression on the scale of the processing of emotions as per the hierarchy of emotions. It would naturally not be helpful to remain in this angry state for the enjoyment of the person's life.

When I go through the symptoms of depression with clients I usually ask them to answer the related questions in whatever way feels right for them, without thinking about the answer. However, this is not advisable if the client is in the throes of severe depression or is very inarticulate. Let your energy treatment speak for itself in the development of the person's life.

With depressed people, each person will be at a different level of energy that they will be able to engage and relate to you. Each depressed person should be treated as an individual as each case is unique. Therefore you let the person talk and come to you. Do not set the tone or pace of the sessions but give the client permission to find and feel their own level of engagement within themselves. Use the outside world as your focus on rebuilding energetically the lower three 'human' chakras i.e. base, sacral and solar. After three sessions the person usually comes in and starts to discuss a very specific aspect of their life. It may be an aspect that never dawned on you to discuss in therapy but what is important is that you draw out the feelings and new cognitions in relation to this aspect of the client's life. On no account tell or advise dependant clients as to what action to take in their life as what the person is really asking is permission to think and feel for themselves in their life. By all means if you are asked a straight question, give a straight answer as this will build up trust in your therapeutic relationship. They will sense your honesty and will reward you by reflecting back that honesty. This is a major opportunity to tell the person that they are turning their life force outwards as in reality there is no such word as depression.

I have yet to meet a client who was explained the definition of the word depression once diagnosed by a medical professional. Always explain to the client your concept of the word depression as their focus will turn away from suffering from a word called depression to an expression of what it means to be their own person within their own life.

People with lower-back pain, who are dissatisfied with their position in life, may correspondingly suffer from depression. If a client bites his nails it means there is tension within the subconscious. If he looks down to the ground along the centre line of the nose it means he is indecisive. These are clues to what the person is emotionally withholding within their subconscious.

If a male client is in the grips of the anima complex then he will be grumpy and moody. His moodiness will be originating from his weak male side which is internalising his power rather then projecting his power externally. His anger will stem from his dominant female side which will be angry at such little support from his male side. Possible energetic states that this male could find himself encompassing could be:

parent child relationship with their spouse,
energetically stuck in the past,
energetically married to his mother,
paralysed as an eternal 'son' due to his Fathers harsh energetic vibration,
stuck in mother energy as a stay at home father to his children.
positions himself as a rescuer or 'father' energy to women in relationships.
Is the eternal youth in that he is afraid of intimacy and destroys relationships once they get serious?
Stuck energetically in the anima role.

It is very common for men to be stuck in the grip of the mother energy complex of being castrated by their anger and rage at being dominated by their mother or father when as a child. These children were not individuals in their own right but were extensions of a function of a parent. The parent had no real sense of self or 'I' but existed according to the functionality of the exalted position of being 'a mother or father.' Thus Jonnie wearing clean clothes for school became a measure of how wonderful the provision of the functionality of being a mother rather then providing the clothes that Jonnie deserved simply because he was Jonnie. The second synario gives rise to the fact that Jonnie was not able to exist in his own right and therefore will not have developed his individual essence to express his energy as an adult.

For a female who suffers depression look at the energy she embodies. Has she circumnavigated the mother or father complex? Is she jealous in that was she 'seen' by her father when as a child? The opposite could also be true in that was she a surrogate 'lover' to her father whereby no love existed between her parents. It is likely as an adult she would be attracted to much older men. Is the woman stuck in Aphrodite energy in that she embodies the essence of the God Aphrodite? This will probably manifest as being the eternal femme fatale too delirious in their own magnificence to mature into being an adult woman. Marilyn Munroe was one such embodiment. Examine if the woman is:

Energetically stuck as a child due to trauma.

Imprisoned by their mother's harsh energy or treating men as per her mother's harsh male aspect (animus).

Eternally stuck in Mother role to their siblings as the eldest child.

Married to their father as their surrogate spouse.

The eternal daughter who refuses to energetically grow up and become their own woman.

A surrogate husband/male to their effeminate spouse.

The composed 'old Hag' content to enjoy such barbaric power to all that cross her path.

The voluptuous young woman who will not be 'tied down' for anyone.

Stuck in animus role incapable to reflect on their actions in life.

Through relationships the causality of their energetic states emerges. What is common is the fact that both parties had similar childhoods which caused the attraction in the first instance. However, the mask of the persona will fuel tremendous conflict which will hide the fact that both parties decided to handle their trauma in completely different manifestations. Thus the circle of the complete essence has being formed i.e. introvert/extrovert, depressive/aggressive, male/female etc. Relationships are perfect even in their level of dysfunction as an expression of the essence of the couple.

Gerard

An engineer by profession, Gerard was in his early thirties when he came to see me with regards smoking cessation. He was a mild, pleasant man but I sensed that his mind was working ferociously in the background. He lived his life from the viewpoint of his mind and at times couldn't express what he was feeling. He had a very long gaze. He picked at his nails and shuffled his feet on the floor. He rocked his knees gently from side to side. He constantly looked at the floor before giving an opinion and at times talked in circles. He would change his opinion often and always ended up taking the other person's point of view at the expense of his own. He was a workaholic who loved solving problems who enjoyed nothing more than to be confronted with an work problem. He had risen to the position of manager of his division which resulted in him devoting more time to paper work and management than to actually solving problems. This caused his feelings of depression to return. His best friend lived on the other side of the country. When he was with his girlfriend he felt guilty because he wasn't giving her his full attention. He spent money on gadgets he thought would amuse him but they were now left to one side. He had no energy and didn't sleep well.

I outlined the gifts of a sensitive person to Gerald. He was amazed to find that someone could 'read' him so well. We focused on the fact that he would be happier at work if he could tackle his mounting paper work. I outlined the basics of time management to him which, if he adopted the principles, would make a difference to his workload. We talked about him spending quality time with his girlfriend and finding hobbies that suited him. He remembered how he used to enjoy sport because it took his mind off his problems. We talked about the possibility of him getting involved again in sport/exercise and he agreed to take a homeopathic remedy from a qualified homeopath. After 3 sessions Gerald was more grounded and had decided on a definite plan of action for his life. He felt in control and was valuing himself.

Sinead

Sinead was a successful business woman in her thirties. She worked very hard but her growing business was proving stressful to manage. Sinead suffered from depression since she was a teenager. At times she would stay in bed all day unable to face the day. She was aware of having a soft, gentle side that was very generous to people, but that she also had a hard warrior side that could be critical, ruthless and aggressive towards the men in her life. Sinead had met someone special and desired the relationship she always had dreamed of if only she could stop being aggressive.

The second session saw Sinead accessing memories of her youth using breath work. She recalled a memory in which she felt her mother didn't acknowledge her courage in a task that was beyond her skill at the time. Sinead did really well in the task but this wasn't good enough for her mother. The next memory was of an argument at home when her drunken mother was hitting a younger sister. Sinead jumped up and slapped her mother, stopping her in her tracks. Sinead then went to bed and after about an hour her mother came to her and apologised. Before she left the room, Sinead's mother hugged her. At this stage Sinead began to get emotional, feeling guilty for slapping her mother but she was confused about being rewarded with a hug for being aggressive. I asked Sinead to compare those feelings with her previous relationships when she loved someone. She described the same emotions and her need for clarity. I asked her to think about those mixed feelings she had as the young girl who had slapped her mother, and when she was aggressive towards a partner or loved one. She then saw that she had come to associate love with aggression as per her mother's parental influence. We continued the session, separating the emotions and removing the guilt. I asked Sinead to think about her actions and feelings when she would be with both her mother and partner over the following week

Energetically I find people with depression have a light body with one or more of the following conditions.

1. A energetic hole in the abdomen of the aura.

This energetic black hole is literally a black hole swallowing life force energy that is usually positioned over the sacral chakra or solar plexus. As the earth energy enters our light body, the energy comes vertically up the body and is then swallowed by the energetic black hole. No energy can enter the power centre or heart chakra of the person's life. Life will be meaningless and the person will act as if in a daze. This black hole can be caused by drink, drugs, negative thinking, psychic attack and present or past life issues. The key is to remove the black energy mass over weekly sessions, strengthen the aura's defences, connect the chakras and their functioning, challenge old beliefs and attitudes that contributed to such behaviour in the first place.

2. A blockage in the emotional layer of the client's aura.

As a defence mechanism if we find life challenging we may decide to shut off our emotions and therefore live solely within our cognitions. The Celtic tiger unfortunately positioned many of us in our head and thankfully this is currently being reversed through the experience of the economic recession. You may feel this blockage approximately 24" out from the body over the tummy or heart charka. Ask the client to breathe deeply, connect to a time when they decided that it was a good idea not to feel with their emotions. Tell them to release that blockage through letting go of that fear or anger etc. You will be able to feel the blockage dissolve within your hands or simply remove it totally to the light of your candle in your alter for transmutation. The energy of the power of the chakras can then be felt to vibrate through the aura into the other aspects and layers of the client's life.

3. A closed heart due to Heartache.

Behind every negative emotion is heartache which is lack of self love. This may stem from fear, powerlessness, anger, resentment, guilt shame or despair. These are the primordial emotions that God experienced when he decided to split himself into monads or us humans. As a manifestation of God we too possess these emotions that require transformation through the expression of our life. If we experience a trauma that is too painful to process then our heart chakra can close down or become swamped in negativity. This will stop us feeling in our life, will stop love coming into our lives but more seriously will stop us giving to others in our life. If we cannot give, therefore we cannot receive which is the operation of the law of attraction and reflection. The heart chakra is the link between our physical body and the astral plane where we hold our emotions. If there is a blockage in the heart then no emotions can be burned up or transmuted from within the astral plane. Emotional life will shut down as if the person will be in no mans land. Proceed by energising the body from the earth upwards thus alleviating the intensity of their negative emotions. When the heart reaches critical mass of receiving healing emotion you will see the client gasp for air, gulp or cough. This is the restarting of the heart chakra akin to using electric shock paddles on the heart. Expect the client to be sad over the following days as all the other negative emotions will start to flow upwards to the heart to be transmuted. When a heart chakra becomes closed it is then that even good relationships break down as no love can be expressed or received. As a person continues on their therapeutic journey many past lives, ancestral and primordial traumas are brought from the astral plane into the heart chakra. At this level of healing you are no longer conducting therapy on your clients. You are helping them evolve as spirits. This is why I rarely attract clients that are dealing with a specific fear of phobia. They may attend with such issues but once we look at their psychological history and proceed with examining their light body energetically then nearly all clients enter the process of soul evolution through energy psychology.

4. An energetic imbalance between the couple in a relationship.

If the male and female energetically switch roles, then both will express their soul's essence in a dysfunctional manner. This can work very well for people as a status quo is created for all concerned due to the fact both parties will be willing participants in the energetic stalemate. Unfortunately their children will inherit the parental dysfunction with regards their expression of their essence in their adult relationships. On a soul level this is possibly undesirable for the couple as Earth is a training ground to find and express our true selves. You will not evolve as a man living your life energetically as a woman. Conflict arises when a particular party starts to look inwards and asks 'what type of man or woman am I.' Their focus will then shift to their partner and their shadow will become depressed or angry due to the competing nature of that expression within their relationship. There is only room for one woman in a relationship. There is only room for one man in a relationship. I describe this aspect to people as two people kicking the shins off each other at the oven because they both want to do the cooking. If the male starts to develop his masculinity then he will resent his energetic masculine wife for being unfeminine, unsexy or boring. Worst of all she may resent his newfound maleness and refuse to hand over her masculinity due to her fear of her own femininity. The male may be afraid to trust his own maleness and may want to remain in his own old fashioned role as 'the mother of the family.' The woman may feel crowded out in her own home or even be forced to work externally to pay the bills. This is all conducted on the astral or energetic plane and replicated on the physical plane. A power struggle between the sexes always results in depression for the weaker or more feminine soul.

5. Energetic chords between energy beings, a deceased being or energetic parasite.

Depression may originate from one person being energetically attached to another person through a parasitic relationship or a psychic attack. This may occur because a deceased spirit that has not gone to the light, an energetic entity living off their energetic host an old relationship that needs to be severed or the moving on from an old home/house etc. There will be a drain to the other energy will show itself in dreams or obsessive thoughts about the other energy.

6. Trauma resulting in a splitting of the ego or soul essence.

If a soul becomes fragmented then that person is emotionally stuck in their past. If the event occurred in their childhood then that person will energetically be stuck at the age that they experienced the trauma. This will the level of developmental energy in the astral plane that the person will use to attract, create or project their experiences and emotions in their so called adult life. The person's life will be full of anxiety and emotional pain. If the event occurred due to a shock or accident then the aura will be damaged i.e. a crack in their crown chakra. It is highly likely the person will keep attracting into their life the very same experiences in their future. The person will probably attract in a partner of a similar energy that originally caused the sensitising even as per the law of attraction. Co-dependent relationships are sometimes formed in this manner.

This person will not be able to stand their ground whereby they will retreat in times of conflict. They may never have an opinion on any subject and may only express their opinion in rage or outbursts. This is the hidden anger at the loss of their soul essence and the way they live their life.

7. Depression due to Geopathic stress.

The earth releases energy which is negative to us in nature from what we call lay lines. These lines are like an electricity grid on the surface of the earth that breathe out what we call geopathic stress. Houses are naturally built upon these negative lines and in some instances there is an excessive amount of these lines which can be detrimental to people sensitive to energies. An earth healer is necessary to heal the earth and change the land from negative to positive.

When a client attends therapy for depression, I simply let them talk. I know before they ever consider attending a hypnotherapist or energy healer that they have read many books, gone for counselling or taken anti-depressants etc. They have probably been told by lots of people what they need to do in order to 'fix themselves.' I require for the first 2 or 3 sessions to let them feel themselves emotionally and indeed physically in the chair. Many people are out of their body in that their emotions and body are not in sync therefore I advise them to receive a massage before the second appointment. I let them decide whether it is advisable to schedule a second appointment. I always conduct an energy treatment on their light body and am sometimes sparse with the information I tell the client about the treatment. The past or the energy they are carrying is not important as it has changed during the session. I prefer to tell them about the future and how the energy they are transmuting at this moment will affect their life.

Client: What was that all about, Gerry?

Gerry: You are going to be fine, Mr. Client. Your body is reacting to the treatment very well. I want to tell you what you are dealing with now and how it is going to affect your life in

> *the coming weeks. You are dealing with emotions such as sadness and powerlessness in your abdomen…down here. (Indicates with hands). That is lifting quiet fast at the moment so well done. But…you are also dealing with anger because there is a part of you that is hopping mad at the world and probably at yourself for feeling and being this way. So, you are going to get angry. You are going to forget I said this but you are going to project this anger outwards onto others. The smart thing that you really need to do is channel that anger into power and not destruction. I would like you to determine that difference over the next few weeks.*

At the next session I ask the client did you get angry at times with a little smile on my face. They usually reply yes. I ask them was it with your family or just stupid things that frustrated you? They reply just the ordinary stupid mundane things in life. I then ask 'I wonder if it wasn't the mundane things in life that was really bothering you? It is immaterial if we go into their past or wait dealing with the present at this stage. The client knows the treatment is now a science that can be proven and that there is an action plan in place to change the future. Since 95% of therapy takes place between sessions the client will answer their own questions as they develop their energy.

Anger in the liver comes into play when energy reaches the power centre of the solar plexus and proceeds to then enter the right hand liver masculine side of the body. Anger is a better emotion to feel then depression as we only get angry about what we care about. The key is to turn those angry feelings from a destructive energy into a positive energy. Cognitive restructuring may be necessary to help the depressed person think in an emotional mature fashion. This is a skill that many of us have to learn. We must also face the fact that there is no right or wrong way to practise this skill as it is a guideline to structure happiness in our life. The following is a structure of cognitive processing:

What we value in our life,

Forms our beliefs about aspects of our life,

Which gives rise to our thoughts about our self and our life,

Which is the foundation of our feelings about us and our life,

Which leads to our behaviour in our life.

Which ideally should give meaning to our life.

Values are subjective. If you do not value anything in the outside world then that means you do not value anything within your inner world. Values give meaning to life. They form the pattern to the fabric to the cloth of our life. The belief in our life will highlight the risks we must take to enjoy life, to face our past, to envisage where you are going and to fight for the quality of our life. The more we value our self, the more we think well of our self. We may become aware of our inner dialogue and thought process which will remind us that we are not the thoughts that our brain thinks. This allows us the opportunity to compartmentalise aspects or qualities that we need to develop in our life. This means that we should become more aware, circumspect, forgiving and accepting about life and develop discernment. This allows us choice in our behaviour and the behaviour we share with our family and friends. Many people are sad to leave relationships but realise the price that their soul essence or children will experience will be too great if they remain in the dysfunction of the past. The dysfunction will only be carried forward and perpetrated on the next generation.

When working with depressed clients, the first goal is to remove blocks to their happiness. Start with the client's present life situation and use cognitive restructuring to challenge beliefs, attitudes and thinking styles. Use energy healing to structure the lower three charkas as these correspond to our human functioning on earth. The individual will start to get angry as the energy will have reached their solar plexus. Then you know their energetic power has started to be channelled into their life. They will emotionally alternate between sadness and fear, these emotions being projected on to their loved ones possibly in a passive aggressive fashion. Then the depressed person will realise that equilibrium should be struck as to how they should live life. They will start to distance themselves from their anger and sadness which will formulate the emotional control to distance them from other vibrations of a depressing nature in their life. They will stop meeting their 'best friend' they met at a day care centre or they will avoid their smoking and drinking buddy who 'just seems to annoy them all the time.' They will then make tentative steps in socialising such as going shopping on a tuesday morning or while still not going to a night club they still 'bought that new dress that was just a man killer.' They will have greater perspective with regards their home life and will start to see through family relationship patterns from past conditioning.

While depressed people are excellent at observing people they will now have stood back and begin to see patterns in their life. Rather then being immersed in the life of other people they will begin to see clearer boundaries between themselves and others. I do not believe in full analysis of a person's childhood. Session by session I let the law of attraction illuminate their past through the examination of chance occurrences in their life as they develop their true 'self.' Usually the client will rebirth their true self by dealing with the feminine mother complex as derived from Spirit or through their relationship with their own mother. Their masculine side will then be developed through the paternal complex. Greater challenges will be surmounted as they develop in therapy which will further illuminate their past. This may be viewed as a setback but on another level this is a final viewing of the cause and effect of past behaviour.

8. Depression due to inadequate parenting.

If as a child you did not receive adequate or compatible love and affection then as per ego state philosophy and attachment theory, you are likely to endure low self esteem, guilt, shame, poor boundaries, a damaged inner child and poor adult relationships. The child will internalise these feelings in the astral plane in the same manner as a sponge absorbs liquid. If a male child feels insecure because of a weak father figure or excessive dominant father figure then that child will not know how to freely express their life force in maturity. They will have to discover their masculinity in adulthood. A masculine or emotionally absent mother will result in sensitivity being absent which will mean the child will not be able to 'feel' or express their own life force. The birthing process from Spirit to their Mother and from their mother to actual independent person will not be adequately completed. They will have a monkey on their back on the astral plane which will dog their masculinity. This will show itself in the actions of their children. Their children may be angry, have outbursts of temper or may break their toys as the energy given with their toys from their parents was not given with an open heart. This toy will have no currency with the child as it's akin to bringing a child into a sweet shop, showing them the sweets but telling them that they are not allowed any treats. Look but do not touch. Love is the currency that children need. There are conditions attached to this toy of which the child can unconsciously read. If a child turns on radiator valves, taps etc he is in reality describing the tension in the home. If a child wants to escape they are energetically trying to break out of prison. Children need to feel secure and be protected from the world. This means boundaries. If a dog has no master or a weak master then he goes insane. He needs to feel the security of the pecking order of the pack. A child should not be the adult of the relationship. Like wise a child should not have the responsibility of buoying up their opposite sex parent if the paternal relationship is poor or non existent. Addressing the child's experience of their parenting through inner child work will free the adult emotionally.

Emotions ebb and flow. There are energies coming into the earth at present that are causing great turbulence on every level of our being. This is all good for those who see the big picture and taking action to learn what life is about here on Earth. The flow of emotions within our bodies, which comes in waves, can only be healed through the flame of the heart chakra. As the heart chakra governs the happiness, success and fluidity of our lives, then we can only expect that our life will feel as if it shuts down every once in a while. As you progress in therapy, the bouts of greater darkness within our being will be pulled to the surface and transmuted through our heart chakra. The bouts will probably be of a shorter duration but possess more intensity. That is why you need to work with a therapist on your journey because if they are of a greater vibration then they can see through your negative vibration and tell you what is really happening in your light body.

There is nothing worse then self-deception where the deceiver is always with us.

Plato

19. Understanding and Treating Bereavement.

The emotional pain of losing a loved one is considerable. For people who experience the death of a child, the emotional pain can be crippling. The trouble for couples who encounter bereavement is that that each person grieves in their own individual way. One person may want to talk about how they feel and their spouse may not be able to express their feelings about their grief. These entrenched positions may alienate each other in that both parties may not know how to begin to communicate to remedy the situation. Communication is vital and external therapy will be necessary to move the couple forward.

Bereavement from an energetic viewpoint involves the chords of the relationship between the people being destroyed. If the death was heralded i.e. the person had a long terminal illness, then the chords have been given the chance to dissolve naturally as the realisation of the impending death automatically dissolves the chords. The person then has the sadness of the loss of the person in their life to transmute. If the person's death was unexpected, then the chords were abruptly pulled from the living persons light body. This will leave a gaping energetic black hole of sadness which means to successfully deal with bereavement on an energetic basis, that black hole of loss within the chest area must be transmuted.

A parent provides the safety and security aspect of a child's life. If this security is disturbed then the inner world of the child reflects that disruption. For most children, the day their parent dies is the day of two deaths, that of their parent and also the death of the maturing of their inner child. One person described it to me as such;

'The day my Mum died was the day the singing stopped, the baking stopped, the hugs going to bed stopped. It was the day my world ended '

For others it is a day that their childhood ended whereby they were given the responsibility of caring for their siblings because 'that was the way it had to be. We all had no choice.'

Healing Bereavement.

The energetic severing of the chords of the relationship results in a feeling in the chest area of coldness, emptiness and hollowness as if your heart has been just pulled out and ripped to shreds. The truth is, it just has on the energetic level of the astral plane. People can cry tears of sadness for years from this energetic creator in their chest but unfortunately they will be crying the same tears from the same energetic trauma until it is energetically removed. What is required is that:

> 1. The bereaved person is allowed to complete any 'unfinished business' in their conscious mind with the deceased and,
>
> 2. The energetic creator in their chest from the severed chords is healed and their chakra system returned to normality.

Always allow the bereaved person tell their story in their own way. Let them exhaust all avenues of cognitions until the client address's you with how you should proceed in relation to the therapy. With such clients you have to build a picture in their mind of the process of this therapy but in such a way that they have confidence, faith and belief in your handling of their great emotional pain. Your delivery should be confident in that your inner belief of what you do should be reflected in the communication to the client. Subconsciously you will be saying 'Leave this to me, I know what you need and I will take you by the hand and show you the way of releasing this great pain.'

I then proceed to tell the client about the process and ask them to visualise the pending therapy. Whether they agree or not is immaterial as by processing what I am saying to them they are inadvertently completing the exercise. It's a little tricky but most of us are scared of change and fearful of our hidden emotions. Remember no surprises with bereavement which is why I tell them where I am about to lead them within the therapy. I proceed with the full length of the visualisation as follows;

'I am going to ask you to imagine going into a beautiful garden where there is a church in the centre of that garden. You go into the church, close the door behind you and see everyone busily going about their business. As you walk up the centre aisle of the church, see three people standing in front of the altar. The person on the left is a favourite Saint of yours, on the right is Jesus. Notice how he looks to you…..he's different then you thought he may have been. In the middle is 'first name of deceased person.' Always use the personal name of the deceased. If a person describes their friendship with Timothy ask 'what was the actual name you called Timothy? Was it Tim? Quiet often you may get a reply such as 'No, it was bubbles?

The visualisation should proceed as follows:

> Open a chord between your chest (the heart chakra), and 'Bubbles.' Open a chord between your eyes and 'bubbles' eyes. Breathe out now, all the things you need to say to 'Bubbles.' (The eyes are a gateway to the Soul).
>
> See all those emotions leaving your body as you tell him everything. (Pause).
>
> See what 'Bubbles' is saying to you, saying 'Give it to me, give it to me.' (Repeat these words in a whisper).

Now see the chord between you and 'Bubbles' turn red as 'Bubbles' beams their love back into you through that chord. Breathe deeply as you fill yourself with the knowledge and energy of the love you both have for each other.' The returning energy is the client accepting healing energy into their heart chakra.

Notice how I describe the spirit world within the church as people busily going about their business indicating that life has a defined purpose after we die and that death is not what we may invision.

This method of healing has the wonderful benefit of protecting any embarrassment that the client may feel in that the client is not required to speak. I have had many clients, especially male clients who have told me that they would never go to counselling because they felt unable to speak about the experience of the death of their loved one.

If a person has multiple deceased loved ones to meet in the visualisation then deal with one deceased person at a time. Ask them to nod or tell you when they are ready to move on to the next person. I advise clients to open their eyes if the visualisation gets too emotional for them. Give the client the opportunity to decide for themselves who should be the first person they should meet or, you can decide whom you feel is the deceased that caused the greatest sadness and commence working with that person. You will usually see tears stream down the clients face as they grimace in heartache. When they shift position in the chair I usually take it as a sign that they are ready to move on to the next deceased person or stage of therapy. Always remember to tell the client to breathe out their words and emotions as therein lies the cure. Often I just sit in my chair in silence, sometimes for thirty minutes of the session somatically linked into the client's energy field waiting for the client to move or tell me that the session is complete. Its takes courage to do this as your mind will battle with you to do or say something. Remember that therapy is about the client and not about you the therapist.

Quiet often the client will fall asleep during the session as their consciousness leaves their body and travels to the astral plane. The pain of experiencing the release of their sadness would be too great to endure so their consciousness is hidden from conscious awareness by their guides.

After the visualisation, conduct an Astral trance healing session on the client. Bring the Earth energy into the person and channel it into the black hole in the chest area. The sacral chakra will need lots of healing and their roots may be displaced due to the uncovered trauma.

Advise the person to attend in a few weeks time. When they attend, start the session by asking them 'how were the last few weeks for you? Do not be specific; let the session go where it must. If the person, when as a child stopped growing energetically, then issues in relation to their maturity will surface. It is common that the client's burden of responsibility from their youth will emerge in the second session. Often a child will not express their sadness to their remaining parent as they sense the emotional pain that parent is experiencing and they wish not to add to their heartache. They may have had to energetically take on the role as a parent to their parent which may emerge during the second or subsequent session of therapy. If this emerges then you know the sadness of their loss of their bereaved is transmuting and your client is now taking back their power. The visualisation required by the client in session two may not include meeting any deceased person but may encompass inner child therapy. Allowing the person to enjoy life, not to feel guilty about being left behind or removing the burden of responsibility of having to care for their siblings are such issues commonly addressed in session two.

When dealing with bereaved clients it's important to ask the client about the process of finding out about the death of their loved one. Many times I have come across people explain to me that when their parent died that they as a child were:

- not told that their parent was unwell before their parents death.
- knew for days beforehand that something wasn't right but only found out about their deceased parent before the actual funeral.
- The local nun or priest was drafted in to tell the child of their parent's death. This has the double stigma of the child not

> trusting the parent left behind to be honest with the young child.
>
> - Not allowed go to the funeral but saw the coffin proceed to the cemetery after the funeral mass from watching in their neighbours house.
>
> - Had to go away and stay at a relative's house that was ill equipped to deal with emotional problems and therefore channelled their own sadness and insecurity into anger towards the child.

The inner child knows on an energetic level from within the astral plane when their parent is dying or deceased. This knowledge does not follow the chronological time sequence that we envisage that governs our lives. If a child needs soul retrieval you will need to reintegrate the child from the time they tell you they experienced the collapse of their young world. This could be days before the passing of their parent. I have had one client who went through many sessions of therapy that failed to build the integration of their lost soul essence from the correct sensitising event. That therapist tried to integrate the young child from the time of their parent's funeral whereas the splitting of the soul essence of the child occurred three days prior to their parent's death. That was when the young child spent the day curled up in a ball under the kitchen table in their relative's house. That client in subsequent sessions of therapy projected the neglect of their surviving carers onto that therapist for not correctly identifying the sensitising traumatic event.

Dealing with bereavement issues takes time and patience. This healing cannot be rushed. On one level you never get over the loss of a loved one but manage to live with the loss in a more productive and accepting fashion. Many times when we hold on to the past we are really trying to hold on to ourselves.

Abortion.

Clients who attend for emotional healing as a result of a termination should be handled with two distinct methodologies:

1. Clients who are concerned with the loss of their baby and their own remorse for making that decision at that time and,

2. Clients who are solely concerned with removing the trauma from the procedure of the termination.

The difference between the two clients being that one regrets the death of a child while the other may be dissociated from the procedure and has no remorse with regards the actual termination.

Before the actual visualisation I advise the client as to the procedure of the visualisation. I ask the client to go to the astral plane (heaven) and meet a deceased loved one who is with their baby. I ask them to see how happy and loved their baby is with their relative.

I then proceed to ask them to fly back in time to their younger self to integrate their lost essence back into one body. This involves the client lovingly talk to themselves back in the clinic. I ask them to give themselves permission to release all sadness and grief and to realise that they made the best decision that they were capable of at the time. This opens the door to forgiveness and self acceptance.

I ask the client to say goodbye to their baby and to come and visit each other in their dreams at night. After ensuring all light bodies are fully integrated I ask the client to come back into the room.

With the client who is concerned with their own essence with regards their experience in the clinic, I ask them to go back with a big ball of white healing light and circle it around their younger self at the clinic. I ask them to talk, release and when ready merge with their younger self at that time. This releases fear and sadness which integrates any lost soul fragments displaced at that time. I ask the person to fully integrate and when ready move forward to the present time and space.

In both cases the session is but a re-orientating of their energy which will allow more sadness to be released over the following weeks. Acceptance and a non judgemental attitude is what you desire to develop within the client.

Trust is the energy of the Spirit and love is the energy of the Heart.
Unknown

20. Understanding Abundance.

In energy terms, when ever you declare yourself as something to the universe, the universe will immediately respond. You say that this is who you are so as the energy of that belief flows through you out to the world to accept, the world will answer back in answer to that belief. This is the writing of that cheque with your inner belief but now the question remains can you cash that cheque in the physical world. There is nothing wrong with growing into the job once you are nearly ready to be competent in that task but if you are a fake, then you will be found out. There is a difference in that making an honest effort will provide challenges that will stretch you in developing you in all that you are. Remember the saying be careful what you wish for as you just might get it?

Many people write energetic cheques thinking it is their belief system that matters in the image or words they express to attain their desired result. The fact is that it is their inner belief infused within their inner emotions that provides the manifestation of success. Nowhere is this fact more acutely demonstrated then the status of a persons finances. Many spiritual people have the notion that money and spirituality don't mix. The sad fact is that lack of money or scarcity is like a rope around your neck. It prevents you attaining spiritual growth in that you can only achieve growth in the physical plane to advance in the spiritual plane. You are human first and spirit second in that you have to live in the unreality of the physical plane and live by its rules. Remember the spiritual rules: you cannot complete this journey by yourself so you will require investment in time and money to attend to your particular type of therapy. You don't play by the rules then you don't get to play the game. That means game over in relation to advancement of your spirit.

For many years I had great difficulty in reconciling my hang ups with money, being spiritual and my low self esteem. When I dealt with my self esteem (by going to therapy, learning my craft and therefore bringing forth my gifts), I had to turn my attention to my financial growth. This was a challenge but I knew my principles had to change within my inner belief system which would then filter to my outer beliefs and world.

I asked myself to describe my work. I saw how many people found their true selves through my work with them. I realise how much money I saved people in that people only need to attend my sessions monthly rather then weekly as with other therapies. I realised how people attracted relationships and employment through the development of their vibration. I realised that if people did not see through my work after the first session that they were not yet ready to attend to their souls development. It eventually dawned on me that a person not continuing on their journey with me was not a reflection of poor work on my behalf. It was not down to my fee being too expensive or valuing myself. It was down to the individual themselves.

After addressing these issues, my work changed. My number of appointments increased but I kept my fee the same. I developed a self development course that could be given to groups therefore growing my exposure to a greater number of people rather then one to one therapy. My spiritual gifts developed in that my confidence in myself was the anchor of my gifts.

Life can be a heaven or a hell. Once you have the knowledge of self and your profession you need to develop you niche of your work. Be professional and above all like what you do in your life. Life is too short to spend it in employment that you dislike. View the world as a flow of energy and you are simply looking for your rightful remuneration for that flow of energy through your life. We are meant to be creators as Gods in our own right.

The energy I am talking about is the feeling within your being with regards money. This will be interpreted by the world as per your inner beliefs. The lesser the congruence between your inner and outer worlds the more successful your life will be. The key is to bring your life into alignment with your inner world.

The heart chakra governs the amount of love in your life which equates to success in your life. Abundance comes with being able to hold the vibration of money and acceptance of money in your life. When you bring healing energy from Mother Earth up through your body into your throat chakra you will find the chakra will go into spasm. That spasm will be felt in your physical life as having money one week and being broke the next week. It will be your mind getting accustomed to the fact 'will I throw away my old programmed beliefs about success and money? This will be a very bumpy time in your life but a necessary one for forward movement.

Saturn is the astrological planet that governs our attitude towards money, self esteem and self worth. He will visit your astrological house to destroy any old worn out beliefs that needs to be purged from your consciousness in order that new growth can emerge. It's a matter of aligning your inner world with the flow of the universe and allowing success come to you through the law of attraction. Removing the fear of success is akin to the story in the bible of the servants who were given money by their master to invest for profit. All but one servant doubled their money through work and belief in their own intelligence. One servant buried his money in the ground and when his master returned, handed back exactly what he was previously given. He was punished for being so uncreative and lazy as per the law of attraction.

The moral of the story is that we are creators and should not hide our gifts and talents. Fear is darkness, the symbolic meaning to the method by which the servant hid his light that could not manifest as a God living in the physical plane.

Motor car as an expression of inner world.

After some time developing myself through energy psychology, I decided to buy a luxury car. It was a gem of a car, fully loaded with all the gizmo's you could dream of and some you would not even want in a car. I bought the car for myself, not to show off to others. After the warranty was up in the car, mechanical problems started to emerge such as the suspension on the right side (masculine side) failed. The engine as a protection mechanism shut down the right hand side of the engine due to the failure of two mechanical parts in the engine. It cost me thousands to fix even as I decided to sell the car. I realised I was premature in buying such a car because my inner world could not cash the cheque of owning a luxury car. I did not mind selling the car as a car is just a car. I was disappointed to have not understood the relationship between success and my inner world at that time and also to realise that my inner world needed further development.

Career change manifested as a new car.

Fiona decided to change career as her old career was not working for her any longer. She was very successful in her old job for a time and had purchased her new car from a main dealer. As her new career took off, some old friends left her circle of friends and her car started giving trouble. It ended up that the car was in the garage three times within three weeks and the trouble was only beginning with the mechanical problems. Fiona decided to trade in the car as she realised that her new energetic light body was repelling her old car that represented an old way of life that was not Fiona any longer.

Once you realise that money is simply a vibration, you need the flow of the vibration through your heart chakra to feed your life with what you need. You may need a plan of action which will at times, test your desire for what you want to achieve in your life. You may need to remove obstacles in relation to the achievement of your goals i.e. if you have friends or a habit that is not interested in the development of your work but may be a hindrance to your future. You must act to protect the energy of your future. Avoid blind spots and seek help if necessary. Realise that life is what you make it and that belief is the cornerstone for your success on the astral plane. Follow your heart and all will be yours.

Remove the fear of success which is located in the kidneys. Meditate on the meaning of the word 'success' realising that financial success does not have to equate to being successful. As we approach 2012, many people are realising that we have no choice but to live and trust our energy of living through the heart chakra. This will illuminate our true self esteem which has the added advantage of aligning our lives with Spirit.

I use a mantra to bye pass the conscious mind and my belief sand attitudes. I meditate and gently repeat the words 'I release the past and align my soul with Spirit.' I feel the words and let them sink into my consciousness. This always produces results within a few days of showing me the next step on the evolution of my Souls journey.

The fear of failure is but the flip side of the coin 'the fear of success.' Transmute the fear in the kidneys, open your heart and throat chakra. Let success come to you as you align your Soul in the expression of Spirit on earth.

It's only at the pit of hell that we find the gates of purgatory.

Dante's 'The Inferno'.

21. The Magic of our Inner Child and Soul Retrieval.

To enter the kingdom of God we must become as children. Jesus was talking about psychology. He was explaining the requirement that in order to develop as a person we need to reconnect to the childlike innocence of life before conditioning was forced upon us. We are energetic beings. We create our life through emitting the energy of the emotionality of our experiences that we hold in the astral plane. Our task through surmounting our personal and world tasks is to find the answer to the questions what type of man/woman am I? The more authentic a life you lead in relation to your individual essence, the greater the expression of your souls essence in your life. You will then be a God in the expression of your God essence in your own right. You will have released the negative emotions and be a creator for positivity in the enfoldment of your life. Yes, the Kingdom of God is within you. You have the power to make your time on Earth a paradise or a hell. If we fail to develop emotionally, this also means energetically and spiritually. This means our foundation has not developed correctly. Inner child healing utilising soul retrieval is one of the most comprehensive healing methodologies to reclaim the foundation of our personality in order to rebuild a fragmented essence. This methodology heals on an emotional, spiritual and mental level.

The approximate age of the subconscious is that of a bright seven-year old. One only has to examine a person's language and body language to realise that it is the subconscious that is in control of our nature. You will often see a person move his feet together, swing his legs, adopt a childlike pout, twiddle his thumbs, shrug his shoulders or bite his nails etc. What is happening is that the adult is accessing the hurt or vulnerable part of his childhood essence and projecting that energetic state in adulthood. The words utilised by the client as per analytical psychology is but the chance occurrence of the subconscious telling us about the emotionality trapped within the subconscious. We listen at the front door but hear at the back door.

We wear many masks. Which one do you normally wear? Is it one of sorrow, resentment, anger, stress or anxiety? Many times you will find that a person has to heal a variety of these masks before finding their true self. For instance, always hidden behind resentment is anger and behind anger is heartache as per the hierarchy of emotions and the path of the serpent. We channel our emotions according to the dictates of our emotionality which, for most people involves the expressing of the duality of fear and anger or fear and sorrow. Anger can give way to bitterness which originates from our hidden anima/ animus complex. It is only in the latter stages of therapy that we are able to differentiate the various identity states that we emotionally operate from.

The only truth in a damaged person's actions is that his language and deeds are that of a hurt little child with a stunted psychological maturity and whose feelings are very real indeed. Self development requires that we connect to those inner feelings and free yourself from this internal bondage utilising understanding, emotional release, forgiveness and then acceptance. Once we forgive and release we can then accept and take responsibility for ourselves rather then play the role of the victim and 'poor me syndrome.' Being a victim also implies blaming others for their actions or inaction which hides the fact that we create our reality. Forgiveness has little to do with the other person and to some extent it involves an element of judgement on behalf of the victim towards the perpetrator. Acceptance allows freedom in that the emotionality of your past concerns only you. Forgiveness and acceptance must also occur on an inner psychological and energetic level through accepting themselves for experiencing such a childhood. The fact that it has taken so long to discover, feel and release their childhood emotional pain means that our inner child needs to forgive that part of our adult self that hid from our true essence for such a long time. This work involves visualisation and releasing self blame/responsibility for their past.

In a meditation if a client first presents with a childhood memory from age twelve or thirteen (adolescent), I deal with that memory but ideally you need to find the inner child before age seven. Being presented with a twelve or thirteen-year old inner child can be regarded as a defence mechanism or simply the child felt that they had no right to exist in their own essence before that age. We have no filter over our chakras before the age of seven therefore the energy of the inner child by this age will have been immersed with the atmosphere of his surroundings. This means the inner child that was immersed or emotionally stuck in the past would have been unaware of living in such an energetic state. This lack of awareness and disconnection can continue until awareness and integration occurs and felt within the psyche of the adult person. To reconstruct a childhood means to access his old hurt and rebuild from the base chakra upwards utilising the healing energy of Mother Earth. The base chakra deals with our identity and right to live and exist which is formed by age one. The sacral chakra stores and operates our emotional, sensual and sexual world which is formed by age six. Therefore inner child healing involves healing the base and sacral chakra.

When a person is unaware of the cause of their neurosis, this can often be due to a dissociate state. This is why many therapies dealing with obsessions, compulsions, anxiety states or eating disorders usually fail because they do not allow the client to connect and let go of the sensitising emotion that is hidden and trapped from their past. To be free means to break down barriers and not just skim the surface of the trauma. Many therapies simply deal with changing cognitions which is necessary at some stage during therapy but the cellular, subconscious and soul level requires healing to completely eradicate the trauma of the past.

There are two schools of though with regards letting go of the past through therapy. One school states that the methodologies to self actualise is to analyse the past, release the repressions through abreactions and move forward a new and free person. Another school of thought states that analysis is paralysis. They believe that the key to moving forward is to avoid pain and move towards pleasure. If something feels bad – avoid it and move your life to something that feels good. No analysis just simply live in the now and that the past is gone forever. Which method is correct? The answer from my experience is that they both are correct which is the methodology behind the process I utilise to practise inner child soul retrieval.

Jung talks about the fact of 'will to life' in that an aspect to our life involves our soul essence deciding to mature spiritually. It raises the concept of what degree of control or free will we can exert in our life if such a development programme can enter our lives and turn us inside out. The fact is there is no other show in town but is a matter that our higher self wishes to evolve by merging energetically your inner and outer world. For many people this occurs between the ages of thirty six and forty two. It may mean you have to give up a life in order to gain a life. This tension is expressed psychologically between the shadow and ego which gives birth to the true self.

Inner child work can heal a damaged childhood. No physical trauma need have been inflicted upon the child but, in most cases, simply having been born to their particular parents was sufficient to provide the necessary environment for such a condition. US self-development expert Dr. Wayne Dyer states that up to ninety-five per cent of all marriages or partnerships are dysfunctional. This invariably leads to an unhealthy atmosphere in the home. The sensitive child will feel the pain of carrying his special gifts in an unpredictable world never mind such a house with an unhealthy vibe.

How to recognise a person with a damaged inner child?

- The person is insecure about his sense of self?
- Does he appear to apologise for his existence?
- Does he continually repeat words such as 'I'm sorry!
- Does he constantly let people jump ahead of him in a queue?
- Is he bullied?
- Does he always look on the bright side even when there is little brightness to recognise?
- Does he smile? Is he cheerful with everyone, hiding darker feelings?
- Is he afraid to lose his temper?
- Does he wear clothes that do not fit, that are unsuitable to his age or position? For example, does he dress in the clothes of an older man (father issues)?
- He may be 'intense' and find it difficult to engage in small talk.
- He may remain in the same job for years, well past its sell bye date.
- He may be a people-pleaser, unable to say 'no'.
- He may have a sixth sense that he trusts (indicating a child who had to grow up quickly).

- He may have stomach, ulcer, irritable bowel, intestinal problems. (The seat of power in the light body is the solar plexus, indicating powerlessness.)
- He may tell white lies in order to put on a good face.
- He may have a slouched stance or rounded shoulders or stand with one shoulder lower/higher than the other indicating influencing energies.
- He may over-sympathise with people and be unable to differentiate between others' and his own emotions.
- Does he know where to draw the line with regards boundaries? Does he know when enough is enough or carries on regardless?
- He may have addictions in order to stop feeling the pain of his childhood.
- He may conduct his life on a grand scale e.g. have a minimum wage job but still drives a executive car with little or no money for petrol.
- When drunk or making love to a partner, his Mother or Father may come into his mind indicating his energy is immersed with that parent through the father/mother complex.

Alice Miller in her book 'The drama of the gifted child' describes the pattern of adult life the gifted child will experience as a result of a dysfunctional childhood. If the child wasn't allowed to feel their own emotions during their childhood then the child will grow up unable to express their energy in adulthood. This situation is very common as not only do we run the risk of being rejected as a child but our parents may not be of the same essence as us therefore, we can be rejected energetically. If as cars, our parents were 'Toyota's' and their children were 'Fords', would they be able to talk to each other, fix each others problems let alone understand how the other operates? The answer is no. Spiritually we would choose our parents to learn a particular lesson in a particular fashion. This may be poor comfort to a person in the early or middle stages of therapy but it is certainly a topic for discussion towards the end of therapy. If the child felt emotionally trapped in that they could not trust their own feelings and essence, then their life force or energy had to be introverted. This gives rise to depression which I describe as a person's life force turned inwards. The law of cause and effect will emerge in that what goes in must come out. The swing will emerge in what Miller describes as 'grandiose' behaviour. Grandiose behaviour is the little boy in the sweetshop grabbing uncontrollable at the treats of his hearts delight. It will show itself as spending money that is borrowed on a credit card, booking two holidays a year in the middle of a recession or constantly dining out at weekends. It is behaviour that overcompensates for his depression. The realisation that money cannot buy happiness comes when he gets his monthly credit card bill but still feels in a depressed state. This is the reason as to why so many people have addictions in their adult life. The addiction exists and is being supported by the failure of the adult to engage with the hidden inner childhood feelings of being alone, abandoned, misunderstood and unloved. To avoid their internalised feelings they identify with their addiction in that they are powerless to avert the descent into their behaviour until after the very act of the addiction. Reflection brings self loathing and the fact that the cycle of their behaviour is build on the foundation of inner isolation.

Miller goes on to talk about the feelings of contempt that arises from the introverted feelings of lack of love from their inner child. I describe this emotive behaviour energetically as the persons female aspect being scared of getting angry (liver), which is then expressed as 'bitchieness' and then into sadness (spleen) and opening to the heart chakra. (heartache). See the chapter The Emotional light body and the path of the serpent. Their female side will feel alone, cold and exposed by their weak male side and will say to themselves 'if my male side is no good at protecting me then I better do it myself? Then the bitchieness of the unsupported female side will raise its head. I tell clients that at this stage they are learning how to integrate their male and female aspects while the universe is tempering their education through the spiritual laws of the universe. If the person can find middle ground within this psychological matrix then they can answer the question 'what way do I feel is the correct response to this situation' or still hold their ground when a woman chat's them up even though they feel really nervous.

I describe the inner child matrix as follows:

Addictions/Stress/ Avoidance/O.C.D

Depression _____ Grandiose
Behaviour

(Life force turned inwards)   (Going over the top)

Male /Female Balanced

Bitchieness/ Contempt from Female/ feelings aspect

The practise of ego state philosophy states that we shift energetic positions according to the defence mechanisms we adopt in order to protect ourselves. We can revert from the energetic state of an adult to that of a child in a thirty year old adult's body. This is to avoid the re-experience of a threat that we previously experienced as a child. The shift is so subtle that it can almost be indiscernible. On an energetic level the results are explosive as per the identification of a damaged inner child. Soul retrieval is one method to reclaim the inner child which I complete utilising energy healing and psychology. The method I use to complete inner child healing is as follows:

1. **Identify the inner child's ego state** communicating with the adult through words, actions, thoughts, emotions or the laws of attraction.
2. Ask the person to **connect cognitively, emotionally and energetically** to the same time that they previously experienced the same emotion when as a child.
3. Ask the person to wait in their body and identify what they feel. This is **the understanding** of the process of their utilisation of their defence mechanism. This will illuminate any fear, stress and anxiety and identify the flight or fight syndrome that they may use to leave their body in times of stress.
4. Connect your eyes to the **radar screen** of the clients light body and notice the shift in energies. Usually the **lost soul fragment** can be seen floating around the eyes of the radar screen of your closed eyes. When the cognitions are correctly understood the person is then able to **integrate** energetically the lost soul fragment by **releasing the other person** for their actions. This allows forgiveness and acceptance of the situation. **Acceptance will allow freedom** and choices to emerge which will support the client's male side thus avoiding the flight into fear or a negative ego state. This is the emerging male essence of the client and the **realisation** that the client was in blame and victim mode as a result of their **perception** of their past. The energetic soul fragments can be seen merging into the energy field of the radar eye vision as the lost

fragments are integrated energetically and emotionally through the inner child. Adult behaviour will develop through the adult realisation of the changing cognitions of their desired adult behaviour.

5. The emerging male side now channelled into their psyche may provide the **foundation** for the integration of a female essence to return 'home' to the client. In this instance the female essence would have been fragmented in the past and requires the male side to support its expression in his life.

6. In future sessions of therapy check in with the client to identify how they are processing the new cognitions, behaviours and developing attitudes in their day to day life.

7. The mergence of the younger self into the older self will reclaim any energetic emotional vibration invested in that situation in the past. Therefore if that childhood situation occurs today the person will not have a trigger within their energy system to put them back into 'little child mode.' Therefore the person is now free of their past.

The Inner Critic or Inner Bully.

Many people are not consciously aware of the thoughts they think within their own inner voice. They mistakenly treat the thoughts within their mind as truths that are sacrosanct. The solar plexus energetically formulates the thoughts within our mind which means that if we have a developing energy field we will have constantly developing cognitions with regards our awareness within our life. We can have an inner voice that objectively is called the inner critic. If we endured a childhood whereby we were criticised, controlled or manipulated then the energy of our childhood would exist within our psyche. This creates confusion, doubt, self blame and paralysis in the expression of our adult life. Through the law of attraction we have no choice but to re-experience the same energy as our childhood through our relationships, career or marriage. It is usually a schizoid or oral personality types that possess such an inner critic and have experienced a psychopath, masochistic or rigid subtype parent.

The inner critic will generate an inner voice that speaks the following language to us: 'You can't do that, you should not speak now, you don't know what you are talking about, you will fail at that too.' Usually it originates from a parent or guardian who was gripped in fear who energetically projected that fear onto their children. The child as an ego defence mechanism reinforced that fear which energetically feeds the energy to the voice of the critic. What we perceive as a protection mechanism at aged six will paralyse the expression of our life as an adult. It will bind us to shame as shame is concerned with our identity while guilt concerns our actions or inaction.

If a client responds that they have an inner bully or critic I ask them to float back in time to meet their inner critic or bully. I guide them through a forest to a clearing where they meet their younger self that is the personification of the inner critic. I ask them to befriend their younger self and ask them what positive function the critical voice is providing to the client. I ask them to decipher with the logic of their six year old self as to why they found the need to create such a function in their life. Fear is usually the answer with the younger self not constelled and not feeling safe enough to express their essence during their childhood. I then ask them to formulate a new methodology to deal with the fear and to integrate the critical voice into the essence of the adult client along with their new cognitions. The client is always surprised to find that the voice within their head has been removed after the session.

Gerald

Gerald was in a lot of emotional pain. On the surface, everything was rosy in his world. He was married with children, financially well off and was in the throes of changing career when he came to see me.

Nothing ever went right for Gerald. He described how, through no fault of his own, his career had failed many times even after an effort that was 'above and beyond the call of duty.' He had a happy childhood but suffered from what he now knew as depression and anxiety. He was charismatic and attracted people but as a young man, had never played the dating game.

Accessing his inner child, we found Gerald alone but unwilling to communicate. As Gerald had been a child sensitive beyond his years, we dealt with responsibility, boundaries and guilt during the first few sessions. I explained that as he started to treat himself better in thought and deed, he would earn the trust of his inner child and complete this phase of his life's path.

We realised that Gerald had a lot of buried emotion due to his mood swings, insomnia, nail-biting and fears. He never got on with his father. They had an argument when he was 20 and had never spoken since. To compound matters, Gerald married a woman with the same energy as his father. Their relationship was functional at best and tempestuous at worst. Gerald's soft nature was being dwarfed by the energy of his wife and I advised him that his relationship would change in both positive and negative ways in the future. I advised him that the changes that were happening within him would be reflected in his external world. I told him to stop and think when a energy came towards him rather then reacting as he would have done in his youth. I also asked him to meditate on the meaning 'reacting as per his past.'

Gerald battled to correct the balance within his marriage and his psyche. During that unfolding (after a year of monthly sessions), Gerald grasped his essence. His heart chakra opened. He felt the energetic imprint of shame which he was able to remove himself by connecting to this energy somatically within his body.

His wife, energetically sensing that a change was afoot, reacted angrily at his independence and threatened to leave the relationship. Gerald was continually attacked by negative energies during the course of his work with me to force him integrate his male aspect. His weaknesses were resentment to embrace his masculine side due to an energetic difference between Gerald and his father. He also possessed a hurt scared and rejected inner child who could not find his place in the world from an absent mother bedridden due to ill health. Gerald's freedom came when he accessed his inner child and integrated the energy imprints of those old belief systems of his inner world. We first dealt with integrating his inner child. Then we dealt with the heartache with regards his absent mother. Gerald stopped blaming his mother and accepted that she did the best she could at that time. Lastly, Gerald dealt with the anger of the suppression of his essence by his father's energy. This allowed Gerald to view his wife for the person she was in her own right. This strengthened their relationship to find love again in their lives. Gerald no longer related to his wife as per his inner child related to his father. The session went as follows:

Gerald: I had a bad week at home. Lots of fighting. I was very upset.

Gerry: Connect to that time during the week as you close your eyes Gerald. What do you see when you close your eyes Gerald?

Gerald: A tiny white spot moving around my vision.

Gerry: Good. That's the real you of your past that we are going to integrate into your energy field now, Gerald just relax and keep your attention on that spot. Be back there now last week where there was a lot of fighting at home. Connect to that feeling. Now blank your mind and go back in time to a younger you and connect when you were feeling the same emotion that you are feeling in your body.

Gerald: I see myself as a four year old.

Gerry: What's going on Gerald? Who is there with you and what's happening?

Gerald: There is so much anger. I am just silent and feel squeezed by the anger from my father.

Gerry: Decided now what little Gerald wants you to do, either stand beside him, put your arm around him etc. What feels right for your both?

Gerald: He wants me to stand beside him and hold his hand.

Gerry: Get your bearings on Gerald's aura now. See how it is squeezed back and Gerald is feeling lost. What does Gerald have to do to let that go now and take back his power over his space and aura?

Gerald: He needs to let it go. Stop holding on to it. Release it.

Gerry: Do that now Gerald and as you do so notice the change in the strength and dimensions of Gerald's aura. Notice what happens to your Dad.

Gerald: I feel it leaving now. (Insecurity). My tummy is swirling (The integration point of the soul fragment returning). My aura is growing out to the level it should be. Wow.

Gerry: What is happening to your Dad, Gerald?

Gerald: He's cowering in the corner. He's afraid. That's why he is angry in the first place. He is insecure.

Gerry: Let acceptance enter your mind now Gerald. That is how your dad behaves because that is all he knows. What do you feel for your Dad now Gerald?

Gerald: Sorrow. It's sad to see someone like that.

Gerry: Do you see that white spot now in your radar vision Gerald?

Gerald: It disappeared into a cloud a minute ago.

Gerry: How ever you wish to do it but I want you and little Gerald to see you back in your home last week. Who or what energy is taking the place of your Father at that time Gerald.

Gerald: My wife. Her anger. She is trying to fill the space and home with her anger.

Gerry: Notice how you used the word anger and trying. Who is the person that is in reality 'trying' and where is it coming from?

Gerald: I see it now? She is taking the place of my father or should I say I am letting her take the place of my father.

Gerry: Now you understand the structure of your reality. Let forgiveness into your perception of your wife and father. See now how it's the way you are reacting as a result of

your interpretation of the past. Does it have to be that way Gerald?

Gerald: No. I am reacting in my house as the same way I reacted as a four year old. I just need to carry on in my own space and realise that I don't need to take on board my wife's issues.

Gerry: Good. You got it. Let your new reality sink in now into your mind, thought patterns, behaviours and energy field. See in your minds eye what you will do differently from now on. (Pause).

Gerry: Good. Now what else is around you as that four year old Gerald?

Gerald: My Mother. I don't know where she came out of. She wasn't there a minute ago.

Gerry: What's going on with your Mother Gerald? Notice your vision…see how it's changing.

Gerald: I see that white dot is back again. She's sick. She's feeling sorry for herself. She is asking us to do things for her telling us it's because she is unwell. I see her helpless. She's not really sick just feeling powerless. I can see it now. She is feeling powerless and is using her sickness to get what she wants rather then just getting it herself.

Gerry: Is that her reality Gerald?

Gerald; Yes it is. That's her modus operandi. She doesn't think well enough of herself to get or take what she needs for herself so she uses her sickness to cover for her own powerlessness.

Gerry: Where is little Gerald and big Gerald now?

Gerald: Just looking at her. How do you feel towards her Gerald?

Gerald: I see myself in her. I must be acting out her stuff in my life. I feel powerless at times. I cover up to get what I want. In a way that is funny. At times I am just a function to my wife. She doesn't love me for who I am but simply because of what I earn and do around the house. My Mother only saw herself as a function to get what she wants. She doesn't believe that she can get or take what she wants from just being herself. She was never able to allow herself be loved for the person she was.

Gerry: Breath in that white dot in your radar vision now into your energy field. Throw off your Mother's energy and see how it no longer suits you to act in this powerless fashion. Where in your adult life do you act in this fashion Gerald?

Gerald: In every way of my life. I always leave myself last. I never take or get what I deserve. I usually come from a weak position. I don't accept myself for the person I am or what I can mean to a woman.

> *Gerry: See yourself now Gerald, deciding how to act, believe, think, feel and accept love just because of the person you are. Where is that white dot now in radar vision Gerald?*
>
> *Gerald: It dissolved into the yellow/ greenish cloud in my vision that is right across my eyes.*
>
> *Gerry: That is your heart chakra opening to your life. See how understanding your past has allowed you forgive the people back there as there is never any blame only in reality acceptance of what was a way of life for those people. Notice how you now understand yourself better. Realise that you do have choices and options in relation to how you think, behave, feel and act as the man you are from this moment onwards.*

Sometimes, the pain of the past can be so overwhelming that we decide to shut down our emotions and start to function on auto pilot. We can be very successful, earn enough to enjoy life but this is a pyrrhic victory. The emotional freedom that comes from living in one's own skin will never be contemplated or felt. The person will be living in a daze, driven by their inner child in a frenzied trance, alternating between depression, anger, self-loathing and indecision. Their ego will run riot from time to time, trying to be important to conceal the inadequacies of which they are so painfully aware but afraid to question in case the pain engulfs them. These people will be living in a protective shell. What will be controlling their life will be their emotions through the law of attraction.

This is where the confusion kicks in. The ego, the conscious mind will rebel, saying, 'I've saved you in the past. I've got you to this age in your life so just leave the rest to me and let me make the decisions. I know what's good for you.' Virginia Sitir used to say that the biggest fear we have as people is not death, but the fear of change. Think about your reaction as you thought of a new idea, a new project or the idea to ask someone for a date. Scary! What state did you just access? Will you complete the task just for the hell of it or will you paralyse yourself with cognitive rumination?

The ego will play safe and do what it does best: base its decisions on avoidance of fear with the same logic as that of a seven-year-old. Growth involves challenging yourself, pushing boundaries, asking questions as you enter the silence of your mind. In some instances, our memories are so painful that the censor will deliberately not allow us to process these memories. With such situations the therapist must intervene to assess the trauma as a person may be living their life in an inner child state rather then in an adult state.

As we can see, the spiritual laws are controlling our lives. Esther and Jerry Hicks with their Law of Attraction channelled by the spirit "Abraham" tell us to stop fighting life and go with the flow of what feels right for us. The trouble is that what we are holding onto emotionally will be repeated again and again until we have released this blockage and are living in our true essence. I come to understand what energy my clients are holding by asking them what is going on in their lives. This is a wonderful way to work with clients. Resistance to happiness will surface (the past or emotional blocks) as we create beauty in our lives. You are helping the client destroy and build at the same time.

Advise the client of what emotional charge they are experiencing and what to expect going forward as you see the pattern of energetic laws. It is undesirable for the thirty year old person who has to energetically deal with their mother to start to project these old feelings onto other people. We have a responsibility towards our clients to be honest with them and to protect them from themselves when they embark on their journey. This is the journey back to self. Once the light body starts to feel nourished energetically then all the lower self vices will emerge from the bottom three chakras and come into consciousness. The higher self resides in the top three chakras and can only be activated when the energy of the lower self chakras are transmuted.

If the ego has been split or the person has not grown up energetically, then inner child work is one of the most comprehensive methods to free this client from the past. Utilising the law of reflection and attraction with a therapeutic model of being a mentor or educator will allow you complete really good therapy with clients.

Integrating the female essence through inner child work.

The example of Gerald was an integration of the male essence into a male body. The following is an example of integrating a female essence into a female body.

Gerry: How are you today Tina?

Tina: Not very good. I feel my boyfriend is going to leave me. We fight all the time. Everything I do is wrong. I don't know what I will do without him?

Gerry: How do you know everything you do is wrong Tina?

Tina: He says I cannot cook...the dinner is always awful. He gives out about my weight. He tells me that I am fat and ugly when I go to the bar to buy him drink. I hate being on my own and alone.

Gerry: Tina, close your eyes and float back in time...all the way back to when you were small. Connect to little Tina when you were alone and on your own? Where are you, what's going on?

Tina: I see myself crying in my room. It's a bad night in that the room is being lit up with thunder and lightening. I cry for help and no one comes. They don't hear me. I am afraid.

Gerry: Put your arms around little Tina now. Let all that fear flow away. Feel that fear go as you see it flow away there in your minds eye of your closed eyes. As you are now beginning to understand your feelings a little better, ask yourself how are you acting out that fear of being alone in your life today Tina.

Tina: I am afraid to be myself; I have no confidence and don't want him to leave me even though he treats me badly.

Gerry: See the work you are now completing on yourself. What are you now realising Tina.

Tina: I see the fear that is in my life, holding me back...stopping me from being myself.

Gerry: Breath in the essence of little Tina now, Tina. Take in all that feeling and emotion that was left behind that night and reclaim it for you. See your aura expand now and see how you attract in that same fear in your relationships and life. What have to say to yourself and little Tina, Tina?

Tina: I don't want to feel this way any longer. This is no way to live. I need to see myself for what I truly am.

Gerry: What is that Tina?

Tina: I am better off alone then with someone that will treat me like that. There, I admitted it to myself. He is the one that has to go.

Gerry: With that new found knowledge see your self worth increase as you embrace your masculine and feminine side. See how you walk, dress and relate to others change as you have now taken in your essence that was outside of you? You now have choices Tina. Feel little Tina inside of you know that everyday she is making better and better choices for self love. How does that feel Tina?

Tina: It feels great. Exciting.

In this instance Tina was relating to the world through her fear and displaced soul fragment which was split from her essence the night of her great fear. Tina now has the acceptance, understanding and cognitions to move forward in her life.

Inner Child Healing

with

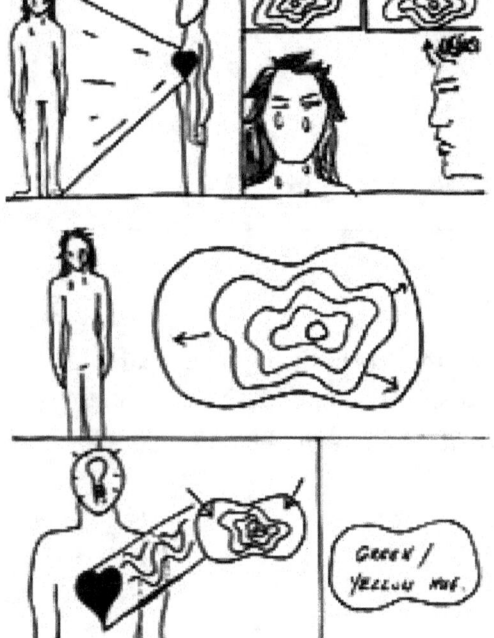

Eye Radar Healing

Soul Retrieval

Integrate the lost soul essence from childhood using

Awareness/ Understanding

Acceptance

Forgiveness

Responsibility

"Where there is love, there is life."

Mahatma Gandhi

22. Dream Analysis: Subconscious and Energetic Dreams.

In energetic psychological terms we find that dreams originate from two sources of psychic energy: the subconscious mind in terms of psychological dreams and energetic healing dreams from the astral plane. Subconscious dreams can be further divided into two phenomenon: dreams of conflict and dreams of wish fulfilment. Wish fulfilment is the subconscious acting out of the ideal situation if the dreamer has his wish. It is the desired result in a perfect world for the dreamer. Wish fulfilment dreams do not help the therapist or the client remove blockages to self fulfilment. Such dreams manifest as flying, succeeding in a task or being rewarded for something. Dreams of a conflict nature are the subconscious methods of telling you that it is working on your problems during the night and more importantly their solution. Subconscious dreams towards the end of the dream always have a method of resolution as to the way forward out of the conflict that gripped the beginning of the dream. There is a latent and manifest aspect to dreams as the subconscious talks to us in riddles. The car journey may not be a journey to be undertaken but may reflect the journey of life or the cycle of life the dreamer is engaged at that moment. Thus there is one golden rule in working with psychological dreams; the dreamer is the only person qualified to decipher dreams. Our work as therapists is simply to illuminate the meaning of dreams by bringing objectivity to an obscure world rich in information and providing options as to the potentiality for the meaning of the conscious analysis of the dream. The ego and shadow will confront each other in most dreams with the shadow presenting itself as the same sex as the dreamer. The male anima/animus complex may also be present illuminating the hidden drives of the balancing of the psyche.

Once psychic conflict has been illuminated through dreams we must realise that the conflicting forces may have been successfully resolved through the dream. It's as if the dream is now nullified as a result of the inner workings of the life force of the client as resoluted through the dream. The client will now be free to progress on their journey to the next level of psychic enfoldment.

We will now examine energetic dreams to determine their healing qualities.

Energetic dreams.

It is usually Morgan that administrates healing energetic dreams. Morgan or Crow energy has three aspects. Therefore energetic dreams can be administrated by any one of the emotionality of her three aspects. It is predominately through fear, anger or sexuality that Morgan triggers the dreamers mind which proceeds to trigger the energetic light body of its negative emotional blockages. The two emotional aspects most utilised by Morgan to trigger the light body are the voluptuous sexually powerful female for the sexual/ confidence dreams and the old Hag for the fear and anger dreams. At the end of the dream Morgan will come in and conduct an energetic healing treatment on the triggered emotions and remove the imprints from the psyche of the dreamer. Energetic dreams are a wonderful method of removing deep and long lasting negative beliefs and imprints which would be very difficult to reach during the normal course of therapy.

Energetic dreams will usually occur between the hours of twelve and four am. This is the time when the veils between the two worlds, Earth and the Spiritual ream are temporarily disengaged. You will know an energetic dream because something will not quiet make sense as opposed to a psychological dream. In an energetic dream, people will have a peculiar look, actions will be outrageous or you will feel that you are half awake so you could not possibly be having such an abnormal dream. As your Guides and Morgan know the particular dreams and emotions that can trigger your light body, I often describe energetic dreams as being better produced then any top movie studio in Hollywood. This is fine with regards the sexual/ confidence dreams after which I usually smile with clients once they explain these dreams during sessions. The fear and anger dreams are a different matter in that your greatest fears can be unleashed within your own mind.

Clients do not usually believe me when I say 'you are going to dream and receive energetic treatments during the night.' I advise clients to remain still and become aware of their light body once they realise they are in an energetic dream. If you get up and walk around the house or smoke a cigarette then you are missing the opportunity for healing that exists within that energetic dream. Remain aware in your body and feel the deep energy gushing through the imprints within your light body. Once energetic dream treatments occur, the dreamer usually comes around to realising the structure of reality and the forces at work in the world.

The following is some examples of energetic dream therapy by Morgan.

Claire and the Coke man.

The female client dreamt that they went to their work in a confident, brash manner wearing a black and white business suit. The suit was peculiar in that the skirt went above the knee showing 'just enough leg to be very daring and interesting.' I was wearing beautiful jewellery; make up done to the last, bright red nail varnish and lipstick that stood out a mile. I had a pair of hand cuffs clasped to my belt. I was also wearing a plastic pair of high heel shoes, something that a porn actress would wear. I entered my work station, looked at my desk and walked straight past it with my head in the air. I entered my boss's office and sitting in his chair was the guy in the coke ad. I tore at his clothes and handcuffed him to the desk. I ripped off my clothes to reveal a leather studded dominatrix outfit after which I jumped on the guy making passionate love…well, I mean sex. The dream ended there with my sacral chakra feeling funny. What was that about Gerry?

Dream purpose: To remove fear and inhibition with regards to the sacral chakra, the home of our inner child before age six, emotions, sensuality and sexuality.

Dream Originator: Morgan. Specifically, the second aspect of Morgan, the voluptuous sexually powerful dominant woman.

Dream analysis: The dream requires little analysis as an energetic treatment was conducted after the dream. Confidence was shown in the way the client went to their boss's office and not their old way of life as per their old desk. They dressed confidently and sexually as per an adult woman in her power. They made love to the man and remained in control of their life and pleasure. Their masculinity was shown in the handcuffs and the methodology of the sex.

Psychological vs. Energetic dream. The client said how the setting or atmosphere of the dream was unusual. The speed of the forward movement was 'brisk', the porn shoes and her 'ideal man' being the coke man. The dream ended with an energetic treatment of her light body in which the client was 'neither awake nor asleep but was aware of what was happening.'

Emotional and Behavioural changes in the weeks ahead: The client became more centred and introspective. She stated after a few weeks that 'men were not some strange alien creatures that she previously thought them to be.'

The essence of Mankind.

When I was healing my sacral chakra through energy healing I encountered this dream one night which illuminated my beliefs about human sexuality. Morgan was the provider of the dream. In the dream I was sleeping in a luxurious four poster bed in a spectacular palace. The room had high ceilings decorated in an ornate fashion with gold and ivory. There were mirrored walls with huge chandeliers. The bed was fluffy and soft. A beautiful, sophisticated confident and elegant woman entered the room dressed in a beautiful dress, diamonds and jewellery. We started to make love which was really passionate and sensual. As I was partially asleep and partially awake I was aware of my light body responding to the dream. My sacral chakra was pulsating vigorously with my kidneys energetically releasing fear and my solar plexus beginning to receive energy.

Then the beautiful woman changed to a man. He was tanned and very refined in his essence. What was so strange was my sacral chakra continued to react as if I was still making love to the beautiful woman. After a while, the man reverted back to being the previous woman. The dream ceased and the healing reverted to an energy healing on my light body.

Purpose of Dream: To heal my sacral chakra/sexuality. Morgan also released fear and powerlessness from my energy system. The dream also served as an educational lesson with regards to explaining the complexity of human essence. I was healing a past life trauma when as a woman and healer was killed for my essence by harsh masculine forces.

Provider of Dream. Morgan, specifically the voluptuous confident adult female.

Battlefield.

The client had a dream that they were in a battlefield. They had a sword in their hand which was covered in blood. As they scanned their surroundings they realised that they were in the middle of a battlefield with dead and dying people lying on the blood soaked ground. There were dismembered body parts all over the field as the vision in the dreamer became awash with blood. The dream then proceeded to enter into an energy healing session which cleared the base, sacral and solar plexus.

Purpose of Dream: To remove fear and develop masculinity.

Energetic provider of Dream: Morgan. More specifically the third element of Morgan i.e. The Old Hag or Crone.

Psychological Dreams.

The most important factor in working with dreams is that the client is dealing with the conflict in their subconscious in a metaphoric fashion. To decipher the dream I ask the person to recall the dream to the best of their ability. I say this as if it doesn't really matter as I want them to go into their own spacey hypnotic trance and to regurgitate the conflict within the dream. You will notice how your presence in the room will subside as if the person is talking to themselves which is the correct atmosphere to conduct analytical hypnotherapy. After the person has recalled the drama I stop, usually ponder the dream in my own mind which in reality is to ask their subconscious 'what's next….and anything else to add to what was said'. I then change tactics to confuse the client's conscious mind which only thinks in a linear fashion and ask;

If you went to the cinema to see a film that was your dream, what would be the name of the film?

Client answers……

What comes to mind when you think of (the name of the film)?

This usually opens up a new avenue of analytical conversation.

Towards the end of the analysis I ask the person If the dream were to ask you a question, what would be that question?

Once again, the start of the dream will illuminate conflict that exists within the subconscious mind whereas the ending of the dream will reflect the solution to the predicament of the dreamer's life.

I explore the energies of the people in the dream i.e. was there a King or Queen in the dream. Was fear present? Was the feminine/mother aspect present or was the person within their own power. Was the person transmuting fear, overcoming obstacles and surmounting challenges? Was the person in adult mode or in little child mode. The possibilities are endless but will reflect the challenges the person is experiencing in their life to date.

The gem cannot be polished without friction, nor man perfected without trials.

Chinese Proverb.

23. Parasitic Entity Removal.

I have been directed to include this chapter in Soul with a Mind by my Guides. Up to and including two weeks before publication I made a conscious decision not to include this chapter in my book. Among the reasons was that I thought the world was not ready to receive this information at this time. My Guides energetically positioned a teachers cane in my hand while administering an entity removal treatment on a client the same day a trusted friend of mine who is an excellent energy healer remarked to me 'why did I see a teachers hat while driving over to your office today Gerry? Then I knew that I have to explain to both psychology and energetic students the facts of entity possession.

All energies exist because God wills them to exist. Some galaxies consist of very advanced civilisations where love and harmony prosper whereas other galaxies are dark worlds where no love exists. At various locations on planet earth, portals exist as gateways to other dimensions that allow energetic creatures enter earth's realm. Just because we cannot see these creatures do not mean they are not real. They exist in various shapes and sizes but do have a consciousness. This consciousness can read our minds and because entities are negative by nature they thrive on such negative emotional energy derived from fear, guilt, anger, shame, sadness, grief, resentment, rage and low self esteem. The emotion of love and understanding is anathema to these entities so as entities take possession within your energy field they will influence your actions and cognitions to manifest negativity within your life.

Entities are devoid of love. They seek only what they can take from you. They do not ask or care about you. Their sole desire is to act like a parasite and live off your energy. The weaker you energy becomes the chances are you will go for therapy or healing in order to boost your energy level. The problem is that the energetic help you will receive will solely go to the entity and you will literally be feeding that which is destroying you. If you are a therapist of any discipline then your client base makes you susceptible to entity attack. Once you connect to a person's energy field then any foreign energy within their field is connected to you. As entities have a consciousness they will try and trick you in order that you do not uncover their presence and remove them to the light. Worse still is the fact that they can divide in two and infect both therapist and client or fool you thinking that the entity has been released.

Possession occurs usually through the following means:

Extreme anxiety and stress in the person's life. The person's defences were low and the person felt vulnerable.

An accident or fall that opened a crack in the person's aura. A car accident or bump in the head is a common incident of the origination of an attack.

Consuming illegal drugs or banned substances.

A serious bump to the head.

Getting seriously drunk and awakening in a confused state.

Administrating therapy while not having adequate energetic protection in place.

Opening energetic portals with no knowledge of the danger of such work.

Entities energetically transmitted through sexual activities.

The effects of entity possession are as follows:

Obsessive and compulsive negative actions and rumination.

Pain under the shoulder blades or lower back.

Pain that stems diagonally across your back from kidney to opposite shoulder.

Being accident prone e.g. burning your hands on the oven or stubbing your toe against the door.

Out bursts of anger and rage.

Feelings of extreme anger manifesting as such thoughts as 'I feel like going over to that man the other side of the road and fighting him?

Suicidal thoughts e.g. I would be better off at the bottom of this river.

Attracting accidents e.g. cars dangerously driving in front of you going to a healing appointment.

Distorted thinking patterns in that life will be a struggle.

Nightmares in which no logic exists.

An abnormal trance like state emerging over the person during love making. The person will revert to demeaning acts perpetrated against their lover.

The persons lower three chakras become strangled upwards into the solar plexus. Therefore the person's humanness on earth becomes distorted.

Entities are waiting for opportunities to take host within our bodies. Drink, drugs and sex are some of the commonest methods to transfer themselves from host to host. Some sexual entities live within the sacral chakra and energetically divide in two and infect the lover of their host. The mind of the host will be taken over by the entity in which the host will act in a sexually abnormal fashion. The host may turn violent, perform degrading sexual acts on their lover, utilise anal/abnormal sex or treat their lover as if they wee nothing more then a piece of flesh. In many such cases of rape and sexual assault entities are behind the attack and the perpetrator is to some degree unaware of their actions.

Using illegal drugs lowers our defences and makes us vulnerable to attack. Many drug user's are but past life healers, shamans and astral travellers. The dawn of the digital age has hidden and blinded their true selves from their heritage so a quick fix of utilising drugs to attain their past is the only option available to them. Such entities distort our perceptions and keep us locked in that endless cycle of darkness.

Many hosts are people who have not learned to handle stress and worry adequately in their lives. This may mean they are emotionally immature but there is a catch. When the person is ready to mature the entity will leave as the soul is sacrosanct onto itself as a creator with God. The parasitic relationship will be no more as the person will not want to hide their essence behind the entity and its related darkness therefore no contract exists between the two energies. The person will be free.

When you read such sad headline newspaper stories of a person killing their best friend with a hammer and drugs are involved then chances are that entities are behind the attack. Many victims of anorexia, obsessions and compulsions are but hosts of negative energies driving such abnormal behaviour. Therapists engaging with the cognitions of such clients are but dealing with the darkest energies in the universe. Unless you remove the entity or entities then the client is trapped in negativity.

<u>Procedure to Remove Negative Entities.</u>

As people are fighting for their essence with the entity, expect the client that comes for therapy to have freak accidents on the way to your clinic. A car driving out in front of them is common as is losing the keys of the car before it is time to leave home would be a likely event. It's as if the negativity of the world will support the existence of the entity within its host. Always drive very slowly when you realise that you are host to an entity.

Entities can read your mind and they will know when you realise that they inhibit your life. They will fluster you with negativity, stress and anxiety. They wish to keep the status quo in place therefore you as a therapist will be seen as an enemy to its existence. As a therapist you will have a higher vibrational charge then your weakened client so the entity will view you as a prise catch for energetic food. The stakes are high in that any doubt on the therapist's behalf will diminish your protection and leave you vulnerable to possession. There are no second chances with this work.

I utilise crystals that I place around the body of the client. This increases the charge of loving light within the clients body which helps make the energetic light body unbearable to the entity. I tune into my Guides and through an old Shamanic practice, I suck the entity energetically with my breath into my mouth. I proceed to the candle in my altar and blow the entity into the light of God in the candle. This procedure may have to be repeated if a second entity is present. If you have negative thoughts streaming into your mind then your solar plexus is transmuting energy and you are not in your power. The entity can latch onto your negative rumination and place a doubt into your mind with regards your work and then you are weakened. The entity will then have a new host…..yes….YOU!

By the way….how is your own therapy proceeding?

Do you see what I mean? Your success in completing this work involves removing fear from your ego thereby building your energetic vibration. It has taken me over five years to be able to complete this work. Yes, five years analysing client's to determine if entities are present and refer them to other competent professional therapists who is aware of the specialised field of entity possession. It is not every therapist's cup of tea and always, always have your own therapist on hand who will clean and repair your light body in times of need. A therapist in my opinion is a person who can remove entity possession. It is not your run of the mill weekend workshop therapist with an ego the size of a building. It is the quiet, unassuming gentle but strong therapist who will treat you with respect and dignity that should be your strength in learning this work.

Entities are negative but are also a part of God. They too need to be treated with respect and dignity. Love is your defence. If you hate them or are fearful of them then you are only feeding them, making them stronger with negative energy. If you get possessed then make an appointment with a good energy healer. Talk to the entity; tell it how much you understand it, how much you need each other and how good it is for you to learn this energetic lesson. Tell it about love and light. Tell it about the wonderful energies of your Guides and Angels when they come and touch your Soul during meditation. You will feel the entity stop moving within your energy field as you are literally starving it of its power.

The Intuitive mind is a sacred gift and the rational mind is a faithful servant. We have created a society that honours the servant and has forgotten the gift.

Einstein.

24. Mediumistic and Psychic Unfoldment.

I use the term 'unfoldment' in relation to the bringing forth of our spiritual gifts in that the emergence of our gifts unfolds in conjunction with our individual essence. Spiritual gifts such as trance healing, psychic and mediumistic awareness, prophecy, therapy and philosophy are natural occurrences to the essence of mankind. The sad fact exists that many manmade organisations wish to blind you to your true essence and therefore rob you of your natural gifts that is your Divine right. I use the words 'gift' in that the power of these gifts is gifted to you if you use them as tools for Spirit. If you pollute your gifts with ego or greed then the gifts can become stagnant or be rescinded. Their power lies in the fact that the more you give the responsibility of your gifts to Spirit then the more power Spirit will return to you through the law of attraction. To take yourself and your ego off the stage and let Spirit take over is what will put you right back on stage in what Spirit wants to do with the gifts given to you.

You are a deathless being. The degree of separateness between you or, more precisely your spirit consciousness and Spirit is the degree to which you view yourself as alien to God. The more you realise your own individual essence the lesser the degree of separateness between God and you. You will realise that you are a God. The ego will stop fighting and you will not ask for gifts but you will simply say 'Spirit, I am here, please use me for the purpose of this lifetime, whatever that may be. Allow me manifest the glory of Spirit on earth.' This attitude will make you an empty vessel in which you will be receptive to the whispers of your Guides, Masters, Teachers and Spirit. Most certainly, you will not be alone.

It is then that Spirit will directly come to you and provide you with a course within your formal psychic or mediumistic educational course. If you decide to go to an international college of spirituality or attend a local class then fine, you can do so. What if I was to tell you that the real reason behind you travelling around the world to that college was to encounter the energy of your father, rejection from your mother, to stand up for yourself to know that a tutor was incorrect in their teachings or to help an amazing light worker realise the power and gifts that exist within him? What would you feel if I told you that the particular teachings within the course would be encoded within your light body and would mature when you were ready to handle the functioning of those teachings? Also that the purpose of those exercises would come to maturity when you have a greater degree of surety with regards the balance of male and female essence within your individuality in own light body.

Spiritual gifts are processed through our spirit consciousness. By spirit consciousness I mean our mind, subconscious, thoughts, feelings and experiences as us as individuals within our own right. This means that the energetic vibrations from the discarnate world enter our aura through our chakra system. Our conscious mind or thought process then interprets the energy from our chakra system. Our chakra functioning as already explained are but transmitters, receptors and interpreters of energy. Therefore it is our purity of our own mind and energy system that is the determining factor with regards the quality and accuracy of the interpretation of the external energies from discarnate or psychic energies. The power of the clarity of the message is determined by the ability of the light body to receive psychic energy from outside the body. A greater ability to channel psychic power rests in the fact that if we have a wider or thicker base chakra to channel the energies up our body then we will be able to channel greater amounts of psychic power. It is similar to being able to flow energy through your light body. Being plugged into the national grid and being capable of handling that frequency will channel more electricity then pulsating electricity through a small wire of a door bell.

I see many students of mediumship who are disconnected emotionally from their own essence. Their psychological growth was stunted in childhood due to their great sensitivity to external energies. This caused them to literally switch off from trusting their emotions and become introverted whereby their sacral chakra never properly connected to their heart chakra. While these people successfully develop their psychic abilities they do not know how to develop their emotional connection within their gifts. The readings they give, while brilliantly accurate can be as emotionally cold as ice. You can feel the other students switch off with the lack of warmth being conveyed within the reading. It is not the students fault but the foundation of their spirituality needs to be explained in detail to the students in order that they develop their essence and therefore their spiritual gifts. These students need to become intimate within themselves by engaging in energetic development. They need to reconnect their sacral chakra with their heart chakra and awaken their true essence as explained within this book.

While in an airport flying home from a mediumship course I went to a shop to buy a sandwich and a drink. As I examined the price of the food I stopped and though for a moment. I had a choice to make. I could treat myself and buy the food or leave it and wait till I got home. It was then that I realised that our spiritual gifts is more dependant upon our ordinary life then the actual quality of our education. If my essence wanted this food and I purchased the food, then I was connecting to a greater degree to my own essence. That is the reality and foundation of spiritual mediumship. Mediumship and psychic development concerns honesty within our own psyche.

Many times I listen to mediums explain how at times no information was forthcoming from Spirit. They explain how they ran home and cried on their bed but yet returned to mediumship the following day. Did any of them every care to ask as to why they were experiencing such fluctuations in their spiritual gifts. The answer lies in the theory with regards how we process trauma. Trauma energetically blocks the flow of energy within our light body and competes with our true essence for the available psychic energy from Spirit. The negativity we hold distorts or blocks our male and female aspects which pollute our spiritual gifts. It is through the process of self development through the energetic evolution of our light body as contained within Soul with a Mind that will unfold our spiritual gifts.

Our male essence is akin to a chalice while our female essence is the liquid that is held within the chalice. Our psychic gifts are contained within our female essence while our masculinity is the power to deliver the message of our spiritual gift. Fear will hinder our delivery and will rob us of focusing inwards towards our intuitive awareness. Fear will lower our vibration to access our ego mind to try and think what is the correct answer that our gifts is trying to unfold. Spiritual gifts are entertaining in that we can never predict what Spirit will bring to our awareness. The lower vibration of the boring, common conscious mind will simply repel the sitter away from the medium as it is a figment of their own imagination.

Your gifts will unfold if you engage in the energetic healing methodologies within this book. Your sensitivity will be regarded as a gift from God towards humanity. You will stop placing a time frame upon the emergence of your gifts and realise that their development is between Spirit and the development of your inner self as understood through your individual essence.

You will not be disappointed when a tutor admonishes you for describing a person's Guides or Angels that was communicated to you. If it was not important why would Spirit give the information to you in the first place? Ego is very deceiving. We work for Spirit first and the rules and dictates of mankind and their manmade organisations come second.

Work for Spirit. You will only be lucky to meet a handful of tutors who will not place conditions upon your unfoldment. They will stretch you to dig deeper into your intuition. They will allow you feel relaxed and to turn your focus inwards to realise that Spirit does not make mistakes in the images or feelings that are dictated to you. They will open your consciousness to feel the answers through your sight, sound, feelings, hearing, smell and kinaesthetic abilities. They will attune your essence to Spirit in allowing your own Divinity touch the Divinity of Spirit. They will introduce the elemental realm to you in the realisation of the creation of beauty on the Earth plane. They will give you the courage to be the voice of those that are voiceless.

Ask your Guides to formulate a team consisting of an Archangel, a deceased medium and a deceased loved one to help you develop your spiritual gifts. Ask a teacher to emerge that will encourage, support and build upon your strengths to become all that you are. Ask for a teacher that has transmuted their ego and their hidden shadow. Place your energetic protection in position to protect your energy in a class room and then have fun within the class. Don't take your spiritual unfoldment too serious as Spirit wants you to have fun developing yourself in this work. Ideally get feedback as to where you are in relation to the development of both your spiritual gifts and the development of your energetic light body. Classify your light body as per the development of your female essence, male essence, constellation of self, the conflict between shadow and ego, the crucifixion and the birth of the true self as per human energetic development as contained within this book.

Ideally your tutor will show you that trance healing is a natural phenomenon of our essence. They will illuminate the four energetic systems that are healed with the mergence of our Guides alongside our physical body. Trance astral healing is a different therapy for each student I teach because who am I to dictate as to how a student should heal? That is left to decide between the students Guides and their essence right from the beginning. Ego needs to be removed from the world of healing and Spirituality. The science behind astral trance healing as contained within this book is explained and cannot be faulted as it is correct and proven as of this moment in time. The knowledge never fails. Only you as a therapist getting in the way of the energetic trance state will disempower a deeper connection with your Guides and hinder the administration of the treatment. If you disregard this science then you must live with the consequences of your actions. That dear reader should be your choice in the exercise of your free will.

Mediums and psychics need to be cognisant of what created their abilities during their childhood was extreme sensitivity that quite often made them feel as if they were living in a dark cave. For the adult medium that dark cave does not go away. The psychic and medium is advised to have a friend or healer available to remove them from their dark cave when it occurs in adulthood.

As of March 2012 a new type of medium is emerging in Ireland. This is the medium that can actually see Spirit manifest directly in front of their eyes. The veils between the worlds as per the dawning of 2012 are becoming non existent. They can actually see and talk to Angels, Guides and Saints as with deceased people. These mediums are not well know yet but will become public when they are told to emerge from their training programme. More importantly, these are mediums that have developed their own essence and being rewarded as one who can see Spirit. More on that subject in my next book.

I wish you well in the unfoldment in your spiritual gifts. I wish you the wisdom to exercise logic in the exercise of your gifts. I wish you the courage to know when to speak and more importantly, when not to speak. I wish you the wisdom to exercise logic and caution either as a student or tutor in the unfoldment of Spirit within your life on earth. God will bless you all the days of your life in the exercise of his work.

Part 2

Energetic Therapeutic Healing Methodologies.

25. Astral Trance Healing

Astral trance healing is the name I have been given to call this new healing methodology that energetically heals the emotionality within the light body in the astral plane and therefore the psychological well being of the client. Cognitive and talking therapies reconfigure thought process leading to transforming the schemata of the psyche. Astral Trance Healing heals the light body energetic systems of the client which filters into the fabric of the person and transforms their world. This is achieved by unblocking, retrieving and developing their energetic systems, the manipulation of the spiritual laws in operation through their light body and increasing their knowledge as the levels of light within their light body develops. The transformation takes place on all levels of our life – emotional, mental, and physical because it heals on the primary level of our existence, our spiritual level. This is the very fabric of our Soul. Why work on just a mental level when you can heal on a Soul level. Before practising this healing methodology it is helpful to know the anatomy of the light body i.e. the chakras, cauldron system, tree of life system and energetic emotional light body imprintation system. To get the best benefit of working with this system, it is also helpful to:

Be able to feel the emotional imprints somatically within your own body thereby identifying your client's emotional imprints that requires healing. This will also show you the level of development to date or between sessions your client has achieved. If the clients light body is examined from session to session you will be able to determine if the client is making progress with their self healing energetic meditations at home.

Trance is achieved through merging your Guides into the therapists light body whereby the Guides move the therapist's body to conduct the treatment. Every client will therefore receive a specific treatment by the Spirit Realm through Astral Trance Healing.

Know the energy of your Guides/Earth Energies etc which you utilise during the treatment.

Be sensitive to feeling the chakra system with regards the different somatic imprints that emerge within the body. This is developed through

meditation and the removal of your own negative imprints through personal therapy.
To complete this treatment you will need:

A plinth or bed for the client to lie on. You will be required to walk around the plinth therefore if possible it is best to position the plinth in the centre of the room.

A stool positioned at the correct height so you are comfortable leaning into the clients head at the top of the plinth.

A throw or blanket to place over the client to protect their privacy and convey the correct message that you are a professional with regards your treatments. It may be suitable to have a blanket and throw under the client to add to the clients comfort.

Two small circular pillows, one to be placed under the persons head and the second pillow to be placed under the persons knees to support their legs and back. Position the pillow under the head in such a way that it allows access to the circumference of the head.

Position the client on the plinth so that their head is at the altar of your healing room.

<u>*Therapist Care.*</u>

Ensure your breath is fresh

No cigarettes before clients.

Have clean nails.

Be professional in your attire.

No chewing gum.

<u>*There are three treatments within ASTRAL Healing.*</u>

1. Healing the Chakra/Cauldron system.
2. Healing the Emotional imprints within the light body.
3. Healing the tree of life – the soul's configuration within the light body.

Some clients will require specific energy treatments such as

Soul retrieval.

Repair of a cracks in the crown.

Cutting any undesirable energetic chords.

Emotional imprints removed from within the light body.

Replacing a person's base chakra or roots back into their body.

Your meditation practise will show itself through your self development when you can somatically feel what treatment is indicate within your own body. This may or may not correspond to which energetic system is presented upon the clients crown when you commence blowing the astral healing 'breath of life' on the clients head. With experience you will be able to determine what treatment the client requires by what they say to you before the energetic treatment begins. Simply see what system is presented to you when you start to work on the head as your Guides will present to you the optimum energetic healing system.

Healing the Chakra/ Cauldron System.

Preparation.

1. Connect to your energy and call in your protection.
2. Place your attention in the Pale Silver Ball of energy at the core of the Earth.
3. Send down your breathe to the Silver ball and breathe the silver energy up to your Earth Chakra at the base of your feet. Feel the energy like a pulsing fire as if you were standing on a spherical ball.
4. Pull the silver energy from your Earth Chakra up to your Hara centre. Hold the silver energy there until you feel the Hara centre pulsates with healing silver energy.

5. Connect to the Father Sky Spiritual energy via your crown chakra. Bring the energy down through your light body into the Hara centre. Merge the silver energy with the Father Sky energy within the Hara centre. .
6. Bring your attention to your heart chakra. Feel the energy flow from your heart chakra into your clients crown chakra. Feel the energy from your heart chakra flow into your hands and from there into your client's body.

Spiritual Help.

> 1. Build your Guide at the feet of the client via the infinity symbol.
> 2. Connect your Guides heart chakra to the feet of the client.
> 3. Merge with Your Guides who will direct the trace healing.

<u>Chelation of The clients Light Body.</u>

1. Connect the pale silver ball of energy in the centre core of the Earth to your clients   Earth chakra. (Positioned at the base of their feet).

> *As you breathe somatically for your client bring the silver ball of energy in the centre of the Earth up to your Earth chakra. You will feel the energy of the earth chakra. It will be like standing on a spherical ball of energy where the energy will 'tingle' into your feet.*

2. Place both your hands near the base of your client's feet allowing the pale silver earth energy into the body of the client.
3. Breathe deeply as you pull the energy from the earth into your body, all the time letting your body somatically be your client's body. Hold that position until the pale silver energy reaches your clients heart chakra. Your client may feel the energy enter their heart chakra whereby they may cough or breath deeply.
5. Swing your hands around the feet to pulse energy into the top of the client's feet.
6. Your hands will now begin to bring the roots from the feet up the **left leg** in a circular fashion until you reach the **base chakra**.
7. Chelate the base chakra upwards (perpendicular towards the ceiling), removing/dissolving any blockages.
Allow the base chakra to emerge upwards if stuck at a particular point. This will allow trauma to transmute. (Trauma can be lifted off through the higher vibration of the therapists light body or can be cleared through the heart chakra).
8. After the base chakra is correctly extended through the aura, connect the **base chakra** to the **sacral chakra** via circular hand motions. You may be able to feel the energy flow up the light body with your hands.
9. Chelate the sacral chakra upwards dissolving/removing any emotional blockages. Determine if any soul retrieval is necessary by the condition of the chakra. (This may have already been achieved through any talking at the start of the session as remember the principle of Energy healing is trigger and release from the Astral plane.
10. When the sacral chakra is completely cleared and extended perpendicularly, connect the **sacral chakra to the solar plexus**.

11. When the solar plexus is completely cleared and extended perpendicularly, connect the **solar plexus to the heart chakra**.
12. When the solar plexus is completely cleared and extended perpendicularly, connect the **heart chakra to the throat chakra**.
13. Chelate the throat chakra perpendicularly, removing/dissolving any negative imprints.
12. When the throat chakra is completely cleared and extended perpendicularly, connect the **throat chakra to the third eye**.
13. Chelate the third eye perpendicularly, removing/dissolving any negative imprints.

Stage 2.

The client is now connected to Mother Earth and Father Sky.
The client's chakras are cleared and unblocked which means they are primed to transmute any trauma being released from the astral plane into their light body at that time. Once you commence the astral healing treatment they will release any negative emotional imprints within the organs of the body which at this stage is now cleared with the chelation of the light body.

1. Sit at the head of client and place your left hand over your right hand. Position your joint hands 2 inches from the client's head pushing the energy through the body and illuminating the chakra imprints on the crown.
2. Find, using your mouth, the base point of energy (representing the base chakra) on the clients head.
3. **Blow gently** into the client's base point on forehead (base chakra) from your hara centre via the breath of life. This is blowing earth

energy up through the chakra system of the client and transmuting negative emotional imprints within their light body.
4. Somatically feel the hara centre gently release the energy and ease into the imprints within the client's body. It will feel like heat melting an ice cube. The flow of energy upwards should be effortless and once you get comfortable with the technique you will realise that the blowing technique is not determined by force.
5. Continue to blow up through the chakras and emotional light body. You will feel a pattern of release of the client's negative imprints.
6. Cease blowing when the Earth energy surrounds and enters the heart chakra.

Stage 3.

1. Go to your client's feet and rebuild your Guide at the feet of the client.
2. Complete the chelation of the light body as in Stage 2. Notice any new developments within the light body e.g. holes, imprints, chords etc.
3. Complete the Astral healing of the client using the clients crown chakra.
4. Cease the treatment when the healing energy heals the heart chakra.
5. Often the cessation of the treatment will coincide with a spark of energy opening the heart chakra.
6. Do not allow the healing energy enter your throat chakra from the heart chakra because it will tear at your vocal chords.

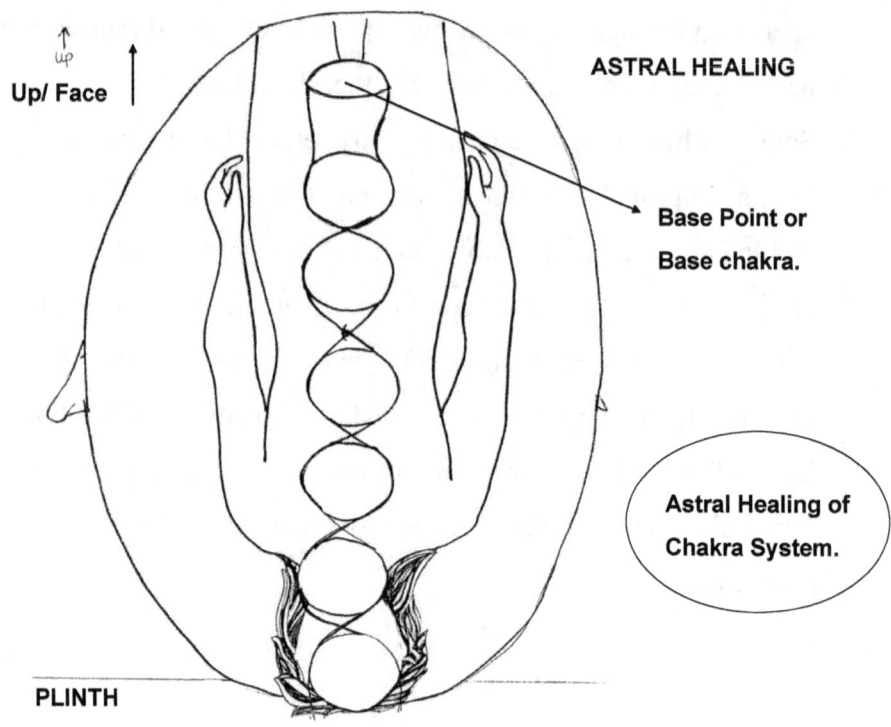

Astral Trance Healing the Emotional light body imprintation system of the person.

The emotional light body is described in the chapter the emotional light body. This treatment is more complex then astral healing the chakra system because it encompasses the chakra system and imprints of the organs where we store particular emotional imprints. This treatment will provide emotional and energetic transmutation of:

Emotional imprints within the light body that influence the chakras and spiritual laws of mankind.

Directly heal the chakras of the person.

Allow the client to energetically mature.

Allow the person merge with their light body if they are the oral and schizoid personality.

Allow the client move to transmute lower vibrational emotions such as fear and anger into sadness and heartache and, finally forgiveness/acceptance.

Stage 1

1. Connect to your energy and call in your protection.
2. Connect to your Pale Silver Ball of energy at the core of the Earth.
2. Build your Guide at the feet of the client via the infinity symbol. Connect your Guides heart chakra to the feet of the client (Roots into body).
3. Connect the pale silver ball of energy in the centre core of the Earth to your clients Earth chakra. (Positioned at the base of their feet).

    As you somatically breathe for your client from the silver ball of energy up to your earth chakra, you will feel the energy enter the earth chakra. It will be like standing on a spherical ball of energy where the energy will 'tingle' into your feet.

4. Place both your hands near the base of the feet allowing the pale silver earth energy into the body of the client as you pull the energy from the earth into your body, letting your body somatically be your client's body. Hold that position until the pale silver energy enters your clients heart chakra.
5. Swing your hands around the feet to pulse energy into the top of the client's feet.
6. Your hands will now begin to bring the roots from the feet up the **left leg** in a circular fashion until you reach the **base chakra**.
7. Chelate the base chakra upwards, removing/dissolving any blockages.

Allow the base chakra to emerge upwards if stuck at a particular point. This will allow trauma to emerge. (Trauma can only be cleared by the heart chakra in the astral plane).

8. After the base chakra is correctly extended through the aura, connect the **base chakra to the sacral chakra** via circular hand motions.
9. Chelate the sacral chakra upwards dissolving/removing any emotional blockages. Determine if any soul retrieval is necessary.
10. When sacral chakra is fully extended through the aura, connect the **sacral chakra to the solar plexus**.
11. Chelate the solar plexus upwards, removing/dissolving any negative imprints.
12. When healed, connect the **solar plexus to the heart chakra.**
13. Chelate the heart chakra.
14. Connect **the heart chakra to the throat chakra**.
15. Chelate the throat chakra.

Stage 2.

Now that the client is connected to Mother Earth and Father Sky, we continue removing the imprints within the emotional light body. This treatment reconnects the negative emotions stored within their corresponding organ to the heart chakra for transmutation. The heart chakra exists on all spiritual levels therefore the heart chakra can disintegrate any negative energy that flows into the heart chakra. Many clients will release emotion during this session and may see images in relation to their past as part of the release.

1. Sit at head of client and place your left hand over your right hand. Place your joint hands 2 inches from the client's head opening the

energy through the body and illuminating the chakra imprints on the crown.

2. Find, using your mouth, the base point of energy (representing the base chakra) on the clients head. This will be at twelve o clock along the hair line.

3. **Blow gently** into the client's base point on forehead (base chakra) from your hara centre. The 'breath of life' by blowing earth energy up through the chakra system of the client facilitates the transmuting of negative emotional imprints within the heart chakra.

4. **Feel somatically the energy moving upwards through the body. Place your attention on any imprints that emerge and let them flow somatically like water down your body (client's body). Do not hold on to such emotions but quickly release as energy follows attention. That it is your task to release these imprints and let them flow, not to hold on to the imprints and remain in physical pain in your body.**

5. **Notice which imprints are being transmuted and which chakras are being compromised/healed by those imprints. This should correspond with the client's lifestyle if they imparted this information to you.**

6. Cease blowing when all negative imprints have dissolved by flowing upwards to be destroyed by the energies within the heart chakra.

7. Repeat the chelation of the chakras starting at the client's feet and connecting their Guide to the client's body. Notice if ant further

trauma has been brought in from the astral plane to the light body for transmutation.
8. Complete an Astral Healing treatment on the client.
9. Close down and protect the clients light body.

At various stages of the treatment your Guides may ask you to connect a beam of energy from Father Sky or your Guides third eye directly to a particular chakra. This will provide deeper healing to that chakra.

Astral Healing the Tree of Life Energetic system.

1. Chelate the light body as per the astral healing treatment of the chakra system.
2. Find the base point on the clients crown chakra which will be the base chakra or foundation sephiroths.
3. Somatically link into the clients sephiroths while connecting to 'the breath of life' from within your Hara centre.
4. Blow gently into the base point noticing the energy move within your body which is representative of the clients light body.
5. Notice if any chakras emerge for healing and how easily the energy flows through the light body.
6. Once the energy flows through the light body and reaches the heart chakra (knowledge sephiroth), the first level of trauma has been released.

7. Go to the feet of the client and rebuild your Guide. Proceed to chelate the light body and tree of life system noticing any new imprints that have emerged from the astral plane.
8. Complete the breath of life energetic blowing technique on the tree of life system on the crown chakra.
9. Close down the chakra system.

The Tree of Life

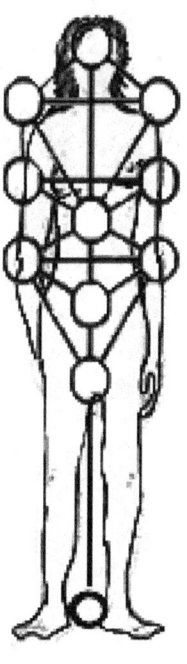

Tree of Life system on crown chakra

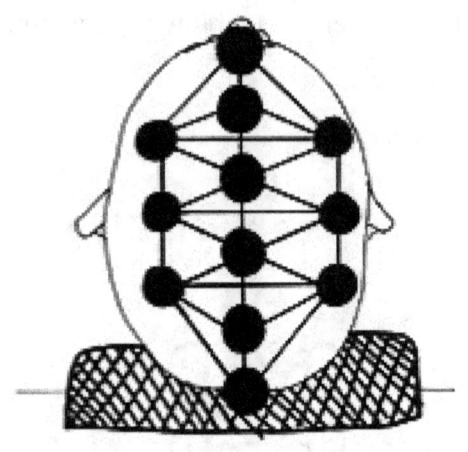

Astral Healing the crown chakra

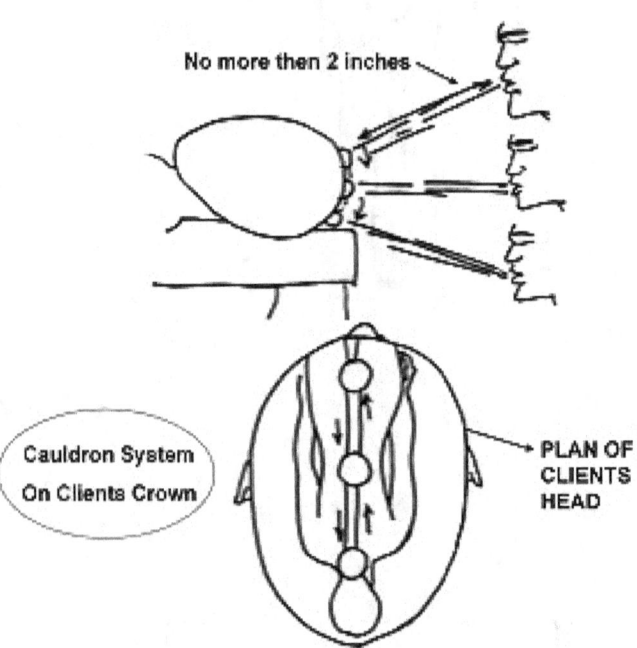

26. Somatic healing.

This method of treatment allows you transmute imprints within a persons light body even if they are aware or unaware of your treatment. Somatic healing is also suitable for distance healing. Ask your higher self to oversee the treatment and to seek permission for the treatment if the person is unaware of the treatment. If you do not have the person's permission your higher self and the person's higher self will accept or reject the healing. Intend that if the treatment is to be rejected then your light body will receive the benefit of the treatment. If a client attends for a healing session/ therapy then they have already given you permission for this work.

1. Allow the client to sit directly facing you. This allows the greatest possibility for you to 'read and feel' their energy.
2. Ensure your protection and team are in place.
3. Call in your roots and bring earth energy (Pale silver ball in centre of earth) up to your solar plexus.
4. Bring energy down from Father Sky into your solar plexus. Feel the energy floating, merging and spinning around your solar plexus.
5. From the energetic beam of sunlight that is entering your crown chakra from Father Sky, allow that beam come down into your third eye and project out like a laser beam into the third eye of the client.
6. Notice such changes as forgetting what they were saying, looking away, scratching their head or their body language changing.
7. That beam will enter their energy system and proceed down their chakras uncovering and transmuting trauma (emotional imprints). This is why their conversation will change to illuminate through

the spiritual laws what imprint is really triggered within their light body.

8. Notice how their language may become displaced as their subconscious will find words to describe their past and pepper their present language with nuggets of this analytical information.
9. Let your body be your client's body and start 'feeling' their energy from the root chakra. Proceed by willing/pulling the energy with your breath up through your light body which will be your client's body.
10. Notice how the client will start to make sense of their world even if you say nothing to them as you are increasing their vibration.
11. Notice where the energy imprints dissolve or are stuck which represents the stage of development the client has achieved within a particular energetic light body system.

Alternative Method (1).

As you complete this healing methodology, in your own mind ask your client a question such as 'How did you get on with your Father?' Notice how they will shift in the chair, cry, laugh or change demeanour. You will be directly talking to their energetic light body and avoiding the filter of the conscious mind. Even if they are talking about their cat, notice the language utilised or how it changes from the time of your question. The emotionality of the conversation about their cat will directly correspond to the real issue of what is lodged within their light body.

27. Removing Imprints within the Layers of the Human Light Body.

As you practise healing and develop your light body, more powerful Guides and Energies will come and work with you. Your methodology of healing trauma will become more efficient therefore, you will be utilised by Spirit to transmute more complex human suffering. Spirit will test you at times but you will have all the resources you require to be successful with any client.

Imprints are simply emotional charges of negativity from the past that come into the layers and chakras for transmutation. The degree to the heaviness of the imprint is the degree to which the imprint can influence the actions of the person holding on to such emotionality from the past. One only has to look at the papers to see how people commit manslaughter and crimes in a fit of rage. The position of the imprints can correspond to the emotional light body map and therefore its corresponding chakra that they affect. I use three methods to remove imprints.

1. Channel Spiritual energy into the chakra and chelate the chakra.

I rebuild the energetic channel of the chakra by channelling spiritual energy into the chakra. As the imprints emerge, I push down the imprint into the chakra to be dissolved with the breath of life moving the imprint up to the heart chakra for transmutation. It is common that you would have to go back three or four times to push down the imprint into the chakra for transmutation.

2. Dissolve or remove the chakra with your hand.

If the imprint is small, then it may dissolve in your hand. As you give your hands to your Guides to work by their direction, they will move your hand to a clinched position indicating the imprint is now dissolved. Always recheck if the imprint has been removed.

Sometimes your Guides will require you to hold the imprint in your hand and remove the imprint to be dissolved in a candle in your alter. This may be required to be conducted a number of times. This is a very swift method of dissolving imprints.

3. Dissolving the imprint and flowing it somatically through your arms.

With some imprints, you Guides will ask you to hold a hand each side of the imprint. Your Guides will then slowly move your hands closed together as the imprint dissolves and moves up your arms, into your crown chakra and flows up to the heavens. This may be required to be conducted a few times but the imprint will be getting smaller and smaller as each treatment is conducted. This treatment is usually conducted when the imprints are large and flowing across a layer of the aura.

REMOVING IMPRINTS

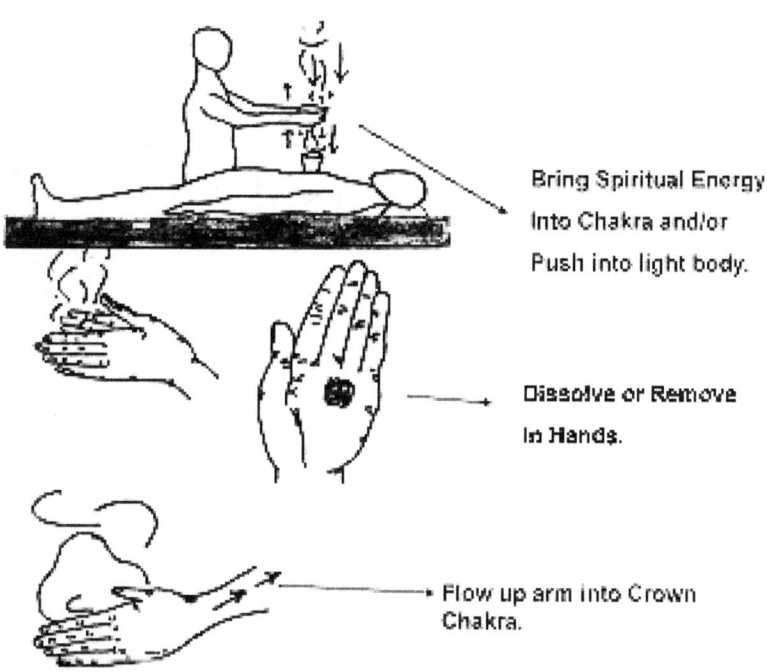

Bring Spiritual Energy Into Chakra and/or Push into light body.

Dissolve or Remove In Hands.

Flow up arm into Crown Chakra.

28. The Eyes as a Radar Screen of the light body.

Utilising the eyes as an energetic radar screen is a simple treatment that the therapist and client can utilise as an effective healing methodology. As energy follows intent, your intention is that what you see within the darkness when your eyes are closed will be the predominant energy imprints that you will be transmuting at that time within your energy field.

When you close your eyes, you will naturally see the darkness in front of your eyes because of your eyes being closed. On further examination, you may find a blue, greyish haze in front of your closed black eyelids. Notice how there is an ebb and flow to the pattern of the haze. You may even notice that in the centre of one of those clusters of haze there may be a concentration of a different colour, a dark spot or a white circle. These are the actual negative imprints within your energy field that are in operation in your life through your thoughts, ego state formations and laws of attraction.

This healing methodology states that if you connect to your energy, bring down spiritual energy into your third eye, then you can transmute those imprints by blasting them with the energy from your third eye. What is even more exciting is that you can see them dissolve right in front of your eyes. As energy follows intent, you can use this method for self healing or for your client.

Emotional Imprints will have a white dot in the centre of a cluster of the hazy imprint which will dissolve as you blast it with spiritual energy.

When the heart chakra opens and releases all it's trauma that has been transmuted from the lower level of the body, the colour of the radar screen will be a green/ yellowish hue. This will only happen when the level of development of the light body progress's to the stage of dealing directly with the heart chakra. This will not happen for instance, in appointment four if you are still transmuting fear within the kidneys for your client as you need to progress upwards in treatment until the heart is opened. When trauma of the session is released then the heart chakra can open.

Entities will appear as yellow/green/brown smudges floating around the radar screen and will not flash or disappear. They will have a threatening feel to their appearance.

Procedure for transmuting imprints using your closed eyes as a radar screen.

1. Relax your body and realise that as with all therapies, you have nothing to do but simply command energy through your intention.
2. Connect to your energy and call in your team.
3. Look into your closed eyes and notice the haze in front of your closed eyes. Make the infinity sign with your vision over the blackness of your eyes. This connects you to the vision of the imprints.
4. Pay attention to colours, shapes, flash's etc as your bring a beam of spiritual energy down from Father Sky and blast it into the centre of the vision of your closed eyes.
5. As you focus softly, notice how the clouds of haze start to swirl at first, then expand outwards as the imprint of the mass of energy starts to dissolve and break up.
6. Eventually after a few minutes you should see a pattern emerge in that waves of energy flow outwards from the centre focal point of the mass of energy.
7. When all that can be transmuted during this session can be transmuted, the energy will stop and you will then notice waves of energy flowing inwards to a focal point. This is your Guides healing the void of the imprint that was transmuted.

Utilising the infinity sign is crucial whenever you want to make a connection in energy terms. This also removes any debris of energy and allows access directly to the imprint.

Eye Radar Healing

 1. Use Infinity sign

 4. Dissolve Imprint

 2. Locate Imprint

 5. Receive Healing energy into light body

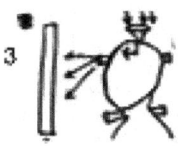 3. Access Spiritual Energy onto RADAR

 6. Finish with a clear heart

29. Connecting the Person to Light and Wisdom during a Treatment.

Occasionally your Guides will require that you bring light and wisdom into the psyche of the client after the treatment has finished. I usually find that they will ask me to do this at the end of a session to a client who has just attended me for the first time. The purpose of bringing light and wisdom into a client is two fold. The reasons are:

1. That the client gains a greater appreciation of the benefit of energy psychology through our work together.
2. The client opens their heart and life to the wisdom and light available to them.

Conduct a normal energy healing session on a client. At the end of the session connect the light and wisdom by the following method:

1. Connect a beam of light from Buddha to the heart chakra of the client. Circle the energy into the heart chakra.
2. Connect a beam of light from the candle to the heart chakra of the client. Seal the energy into place of the heart chakra.

The client will attend a following session and will usually say they 'don't know what happened but realise that something has changed.' This is the beauty of energy psychology in that the development of the person is natural and in congruence with the natural development of the person in their life.

Connecting a client to love and light.

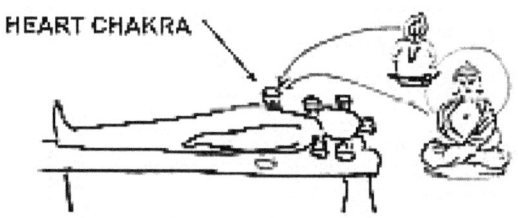

30. Repairing a Crack in a Crown Chakra.

A crack in a persons crown chakra can have very debilitating effects on the person's life. A crack will usually consist of a tear in the outer protective layer of the crown that will allow the energy of the person escape outside their aura. A crack is usually caused by:

1. Excessive worry and stress.
2. A bang on the head such as a fall.
3. Having a black out, fainting etc.
4. Bing drugged, dishevelled or losing control of your senses e.g. getting drunk and losing consciousness, a drink being spiked or a bad reaction to medication drugs.
5. Taking illegal drugs such as smoking a joint, cannabis, hard drugs etc.
6. Not integrating correctly back into your body after a hypnotic session, operation etc.
7. A major traumatic experience such as a car accident etc.
8. A severe psychic attack.

While some people may have experienced some of these symptoms and may never suffer such a crack in their crown others may not be so lucky. You can actually feel the tear or hole in the crown if you somatically tune into a person. As you talk to them you will realise that they hold their head to the opposite side of the crack as the spiritual energy entering their body will flow downwards through the crack and not the centre channel of their crown chakra. The consequences of a crack in the crown to the quality of life can be significant i.e.

1. Insomnia.
2. Paranoia i.e. thinking other people are talking about you.
3. Anxiety and stress.

4. Inability to focus.
5. Inability to be around people.
6. Poor concentration.
7. Physical discomfort i.e. a weight on their head.

The problems listed above stem from the fact that the persons energy is protruding from their crown into the world. This produces the effect that the person begins to read other peoples energy and their thoughts. This culminates in anxiety and paranoia where the protruding energy grabs onto other peoples energy due to no protective boundary in place. Being so open to energies will allow little or no peace in the person's life. It is very common for people with such conditions to agree 'yes, that's just it, people the other side of the room do be talking about me.' As the person holds on to other peoples energy they find that their sleep can be extremely disturbed due to the excessive energy around their head that their brain is trying to read. As their energy is constantly leaking and more then likely the crack was caused by a trauma, their solar plexus is compromised.

The solar plexus governs our mental processing i.e. thought patterns and so produces depression and anxiety. Generally clients tell me that anti-depression tables are relatively ineffective in treating such conditions. This is due to the problem being an energetic problem and not just a medical problem. People can be in such painful condition for years.

Procedure to repair a crack in the crown chakra.

1. As you take the clients history, try and determine what trauma caused the crack in the first place. If the client reports none of the above, check for possible entity attack in that the client could be a drug user and is ashamed to admit such behaviour. The crack in their crown could be masking a more serious energy problem. You can somatically feel the side of the head where the crack is positioned or you will notice the person tilt their head.

2. Call in your energy team and protection.
3. Infuse the body with energy up to the heart chakra. The body will be starved of energy and will not knit together unless an adequate energy supply is in place. (There is no point sowing back a limb if that limb is dead and receiving no blood supply).
4. Ensure the chakras are in place within the light body and not floating above the physical body. This is possible in the case of a traumatic accident where the person was physically pushed sideways and hit an object but their light body continued to propel forwards.
5. Go to the crown and call in Spider energy. Spider energy is excellent for sealing cracks in that spiders form webs and you will require a web or plaster to seal the crack. Also use Gold coloured energy as a vibrational sealant.
6. Blow gently into the crack starting in the top of the crack and move downward along the crack.
7. As you continue blowing the Spider and Gold energy, start at the top of the crack and use the infinity sign of God as a sealant or plaster knitting both sides of the crack together.
8. Complete the seal all the way along the crack and as you bring your palm over the crack. Continue blowing over the crack with the Spider and Gold energy as your palm gently tilts over the crack and completely covers the sealed crack.
9. Once you are satisfied that the crack is repaired, complete an Astral Trance healing of the body by bringing earth energy into the body etc.

10. Ensure the earth energy surrounds the heart chakra from the astral healing, the seal is in place over the crack and any traumatic imprints are removed before closing down the clients light body.
11. Advise the client to abstain from alcohol and drugs for ten days and to attend an appointment in two weeks to determine progress on the seal.

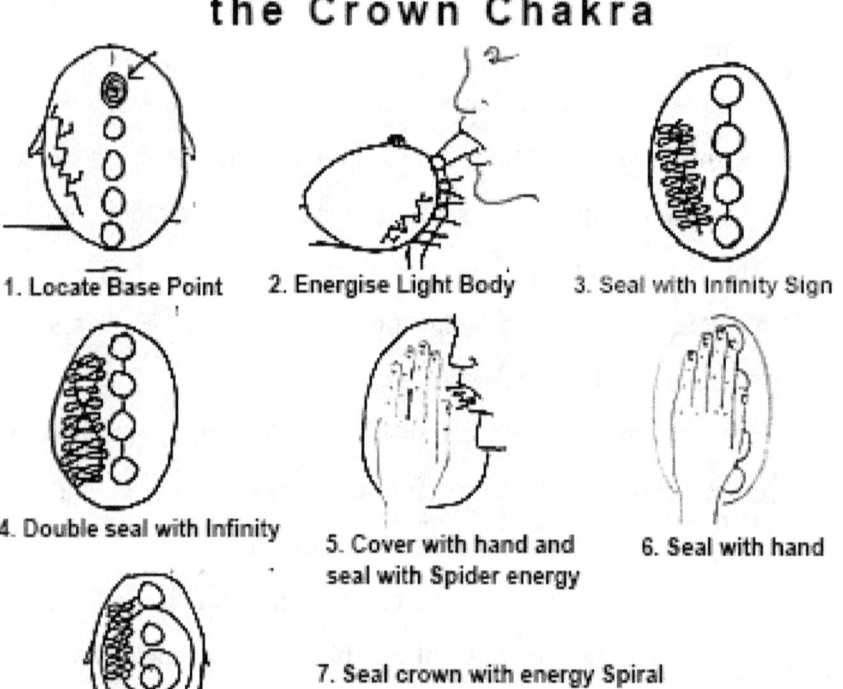

Repairing a crack in the Crown Chakra

1. Locate Base Point
2. Energise Light Body
3. Seal with Infinity Sign
4. Double seal with Infinity
5. Cover with hand and seal with Spider energy
6. Seal with hand
7. Seal crown with energy Spiral

31. Dissociation of Light Body from Physical Body.

Our physical body and light body should ideally be centred in such a way that they both share the same central point. This will mean that any energy flowing through our chakras can be utilised by our physical body and life. Most people are either feminine or masculine dominated with regards personality and energy. This means that one side of our bodies will have a greater flow of energy running through it then the other side. A more flowing right side will mean the person will find it easy to express and utilise their male essence in their life. A more developed left side will mean that the person will be better with emotions and creativity then the action aspect of their male right side. The rare person will be dominant in the centre of their body which means their solar plexus will be extremely powerful. I have one friend whose energy is configured in such a fashion and they can manifest through the law of attraction and intent at will in their life. It is quiet incredible to see in action.

The dissociation between light and physical body I am describing in this instance is as a result of trauma. The trauma was so severe that the persons light body was literally detached from their physical body. It's as if the force of the accident, being run over or hit from one side propelled them forward and, when they stopped, their light body kept moving with the energetic force of the propulsion. The result being that one side of their body is without its energy field or in extreme circumstances the light body in its entirety is floating three foot above its physical body.

Problems that will indicate dissociation of light body from physical body are as follows;

1. History of a trauma such as a car accident, being in a coma, banging their head, being in a fall etc.
2. Will usually indicate that they have never been 'right since that incident.'
3. Insomnia and constant chatter in their mind.
4. Thoughts such as 'what does it feel like to be my dog' will cross their mind. This stems from the energy chords we project to

external loved objects as children when we were growing up hence no barrier in place results in dissociation.

5. A paralysis or weakness on one side of their body i.e. a weak arm or uncontrollable dribble down one side of the mouth.
6. Being constantly cold and unable to get heat into their body even on a warm day.
7. Attracting such experiences as accidents into their life or dreams of being sawn in two etc.
8. Usually accompanies such related traumas as a crack in their head/crown.
9. You should be able to feel the light body hovering three foot above the person's physical body as they lie on your plinth.

It is one issue being thrown from your body but the factor that prevents your light body returning in sync to your physical body is the cellular memory of the trauma. The emotionality of the trauma will be re-experienced via your cellular memory of the trauma if your light body returns in sync with your physical body. Therefore the trauma of the accident needs to be partially removed before any integration of the light body can successfully move back into its correct position.

Procedure to integrate the light and physical bodies due to trauma.

1. Connect to your light body and call in your team and protection.
2. Bring energy up the body of the person.
3. Conduct energy healing **on the chakra system as per the Astral Trance healing methodology**. This will remove some trauma of the accident. The light body will know that some trauma has been removed and will sense that it is safe to return back to its natural position.

4. Check if there is a crack in the crown. Repair the crack in the crown before integration of the light body.
5. Move both your hands above the light body and gently move the light body back in place. You need to move your hands in conjunction with the light body and not proceed at the speed you think you need to work.
6. Reconnect the light/ physical body to Mother Earth.
7. Conduct an astral trance healing treatment on the client. Expect trauma to be released during this part of the session as integration occurs.
8. Seal the person correctly leaving the base chakra half open into Mother Earth as the person requires energy to complete the integration over the following days.
9. Advise the person that they require an appointment within two weeks and not to drink alcohol or take illegal drugs within that time frame.

Dissociation of Light from the Physical Body

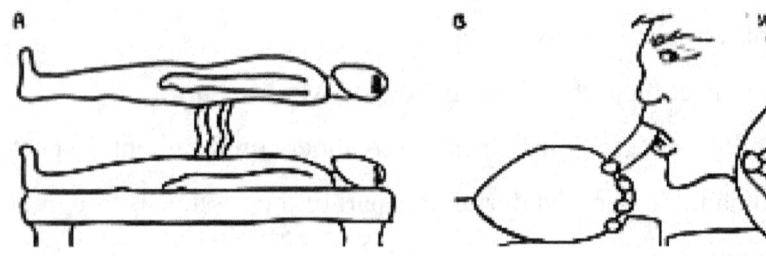

A. Dissociation of light from physical body

B. Energise the body and remove fear.

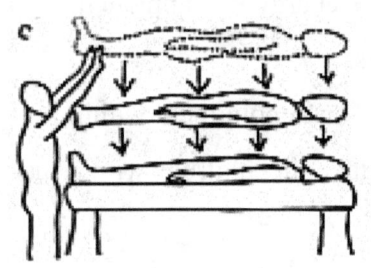

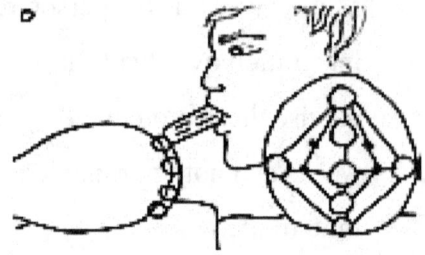

C. Integrate light body with physical body.

D. Complete Astral healing on the integrated body.

32. Dismantling Energetic Chords between People.

As everything is energy, energetic chords connect all people together once they make a connection. These relationships exist as chords of energy that connect from the chest area or knowledge chakra. This is the chakra that once it receives energy, it provides the 'a-ha' moment when everything starts to make sense. Talking to someone about their relationship will provide little insight to them until this secondary chakra starts to operate positively. Some energetic chords are welcome such as family, friends and work colleagues. As relationships ebb and flow due to the law of resonance, people will invariably leave your friendship once your vibration does not resonate with a person. Such is life. For example the sudden yanking of the removal of a chord when a loved one dies can be the cause of tremendous emotional pain. That pain can be unceasing until the hole in the light body where the removal of the chord occurred is energetically repaired. With talking therapies the same tears can be cried for years. Energy healing is necessary with hypnotic visualisation to reseal the aura. Some unwanted chords can exist as a psychic attack.

The chords that join people are fuelled by the intent of the people involved and the emotion invested in the laws of attraction of those people. Therefore in order to successfully cut those chords you need to see what is behind the connection of those chords. It is only then as one person builds their own proper vibration that the chords can be severed and/or let dissolve naturally over the coming weeks. Sometimes a person will hold energy that their parent or child possessed and wish to partake of that energy. Other times a person will fancy that person in a romantic fashion and will have chords connected to the other person. This affection will be shown in that the person will try to make themselves valuable to the object of their desire. Look for a person who will promise to fix their car but never get around to completing the task in order for the continued justification of that chord. They will also try and be in their house, give them lifts etc.

To sever chords it may be necessary to bring fire energy up from Mother Earth and run it through the body of the client. This will help to sever the chords but naturally you need to find what attachment of emotion is behind those chords.

The strongest chords exist between parents and children and husband and wife. The reason as to why husband and wife chords are so strong is because they publicly demonstrated their chords when they got married or simply exchanged rings as a sign of those chords. In reality the removal of such chords will take months and possibly more then a year to dissolve. It can be successfully achieved but only if one party increases their vibration from the position of their vibration of the time they got married. This means therapy or growth. If they got married upon insecure reasons, (which most people do), when one party matures emotionally then they begin to sever the chords. 'Like is therefore not vibrationally going to like' anymore.

Conflict will ensue because both parties are not getting what they originally signed up for but one party is moving on and can see the logic in the separation. Disappointment can be channelled into anger, fear or sadness depending upon how emotionally mature the person is within their own psyche. When one party matures and finds themselves it is then the time to move on with your life. If the parties split before the chords are severed then they are at the mercy of how they channel their emotions rather then viewing their spouse as just another person that they once knew. This is the only way to handle marital breakdown or relationship cessation as a long term solution but it is never easy.

How to identify that chords exist between people.

1. The person will be constantly tired as the chord will be a drain on their energy.
2. The other person will be on their mind, a pest, bothering them, not really knowing what angle they will be approaching their pray.
3. Unusual occurrences will be attracted into their life e.g. their car will break down and their pursuer will be a mechanic.
4. The person will know from what incident that their life went downhill. This was the moment of attachment of the chord.
5. The person may describe as if someone was in bed beside them at night.

6. Images may flash of the other person who may come into their mind.
7. The attacker may be jealous of the gifts and intelligence of their victim. This is very common among therapists and healers. Fear and a poverty complex are usually behind such attachments in order that the victim helped create the attack through weak defences.

How to dismantle energetic chords between people.

1. Somatically feel the existence of the chord from your client within your own light body.
2. Question the client as to what person/events/occurrences is in their life.
3. Ask them to intuit what they provide to the other person.
4. Ask for external evidence to verify the existence that the particular person is behind the chord i.e. utilise the law of attraction.
5. Ask for dream information.
6. Ask the client how they have made themselves vulnerable to the other person thereby creating a energetic contract.
7. As the client has begun to take back their power, the energy should be swirling around the energy chord (located between the solar plexus and heart chakra). Awareness will destroy the contract.
8. Ask the client to bring fire energy up from the earth and blaze through their light body burning off any unwanted attachments.
9. Ask the client how they think they should protect themselves going forward.
10. With these new cognitions, the chord should dismantle.

11. Complete an Astral trance healing treatment on the client and pay particular attention to the removal of the shreds of the chord from the clients light body.
12. Advise the client to not accept anything from their pursuer going forward and if possible remove all objects they possess from the other person.
13. Advise the client to check their energy on a daily basis and take a salt bath for protection.
14. Advise the client to pay more attention to the protection of their aura and therapy space. Invoke Archangel Michael to continually protect their home and space.
15. Advise that feelings of low self esteem and self doubt are a major cause of weakness of defences when attachments can be formed.

33. Repairing Major Holes in a Person's Aura.

A person who has a major hole in their aura will be in great danger of nervous shock or burnout but will be suffering from fatigue, depression, energy depletion and insomnia. No amount of energy treatments will heal the hole in the aura as such a hole requires to be sealed over a number of weeks. As energy is alive, the person should be taught how to nourish their own light body as well as how to seal the hole. I find it helpful to give such power back to the individual as an energy healer is probably the last person they would have thought of attending for resolution to their problem. I show the person how to use a pendulum to check their chakras on a daily basis so as they can gauge their mindset, the influence of their mind on their light body and the degree to which their energy is increasing. I also take their history as the hole would probably be caused from their past, most definitely from a time when depression was a feature of their life.

As holes generally appear over the sacral chakra/abdomen you know that their emotional state will be compromised and so will all other higher chakras. Inner child work may be required after the client has regained their strength and the hole is sealed. Cognitive restructuring will be needed to influence established negative thought patterns from the outset of session one. Procedure to seal a hole in the aura:

1. Once the problem has been identified, explain to the client the nature of the problem and the role they will have to actively play in their recovery.

2. Explain the consequences of not repairing the energetic hole e.g. nervous shock etc but also stress the problem is common and is easily treatable. All that is required is some effort on their part. If the client does not wish to apply themselves to such self care then advise that regular treatments such as weekly therapeutic energy sessions will be required for a successful result.

3. Conduct an Astral Trance Healing energy treatment on the client and recheck: the spin of each chakra and that the person's roots are fully connected to Mother Earth.
4. Show the client how to use a pendulum to douse for the performance of each chakra. Show the client how to recalibrate the pendulum upon purchasing a pendulum at home.
5. Advise the client to conduct energy healings on their light body daily and to use the pendulum before and after the treatment to verify the quality of their work.
6. Advise the client to rest as much as possible. That means doing nothing but simply lying on a couch or staying in bed. A possible herbal relaxant would be good for the client.

An energetic hole in the Aura.

34. Etheric Crystal In the third eye.

Spiritual gifts will be provided to you by your Guides as you develop your commitment to your journey and career. The gifts you will receive will not be your gifts but you simply have the use of the gifts provided you exercise responsibility in your duty of the care in the expression of your gifts. One of the first gifts that people receive is that of an etheric crystal in your third eye. The meaning of etheric crystal is that the crystal exists on the spiritual plane for utilisation for the person who was gifted the crystal. Such crystals can be utilised for:

1. To direct energy into specific points of the clients body.
2. To open channels like a laser to work on the client's body.
3. To beam energy from your third eye into the clients third eye as they sit across from you.
4. To transmute negative energies.

When a person is given an etheric crystal your hands may be placed over the third eye to bring in the energy of the crystal. The therapist will then be directed to blow directly into the person's third eye in a circular fashion. The circles will generally go from large to small as you build the crystal like the horn of a unicorn on the third eye of the client.

Etheric crystals will not interfere with the functioning of the third eye with regards the development of their spiritual sight. It is a great honour to receive spiritual gifts from our Guides which trough the law of attraction mean that you have honoured your Guides with the development of your light body and their work here on Earth.

Position of Etheric Crystal on Forehead.

Etheric Crystal

35. Energetic Breath work (1) and (2).

As we hold emotional imprints within specific organs of the body, these imprints need to be removed so that we can reclaim our original essence. If we hold negative emotions as imprints, the energy flowing through us will take on the vibration of these imprints, send it out to the world and return back the emotion of that imprint to us. Therefore, many experiences of the same emotion can be stacked within each imprint all because a sensitising event occurred many years ago or in a past lifetime. The client will not be cured until the emotion of the first experience is uncovered and released otherwise the law of attraction will still operate and bring further emotional difficulties into their life. Energetic breath work can allow the person access these imprints and experiences and so release them. The process by which we utilise energetic breath work is:

1. Connect to your energy and call in your protection.
2. Connect to Mother Earth to access the healing energy for your light body.
3. Breathe through your open mouth. Send down your breath with your attention wrapped around the feeling of the breath until it wraps around the imprint in your body.
4. Breathe deeply as you imagine that you are dissolving and pulling the imprint up through your body.
5. The feeling or emotion of the imprint has to move upwards to the heart or throat chakra. Remember the heart chakra releases negative emotion through its link to the astral plane.
6. The imprints may then clear the throat chakra. The throat chakra holds sadness and repressed anger and governs receiving abundance and speaking the professionalism of our career. It's easy to see how such an imprint as powerlessness in the solar plexus will cause financial problems from the throat chakra in the person's life. Everything is connected.

7. The centre of the imprint in your eye radar vision, usually a white or different colour, will correspond to the kernel or phlegm of the imprint.
8. The person should also imagine that they send down the infinity sign and wrap one side of the sign around the imprint within their body. They pull their breath upwards as they will find that the imprint can move and become fluid. They may start to cough like a dog regurgitating the imprint.
9. The person may be surprised to find that they can breathe imprints from as low as their sacral chakra. This is their body releasing sexual or emotional trauma. This may need to be completed over a number of sessions.
10. The earth energy (usually Morgan) will come in and wrap itself around the chakra or imprint and return the body to normality. This can usually be a very physical experience with you body possibly shaking vigorously in an uncontrollable fashion.
11. Breath softly and gently to return to normality.
12. This work is highly beneficial as you will walk away from such a treatment a different person with a better insight filtering into your psyche of who you were in the past.

Energetic Breath work (2).

We conduct this treatment by directly connecting to Mother Earth via your solar plexus. The connection to the healing energy of Mother Earth is very powerful once you get accustomed to breathing from your solar plexus. You can feel the energy enter your solar plexus and flow into your body, igniting all other chakras in an orderly fashion. Emotional imprints will become apparent as you may begin to cough the imprints away.

1. The procedure is to lie face down on the ground.

2. Breath deeply from the Earth into your tummy.

3. Feel the energy flow around your body.

4. Cough or breathe away any imprints from within your light body.

5. Thank your Guides and Mother Earth. Close down your energy.

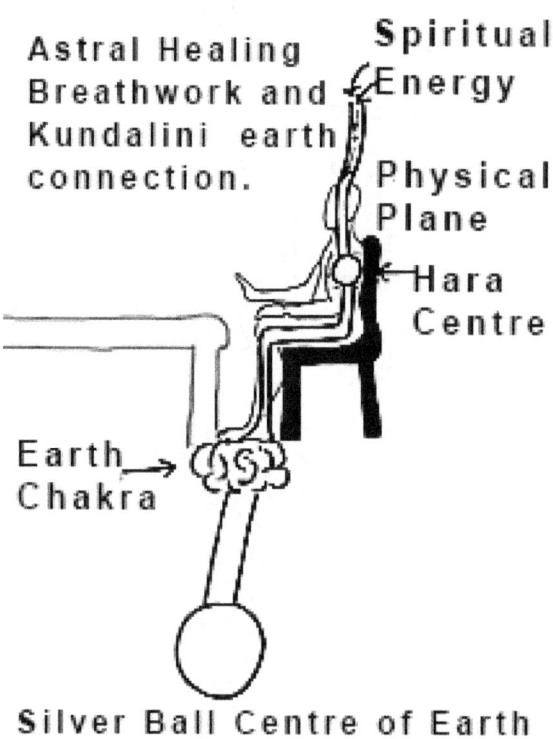

Airflow Through the Mouth

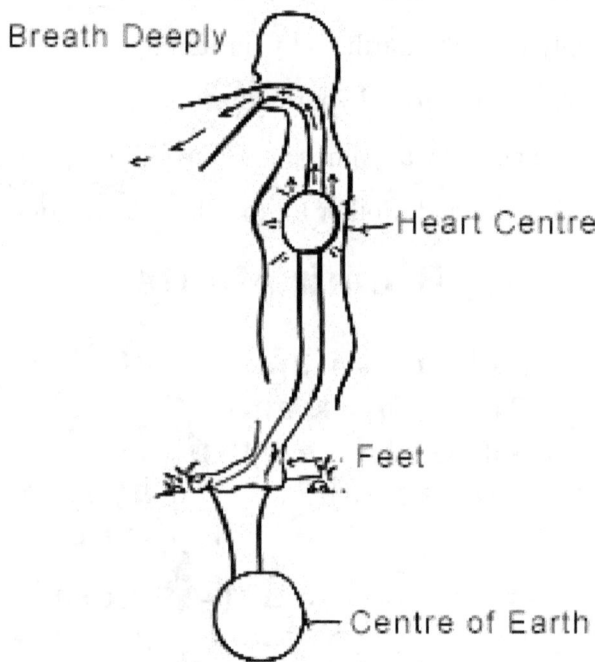

36. Healing the Heart Chakra (1) and Removing Extreme Sadness (2).

If the heart chakra is blocked by heartache, a special treatment may be needed to free the heart chakra. It is vital to have an open heart chakra as it allows the flow of abundance into our life. It allows us to give, receive and trust our world in that all our needs can be met by our belief in our energy flowing through us. It opens love for our fellow man while the back of the heart chakra reduces our ego will or our wish to control others in the world. If we are in unison with our heart chakra then we can take our position with our personal and world task to provide gifts to the world. Therefore we can receive the abundance from the world return back to us through the law of attraction. We will not worry about competition because we have our place in Devine order to fulfil our life's task as co creators in the universe.

The procedure to open the heart chakra is as follows:

1. Ensure the client is on a plinth with a throw or blanket over them.
2. Ensure your protection is in place.
3. Bring a beam of energy from Buddha from your alter to the heart chakra of your client.
4. Place your left hand over the heart chakra and your right hand over their third eye while standing on the client's left hand side.
5. Breathe deeply with your roots going down deep into the earth.
6. Allow the heartache to flow down your body and into the earth.
7. Feel your left hand pulls energy from the heart chakra while your right hand pulses healing energy into the heart via the third eye of the client.
8. Allow your left hand to move upwards as the light enters the heart chakra as you chelate the heart chakra and/or remove blockages.

9. Reposition any blockages or parts of the heart chakra back into their correct position within the chakra.
10. Complete an Astral Trance Healing treatment on the person.
11. Always close down the persons light body correctly; especially the third eye as if this chakra remains open then the person will not sleep at night.

36. (2) Removing Extreme Sadness from the Heart Chakra.

This treatment, up to this point of time, has only been performed through me by my Guides on people who have children passed over to the light.

1. Ensure the client is on a plinth with a throw or blanket over them.
2. Ensure your protection is in place.
3. Bring a beam of energy from Buddha from your alter to the heart chakra of your client.
4. Place both hands directly over the eyes of the client. This will energetically draw away the tears the client is energetically crying. It is likely that you will somatically feel those tears or will physically cry during this healing. You can feel the trauma leave the heart, flow up your arms and away up through your head.
5. Place left hand over heart chakra and the right hand over the third eye. Always position your body facing your client.
6. Feel the flow of energy go from your heart, down right arm, into the client's third eye, into their heart chakra. Feel the trauma being pushed out from the heart, up your left hand and arm, up your head and away.
7. Conduct an astral trance energy healing on the client.

Removing Heartache

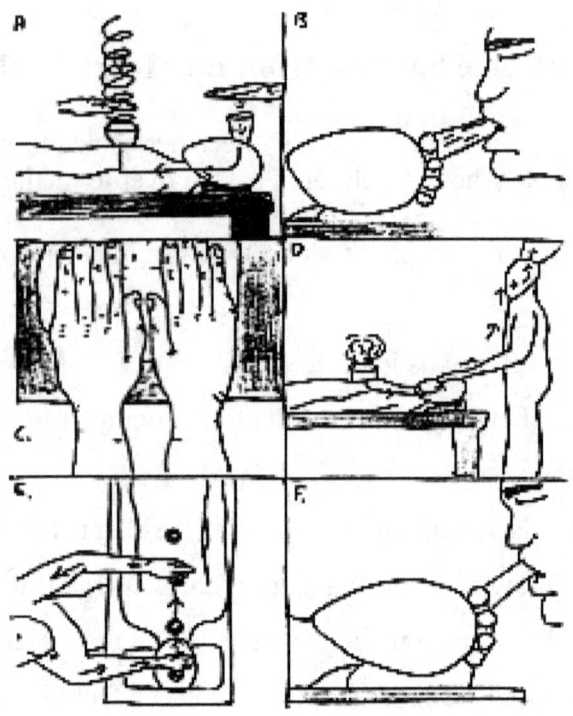

A. Energise Body.
B. Use Breath work.
C. Connect hands to Third Eye.
D. D. Allow energy flow up body.
E. Circulate energy.
F. Complete the healing.

37. Procedure to Rebuild A Chakra.

When a chakra has been blocked for a considerable period of time, the chakra may require a deep treatment to rebuild the chakra. This treatment is not usually conducted in the first energy session due to the light body requiring energetic nourishment to support a new operational chakra. There is no point in putting a new chakra in place when it cannot receive energetic support from the lower chakras and Mother Earth.

The procedure to rebuild a chakra is as follows:

1. Bring energy up through the body. Ensure earth energy is circling the chakra to be repaired.
2. Repair through chelation all lower chakras to ensure energy can successfully pass through those chakras up to the damaged chakra.
3. Thread energy from the base chakra up through all chakras to the damaged chakra.
4. Bring down a spiral of spiritual energy from the outer layers of the aura, down through all the layers of the aura and into each of the seven holes of energy within the chakra.
5. Complete an Astral healing treatment on the person.
6. Notice when a pulse is felt within the chakra and when the energy dissolves away from around that chakra. Notice what negative imprint is fed into that chakra as it could be fear in kidneys, stress in adrenal, anger in liver, sadness in spleen, bitterness in gallbladder that is feeding the dysfunction of that chakra.

7. Your Guides may require that you blow directly into the chakra with a very deep breath. This will retrieve any lost power back into the chakra or ignite the chakra through the energetic breath.

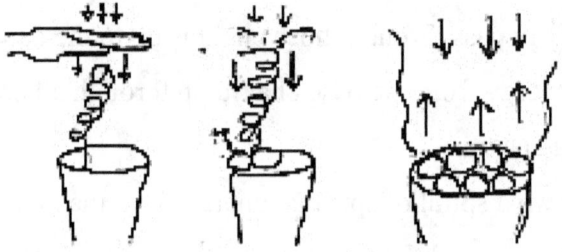

38. Measuring the Functioning of a Chakra through Dowsing with a pendulum.

The energetic and psychological functioning of the chakras are explained in chapter 4, the chakra system: human development in a physical body. If you can determine the spin of a chakra then you can accurately determine what emotional/ psychological state the client is operating in their life at that time. It is also useful to determine the progress that the person is making between sessions. In extreme circumstances i.e. where a energetic hole in a light body requires many weeks of treatment, I advise people to show the person how to measure their chakras to determine the progress of their own energetic work at home due to the serious nature of the attending complaint.

I imagine that as I look at a person's chakras that the face of the chakra is akin to the face of a clock. The spin of the clock should be positive or clockwise. Clockwise indicates that the psychological functioning of that chakra is being felt positively in that person's life. An anti clockwise or negative spin of the chakra means that the expression of the functioning of that chakra is being felt negatively in that person's life. If you bring healing energy into the chakra, then as per the spiritual laws of mankind, the higher vibration of the healing energy will transmute the negative energy within that chakra. Remember that heartache in the heart chakra may be originating from the negative emotions of the sacral or other chakra. Therefore the heart chakra will only become clear when all of the level of trauma is transmuted from its originating chakra. The right side of the body is the energetic male aspect of the person while the left side of the body usually represents the female aspect of the person and their chakras. As either the male or female aspect is dominant energetically within each person, it will be helpful for that person to balance the energy evenly within their chakras and light body.

Positive and Negative spin of the Chakras.

Positive vs Negative Spin?
Male/Female Aspect

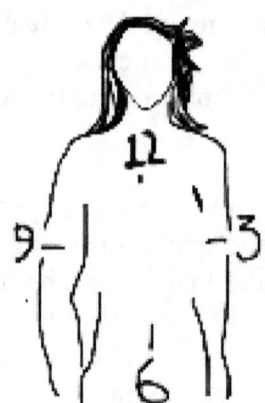

The following diagrams are the measure of the

1. male/ female expression and
2. The degree of positive and negative energy attached to its corresponding chakra and therefore its psychological functioning.

Diagram 2 explains how to 'set' a pendulum for determining a chakra spin

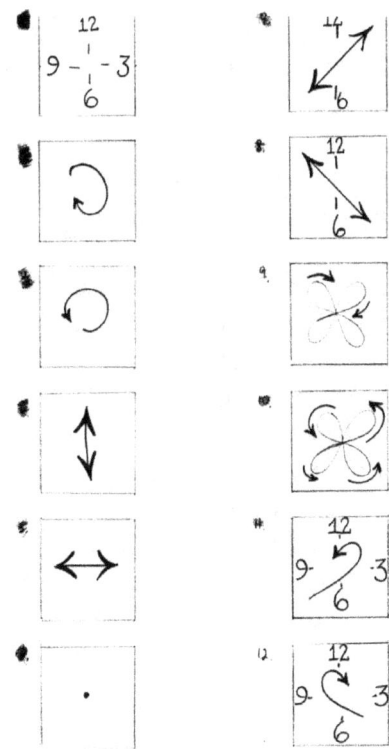

Dowsing with a Pendulum.

Dowsing is an energy trick that can be useful to utilise where time is of the essence. Dowsing should never become a main part of your healing because you are using the pendulum to replace your intelligence, intuition and the development of your skill. My Guides refuse to let me use a pendulum. If I purchased a pendulum it would work for a few days or at worst I would find that it would be broken by the time I drive the five minutes home to my house from the Angel shop. Even if I spin the pendulum correctly so as not to let the pendulum be influenced by my hand, the power of my mind influencing the swing of the pendulum will give me my desired answer. For that reason, I only use pendulums for checking the swing and degree of functioning of chakras. It's a bit like reading your own divination cards in that you just want to give yourself a leg up which will only take from your own power. For all those reasons that is why I am going to focus on utilising a pendulum for checking the functionality of a persons chakras.

You can buy a pendulum in a shop, one that can be energetically cleaned so as to hold a neutral charge is best. Pick a pendulum that resonates with you, one that calls you to work with it. You will know it when you see it. Clean it energetically by leaving it outside in the moonlight during a full moon, bury it in sea salt overnight or run it under a water tap until it feels to be energetically clean. I always shorten the length of the string of the pendulum by wrapping the string around my finger until I feel that the gravity of the weight at the end of the pendulum is a dead weight rather then a light limp weight. This allows quicker and more defined answers by achieving stronger directional swings. The first task to complete with a new pendulum or when using another person's pendulum, is to set the pendulum directions in accordance with your interpretations. Always ask the pendulum if it will work with you. Sometimes they will not work with you or keep giving you negative answers. The setting of the pendulum can be achieved by asking the pendulum questions that you know are either yes or no answers. Always divest of the answers given by the pendulum by blanking your mind after the question is asked to the pendulum.

Procedure to set a pendulum.

1. Wrap the string of the pendulum around your finger.
2. Hold the weight of the pendulum in the air and think or say the question that you wish to ask the pendulum. The answer must definitely be yes i.e. is my name Gerry not am I attractive?
3. Notice the swing of the answer via the direction of the weight of the pendulum. Repeat the process three times with three definitely yes answers. The answers given must be all in the same direction.
4. Ask the pendulum three definitely no answers and you should find that the three answers must have the same directional swing.
5. Alternate definitely yes and no answers which you get clear answers which leave no ambiguity as to the answers given by the pendulum.

6. You should find that the answers communicated by the pendulum are clockwise for yes and anti clockwise for no or 1pm – 7 pm for yes and 11pm – 5pm for no.

Imagine the four cardinal points on a clock. Think of the twelve, three, six and nine points on the clock. The spin of the pendulum going in a clockwise fashion is yes or positive and the spin going anti clockwise are negative. The speed of the spin also signifies the degree to which the chakra is functioning positively or negatively. As the chakras take in information they need a positive spin to accept inwards the energy of the world for interpretation. If the chakra spins negatively then it projects outwards its own negative energy onto the world and therefore is not an interpretation of reality. It is blocked from seeing, feeling and acting in truth depending upon the front chakras (feelings), back chakras (actions) and head chakras (mental processing). If a chakra is blocked it may have no spin in that the pendulum will remain stationary. If the chakra is blocked and functioning negatively then anti clockwise is indicated. If the pendulum swings 12 pm – 6pm then it is wide open in a spiritual fashion allowing energy to flow fully upwards to the higher chakra which will be great for transmuting energy but will provide no nurturance for the physical functioning of that chakras characteristics. If the chakra spins 1pm -7pm then you have a dominant male aspect to that chakra but also a passive aggressive female aspect to that chakra. The opposite is true for an 11am – 5 pm spin in that the chakra will be female dominated but with a passive aggressive male aspect.

If the chakra spins chaotically clockwise means that the persons functioning will be chaotic but at least positive felt in their life. If the pendulum spins anti clockwise in a chaotic fashion then that person will have major trauma and upheaval in their life. It is interesting at times to check a spin before and after a healing as the difference can be significant. As the person pulls in more traumas from the astral plane their chakra may spin negatively again. It does not mean that your work has been substandard. I have come across a few people who have completed two to three years of trauma in a month. Their energy system needed constant healing sessions almost nightly. Each night I completed distant healings on the person. I thought the person must be suicidal with having such an energy system. They were. I only finished the sessions when their energy system returned to relative normality.

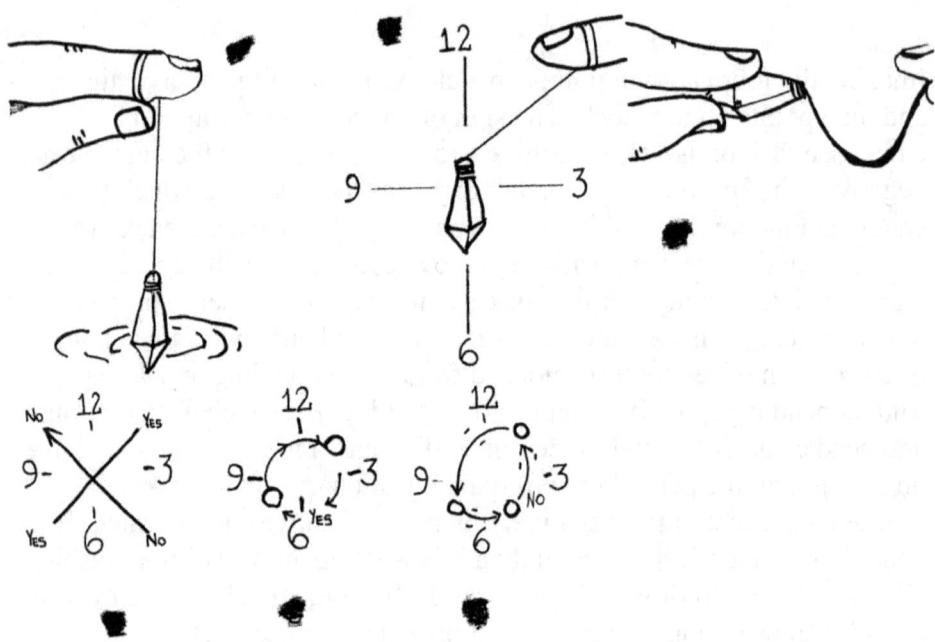

39. Remove Impressions left by living people.

Impressions left behind by living people can usually be seen at the shoulders of your client. Generally the emotionality of the imprint is either positive or negative. If someone is angry they can affect your energy system, particularly the solar plexus. If a person is thinking about you or is falling in love with you, then they will also leave an imprint within your energy system.

An imprint from a living person will feel warm in temperature whereas a deceased person will be cold to the touch. When talking to a person see if the impression will be left in the future or is it a lesson through the law of attraction that the client is experiencing.

I call in my Guides, team and Morgan to remove such imprints. Then I conduct an energy treatment on the light body of the individual.

Imprints left by Living People.

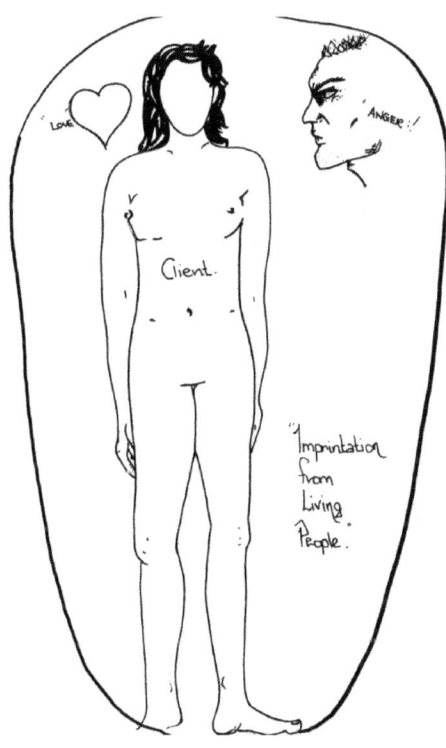

40. Reconnecting A Persons Energetic roots.

Once you realise a persons roots are displaced, the task requires that you determine how the displacement occurred. Through the law of attraction the displacement will occur again in the future so it will be hugely beneficial to analyse the person's life as to determine what energy and emotionality was behind the displacement.

1. Connect the person to Mother earth.
2. Trigger the person to connect to the sensitising event or the emotional imprints that was triggered e.g. their childhood or fear of holding their own masculinity.
3. Once the emotions start to move downwards towards Mother Earth, the base chakra will start to pulsate and reconfigure.
4. Keep sending energy into the persons light body as their roots will proceed to grow downwards towards Mother Earth.
5. Once connected to Mother Earth, the healing energy will travel upwards. This should pulsate the sacral chakra, providing power and usually then the sacral chakra configures.
6. The emotionality of their fear will then leave on a deeper level once they possess the power to deal with the processing of the emotions which exist in the solar plexus.
7. Conduct a Astral trance healing treatment on the light body.

Roots In Place.

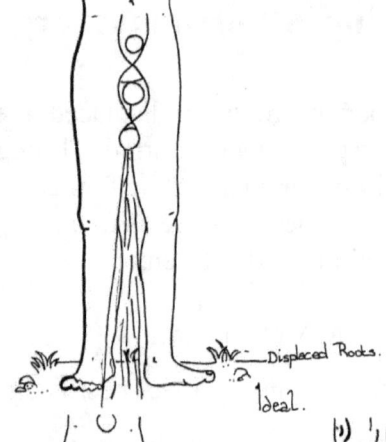

Misplaced Roots.

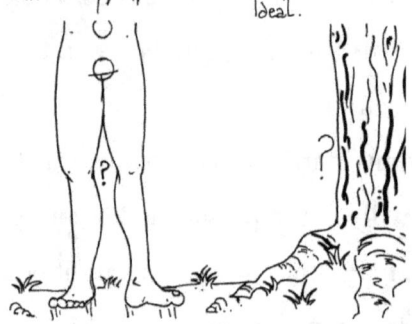

1. Diagnose Misplaced Roots.
2. Determine Cause?
3. Replace & Integrate.

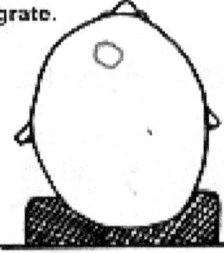 =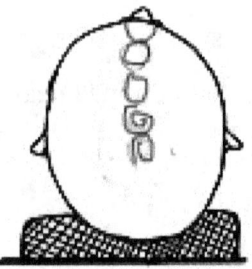

41. Distant Healing.

Distant healing is a useful healing process to utilise when the person requiring the treatment is not present with the healer. The treatment can also be utilised by therapists who agree to train student therapists who will be attending an appointment the following day. This will allow greater progress in terms of transmutation of energies during the following day's session. By virtue of the fact that the person is coming to you for therapy is the permission for the distant healing. It is important to remember that you cannot use any symbols on any individual without their permission. Distant healing is useful where a person is depressed, suffering from extreme anxiety, has experienced a sudden trauma, has recollected a buried incident from their past or where you suspect a person may have self harming thoughts.

The process is the same as if the person is attending a talking therapy session with you but a little bit of imagination is required in order to not block the success of the treatment. Ensure you place your protection in place and that the person's energy field is clear of entities etc. I use three methods to complete distant healings:

1. Somatic energetic breath work.
2. Working with a cuddly toy.
3. Working with cushions.

Because I find that my imagination, trust and somatic interpretation of energy is quiet developed, I quiet enjoy working with the somatic energetic breath work method. The process of working with a cuddly toy and cushions can be faster because you have an anchor point to somatically gage the movement of the energy within your own body. As usual we work from the earth upwards with mother earth energy via the base point.

Somatic energetic breath work.

With somatic energetic breath work you sit on your chair with your hands feeding energy into your sacral chakra by placing your hands over your sacral chakra. You close your eyes and utilise the eyes as a radar screen for the light body. You imagine the person's light body is either standing in front of you or, your energetically create them in miniature form in front of your face. This allows a closer breathe and less energy breathing to the other side of the room. The infinity sign will connect you to that persons light body while also connecting them to mother earth. Usually the persons roots will be malfunctioning to some degree and earth connection is vital for healing to bring the person back to their true nature although possibly temporarily. As I somatically allow my body to be the client's body, I put the roots in place while blowing energy up their light body. I trace the energy up through the energy channels of the chakras and remove any emotional imprints that emerge during the treatment. Allow one hour to successfully complete such a treatment. Once the energy reaches their third eye, I find I maintain that breathe connection into their eye as the energy flows down their light body until the downward energy channels into mother earth. The light body should relax when the heart chakra opens and no negative emotional imprints remain to be fed up the heart chakra at that particular time. Always close down the clients light body especially their third eye so that they are safe and can sleep that night.

Working with a cuddly toy.

Working with a cuddly toy is a simply healing methodology whereby you substitute the toy for the actual physical presence of the person receiving the healing. Remember everything is energy and energy follows intent. As you conduct the treatment, you will somatically feel the energetic channels open and flow within your body to cement your intention of the healing being conducted upon the client. Close down the chakras after the healing. The chakras will be felt on the body of the teddy bear.

Working with cushions.

Some people find it easier to work on a distant light body when they position cushions on their plinth. The shape of the cushions lined along the plinth mirrors the trunk of the body which helps them feel the layers of the aura, chakras and imprints within the light body. The energetic work is still completed in the same manner as the astral healing technique.

Distant Healing Methodologies

Distant Healing

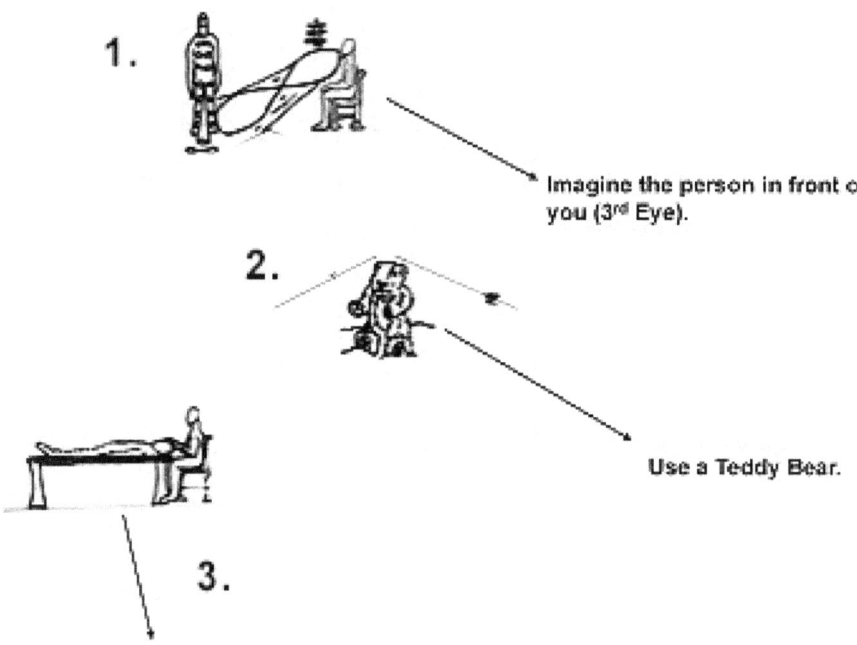

1. Imagine the person in front of you (3rd Eye).
2. Use a Teddy Bear.
3. Light Body on Plinth.

Bibliography.

The following books are, I believe, instrumental in providing the science and physiology of modern Spirituality.

Aivanhov Omraam Mikhael. *You are Gods*. Frejus, France. Prosveta. 2002

Barbara Ann Brennan. *Hands of Light*. New York. Bantam Books. *1988*

John Bradshaw. *Home Coming. Texas*, USA. Piatkus. 1990

John A. Sanford. *The Invisible partners*. New York. Paulist Press. 1980

Adams Bill. *The five Lessons of Life*. London. Rider Books. 2000

Aivanhov Omraam Mikhael. *Golden rules for everyday life*. Frejus, France. Prosveta. 2002

Aivanhov Omraam Mikhael. *Mans subtle bodies and centres*. Frejus, France. Prosveta. 2002.

Bays Brandon. *The Journey.* London. Element Books. 2003.

Beattie Melody. *Co-dependent No More*. Minnesota. Hazelden. 1986.

Bradshaw John. *Healing the Shame that Binds You*. Texas. HCI Books. 2006

Castaneda Carlos. *Jurney to Ixtlan.* Middlesex. Penguin. 1972.

Castaneda Carlos. *The teachings of Don Juan.* California. University Press. 1968.

Cogley Fr. Jim. *The Twinless Self.* Enniscorthy, Ireland. Fr. Jim Cogley. 2010.

Cohen Leonard. *Book of Longing.* London. Penguin 2007.

De Mello Anthony. *Awareness.* London. Fount Books. 1997.

Francis Patrick. *Amongst Equals.* Dublin. Auricle Enterprises. 2003.

Francis Patrick. *The Grand Design IV*. Dublin. Auricle Enterprises. 1995.

Francis Patrick. *The Grand Design V*. Dublin. Auricle Enterprises. 1996.

Frenette Louis Marie. *Omraam Mikhael Aivanhov A Biography*.Liverpool. Suryoma. 1999.

Freud Sigmund. Introductory Lectures on Psychoanalysis. London. Pelican Books. 1973

Freud Sigmund. *The Psychopathology of Everyday Life*. London. Pelican. 1938.

Fontana David. *The new secret language of Symbols*. London. Duncan Baird Publishers. 2010.

Fordham Frieda. *An Introduction to Jung's Psychology*. Middlesex. Pelican. 1953.

Gawain Shakti. *Living in the light*. London. Eden Grove Editions. 1988.

Gibran Kahill. *The Prophet. London.* Pan Books. 1991.

Gray John. *Men are from Mars, Women are from Venus*. London. Element Books. 1992

Gray William G. *Qabalistic Concepts*. Boston, USA. Redwheelweiser. 1997

Hanh Thich Nhat. *Anger*. London. Rider. 2001

Harner Michael. *The way of the Shaman*. New York. Harper Collins. 1990

Hay Louise L. *Life, reflections on your journey*. California. Hay House. 1995.

Hayes Nicky. *Foundations of Psychology*. London. Nelson. 2006.

Hayward Susan. *A Guide for the Advanced Soul.* Australia. In Tune Books. 1984.

Miller Alice. *The truth will set you free.* Germany. Perseus Books. 2001

Morison Jacquelyne. *Analytical Hypnotherapy.* Wales. Crown House. 2001.

O Donohue John. *Benedictus.* London. Transworld Publishers. 2007.

Phatak Dr. S.R. *Materia Medica of Homeopathic Medicines.* New Delhi. B. Jain Publishers. 1999.

Rinpoche Sogyal. *The Tibetan book of Living and Dying.* London. Random House. 2002.

Robertson Robin. *Beginners Guide To Jungian Psychology.* Maine, USA. 1992.

Scott Michael. *Irish Myths and Legends.* London. Warner Books. 1992

Scott Peck M. *The road less travelled and beyond.* London. Rider Books. 1997

Sugrue Thomas. *There is a river, The story of Edgar Cayce.* Virginia. 1942

Weiss Dr. Brian. *Many Lives, Many Masters*. London Piatkus Books. 1994.

Weiss Dr. Brian. *Messages from the Masters.* London. Piatkus.2000

Whitmont E. C. *The Symbolic Quest.* New Jersey. 1969.

Yapko Michael D. *Breaking the patterns of Depression*. New York. Doubleday. 1997

Other Self Development Resources available from Gerry Coleman

Gerry's First Book

Mind with a Soul
Introducing analytical psychotherapy to energy psychology

Divination Cards

Energetic Healing CD's

Inner Child Healing CD's

Astral Healing DVD's

Online tutorials

Skype Therapy

&

Institute of Energetic Sciences

www.instituteofenergeticsciences.com

Visit

www.gerrycoleman.ie

www.astralhealing.net

Mind, Body, Spirit Publications

Are you a budding Author?
Do you want to publish your manuscript but do not know where to start?
Do you have an idea with regards to writing a book?

Mind Body Spirit Publications is a specialist book printing company that combines the best qualities of both self publishing and traditional book publishing companies. The industry of publishing is rapidly changing with the onset of digital printing, self publishing companies and the issues of risk and cost analysis for traditional book publishers. For instance, one of the best selling books of 2011 was a self published book by a thirteen year old girl.

Mind Body Spirit Publications puts you in charge of your career. We are here to help you be successful with a proven business model that is geared for your success.

For Details Contact: Gerard Coleman.
www.mindbodyspiritpublications.com or

gerry@gerrycoleman.ie.

About Gerry Coleman

Gerry Coleman is an analytical depth psychotherapist practising therapy through the medium of energy psychology. He has developed traditional Jungian psychotherapy and energetic light body 'Soul' therapy into a treatment called Astral Trance Healing. He currently teaches this therapy internationally and promotes his two books *Mind with a Soul* and *Soul with a Mind*.

In 2012 Gerry has set up a charity called 'The Institute of Energetic Sciences.' The Institute will aim to promote Spirituality through developing therapies, publications and courses to the general public.

Gerry continues to develop his mediumship with his first courses in the practice and science of mediumship being held in Summer 2012.

Gerry has three children and lives in Kildare, Ireland.

www.ingramcontent.com/pod-product-compliance
Lightning Source LLC
Chambersburg PA
CBHW070306230426
43664CB00015B/2651